Drawn by the River

SUNY SERIES, AN AMERICAN REGION:
STUDIES IN THE HUDSON VALLEY

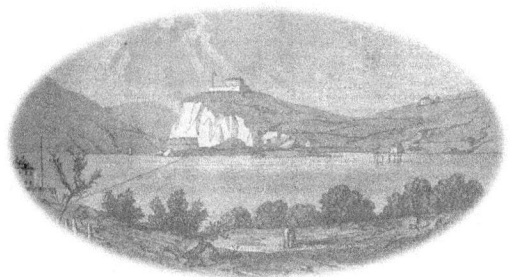

THOMAS S. WERMUTH, EDITOR

Drawn by the River

The Hudson River Valley as a Comics Ecosystem

MOIRA FITZGIBBONS

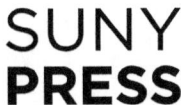

SUNY
PRESS

Cover credit: A drawing of a pine forest along with rocks and a river, created in both vector and hand-drawn styles by Emre Tarimcioglu. Shutterstock.

Published by State University of New York Press, Albany

© 2025 State University of New York

EU GPSR Authorised Representative:
Logos Europe, 9 rue Nicolas Poussin, 17000, La Rochelle, France
contact@logoseurope.eu

For information, contact State University of New York Press, Albany, NY
www.sunypress.edu

Library of Congress Cataloging-in-Publication Data

Name: Fitzgibbons, Moira, author.
Title: Drawn by the river: The Hudson River Valley as a comics ecosystem /
  Moira Fitzgibbons, author.
Description: Albany : State University of New York Press, [2025] | Series:
  SUNY series, An American region : Studies in the Hudson Valley | Includes
  bibliographical references and index.
Identifiers: ISBN 9798855803815 (hardcover : alk. paper) | ISBN 9798855803839
  (ebook) | ISBN 9798855803822 (pbk. : alk. paper)
Further information is available at the Library of Congress.

For Mike

Contents

Illustrations

Acknowledgments

We teachers try to plant seeds in students' minds that might bloom in surprising and helpful ways later in their lives. For this book, though, students have done the sowing. The project's ideas germinated in exchanges with students in first-year seminars, general-education graphic narrative classes, and upper-level courses for English majors at Marist University. Conversations with Evan Fernández and Alexander Close got me thinking about the valley as a locus of comics activity. Kait Dugan, Julianna Gassler, and Amanda Nessel contributed original art to the book, while Isaiah Rettig allowed me to incorporate his ideas and drawing into the introduction. I have cited specific contributions from other students in the endnotes. More challenging to document are the ways that dozens of students' humor, intelligence, skepticism, and generosity have shaped my understanding of comics and the Hudson River valley. To any Red Fox who might read this: it has been, and remains, a delight and a privilege to work with you.

Dialogue with my sister and fellow educators has also played a key role in this project. Gina Brandolino has been a sustaining force in every possible way. Angela Laflen was an ideal collaborator for testing and writing about new teaching strategies. Vincent Lankewish, Penn Szittya, and Susan Crane have long been my academic lodestars. Judy Ciancio, Gwendolyn Moreno, and Martin Shaffer provided key logistical support for this project, and many campus colleagues buoyed my efforts with suggestions and kind queries; I am particularly grateful to Steven Garabedian for his encouragement during an early phase of the project. A Summer Research Grant from Marist University provided financial support for my efforts.

The terrific programming offered by the Hudson River Valley Institute, the Dutchess County Historical Society, and the Poughkeepsie Public

Library District has fueled my interest in regional history and culture. In fact, an exhibit of local cartoonists at the Adriance Memorial Library in fall 2022 provided another prompt for this book.

I am indebted to many other libraries and librarians, both close to home and further afield. John Ansley, Ann Sandri, and Elizabeth Clarke at the James A. Cannavino Library were always on hand to guide me through archival and technological resources, while Linda Furlani provided me with a wonderful primary source in the person of her husband, Michael Calenti. The Wisconsin Historical Society Library allowed me to use its microfilms of *The Westerner*; many thanks to librarian Laura Hemming for her help with this process. Other institutions that shared their resources and expertise include the British Library, Columbia University Libraries, the Franklin D. Roosevelt Presidential Library and Museum, the Historical Society of Sleepy Hollow and Tarrytown, the Libraries at Vassar College, the Metropolitan Museum of Art, the New York Public Library, the New York State Library, the Racine Public Library, and the Yale Library. Thanks are also due to the many individuals at publishing houses, museums, and archives who helped me secure permission to publish the images in this book, and to Michael Barrier and Scott McCloud for helpful replies to email queries. I am also greatly honored that this book includes, in addition to the student contributions mentioned above, artwork created especially for this volume by Alexis Lamb and by Summer Pierre.

Equally indispensable resources were provided by the people who generously agreed to be interviewed—in several cases, on multiple occasions—for this book. To Joe Barruso, Michael Calenti, Jeffrey Canino, Barbara McGue (Jones) Carrington, Bella Dalton-Fenkl, John Decker, Rob Decker, Heinz Insu Fenkl, Linda Fite, Margaretta Friday, Elizabeth Opdyke Jones, Alexis Lamb, Richard Lewis, Ron Marz, Seth Christian Martel, Kayla Miller, Susan Miller, Imani Montgomery, Dennis J. Murray, Summer Pierre, Richard Pini, Wendy Pini, Jim Robishaw, Jon Santana, Pamela A. Scarpero, Harry Sheridan, Amelia Trimpe, Bill Tripp, Jane Tripp, and Sue Turner: I cannot thank you enough for sharing your recollections with me. Hearing reminiscences over lunch with Bill Tripp, Bob Tripp, Linda Tripp-Corbin, Steven Tripp, and other members of their family helped me better understand the achievements of their father, Irving Tripp. Richard Lewis, Ron Marz, Richard and Wendy Pini, Jon Michael Riley, and the Tripp family kindly allowed me to reproduce photographs from their personal collections. At SUNY Press, Richard Carlin has been a guiding light throughout the writing process, Julia Cosacchi expertly steered the book's production, and Caitlin Bean and Camille Hale skillfully copyedited the manuscript. Anonymous readers for the press provided focused and generous feedback. I am also grateful to Carol Scully for thoughtfully responding to selected chapters of the book.

Speaking of support and knowledge, I also want to recognize the environments that have watered, fed, and taught me. I grew up in Ogdensburg, New Jersey, in the watershed of the Wallkill River. That waterway joins with Rondout Creek in Ulster County to form a major tributary of the Hudson. Exploring the plants, animals, and geology of this watershed with the guidance of my parents and our neighbors, Gwendolyn and Harry Slack, and in the company of my friend Michelle Lozier-Teets continues to shape my life and work in the Hudson River valley. Perhaps our living and nonliving companions don't just sustain us but also speak through us.

My social and familial ecosystem deserves a whole separate book, and it would be an entertaining one. To my parents, Mary and Pat Fitzgibbons; my mother-in-law, Christine Petronio; my siblings, Patrick Fitzgibbons, Megan MacMullin, and Kerry Marino; and all others in the far-flung circle of family and friends: there is a reason I do a lot of smiling, and you are it. When it comes to Lia, Tara, and Eliza Petronio, as well as this book's dedicatee, Michael Petronio, I start to run out of words altogether. I am so grateful that we can be part of each other's stories.

As for you, reader: Thanks for picking up this book. Shall we get started?

Introduction

Welcome to our riverside excursion! I hope that this book gives you new ways to think about comics and that it encourages you to seek out intriguing local art, history, and businesses throughout the Hudson River valley or wherever your neck of the woods might be.

Let's begin with a story.

My family and I were delighted to find out back in December 2013 that our local screening of *Frozen* would begin with another Disney production, a six-minute animated short film titled *Get a Horse!* The cartoon's action began in the realm of "early Mickey"—black-and-white images; small, inky dots for Mickey and Minnie's eyes; and an old-fashioned musical score. Chased by a hostile opponent, Mickey broke the fourth wall and unexpectedly landed in a present-day movie theater. Minnie soon followed. She burst out onto the theater's stage, looked around, and asked, "Where are we? Poughkeepsie?" (see figure I.1). Minnie's guess prompted a

Figure I.1. Still from the animated cartoon *Get a Horse!* Soon after this moment, Minnie escapes into the present-day realm and asks if she is in Poughkeepsie. *Source:* © Disney 2013. Used with permission.

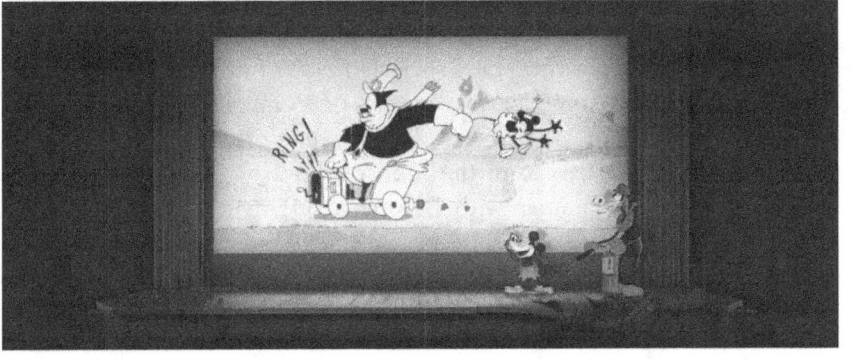

1

particularly big laugh at the theater where we were sitting: Regal Cinemas in the Poughkeepsie Galleria. The cartoon's action had hit quite close to home. At the time, I thought that perhaps Disney had changed Minnie's question depending on the area where the film was being screened, but that wasn't the case. From Seattle to Cleveland to Hoboken, everyone heard Minnie ask about Poughkeepsie.

You didn't have to be a resident of Dutchess County, New York, to find that funny. There is a rich history of people using Poughkeepsie as a reference point, punch line, and byword that is both extremely specific and a stand-in for classic Americana. Maybe you have watched the *Friends* episode "The One with the Girl from Poughkeepsie," in which a potential love interest works in Manhattan but lives inconveniently far away. Perhaps you have read Ursula K. Le Guin's "From Elfland to Poughkeepsie," a brilliant essay in which the city represents the everyday world as opposed to fantasy realms. As we will see, Elfland *has* resided in Poughkeepsie in a fascinating way. Indeed, given that Disney comics for decades were printed at the Western Printing plant in Poughkeepsie, Minnie had good reasons to suspect she had landed in the Queen City on the Hudson.

There have been dozens of other references to the city over the years, as demonstrated by the encyclopedic trove of references in comics, films, television shows, and other media compiled by David Lumb on his Poughkeepsie Pop Culture website. He has also compiled a wonderful video anthology of allusions to the city in films, television shows, and musical performances.[1] What could explain the appeal of this placename?

The sound of the word itself could be a factor. The city's name offers a lively array of consonants: an explosive *p*; another stop of airflow with the *k*; a move right back to *p*; and a sibilant *s*. There is a lot of movement with the vowels, too. If you focus on the *UHH* of the first syllable, the *IP* of the second, and the *EE* of the third, notice how the sound moves from the lower parts of your oral cavity to the higher and more front-facing parts. Moreover, the name's final syllable might associate it in our minds with playful terms such as *tipsy*, *cutesy*, and *flopsy*.[2] More seriously, like other American placenames often invoked for comic effect, such as Kalamazoo or Walla Walla, *Poughkeepsie* originates in an Indigenous language: it derives from the Munsee term for "reed-covered lodge by the spring."[3] Placenames with European origins strike many English speakers as familiar and conventional: there's an "old" York in England, an Ithaca in Greece, and so on. But *Poughkeepsie* exists only in America and reflects distinctly American contradictions. Even as the name represents a point of connection with Munsee culture, reactions to it often reflect unfamiliarity with that culture and its language.

This small moment in *Get a Horse!* has led us to big issues. The interplay between comics and place is the primary focus of this book. How do comics and related media depict particular places? How, in turn, do particular places influence the creation of comics? Our analysis here will home in on one specific area, the Hudson River valley, and all the rich opportunities for place-based inquiry that it provides. We will investigate comics not just as published *products* but also as *processes* involving many different individuals, communities, and technologies. Thinking about the valley as an ecosystem will highlight the connections among natural, social, and cultural environments. It will also provide us with a way of exploring how the same geographic area can support some creators while suppressing or uprooting others.

As a first step, let's briefly consider how several influential comics from the past half century have depicted place in their pages. Connecting protagonists to the places they inhabit has long been a crucial strategy in comics storytelling.

Putting Characters (and Readers) in Their Place

Natural and human-built spaces function as living, breathing entities within many canonical comics. One of the many groundbreaking aspects of Will Eisner's 1978 graphic novel *A Contract with God* is its vivid depiction of Dropsie Avenue, the fictional New York City neighborhood in which the comic's characters live, argue, grieve, and reflect. Eisner's preface (2004) describes the novel's stories as "anchored" in the neighborhood's crowded spaces and interpersonal dramas (xxiv). In the final image of the centennial edition of *Contract*, the novel depicts a teenager contemplating the responsibilities of imminent adulthood while staring at the cityscape below him (see figure I.2). The dark smudge on Willie's back makes his body a counterpoint to the pale moon, and his back's angular shape resembles that of the buildings in front of him. He may be able to gaze critically at the built environment around him, but he is part of it, too.

A very different, but no less significant, urban space emerges in another seminal graphic novel, Marjane Satrapi's *Persepolis*. As the Islamic Revolution engulfs Teheran, Satrapi's austere panels offer few details about the city itself: Characters often seem confined within the panels, just as

Figure I.2. *Source:* From *A Contract with God and Other Tenement Stories*, Will Eisner Centennial Edition, by Will Eisner. Copyright ©2006 by Will Eisner Studios, Inc. Copyright (c) 1978, 1985, 1989, 1995, 1996 by Will Eisner Studios, Inc. Used by permission of W. W. Norton & Company, Inc.

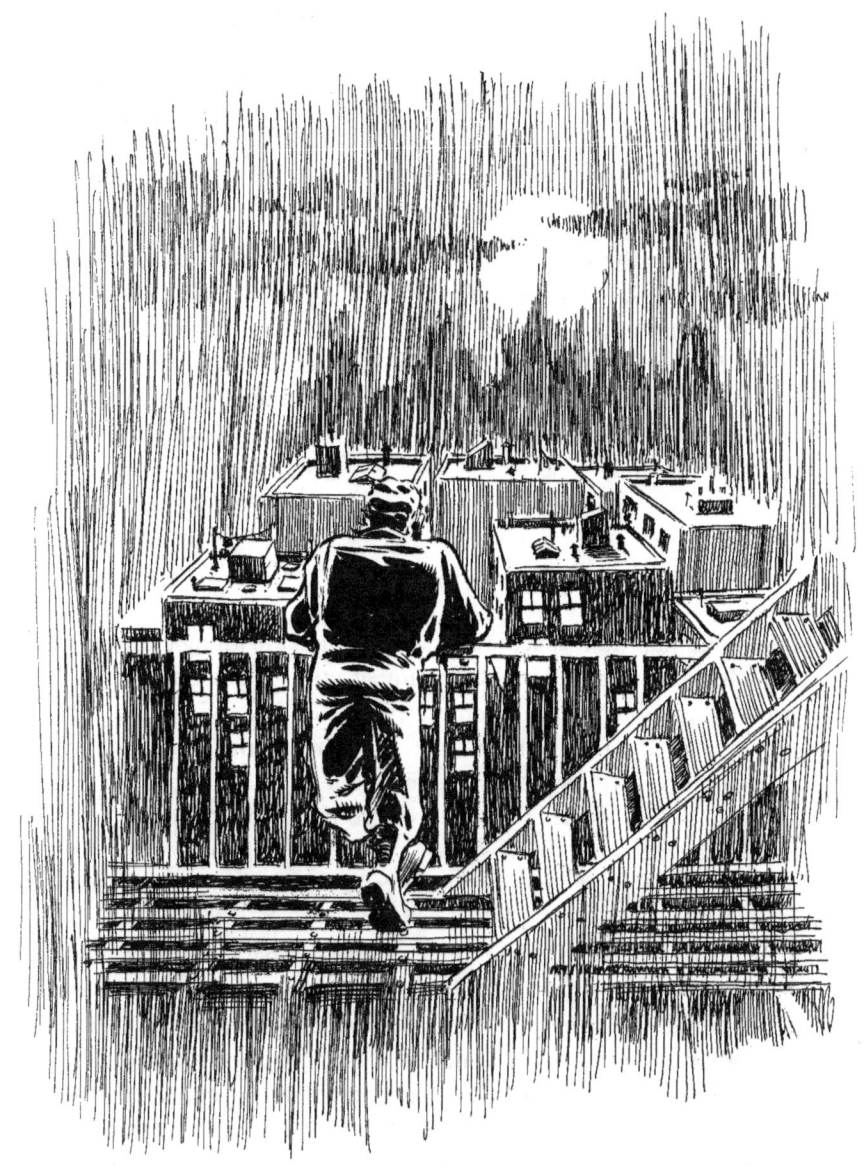

they often are within their homes. A sense of simultaneous connection and alienation also emerges in Ben Passmore's *Your Black Friend and Other Strangers*. As the comic's protagonist walks around New Orleans, he encounters white neighbors congratulating themselves on their brave decision to live in the city and Black acquaintances who regard him as an outsider to the area. In a more rural environment, but with a similarly powerful emotional impact, Alison Bechdel's *Fun Home: A Family Tragicomic* maps key spots in the life of the author's father, Bruce Bechdel. We cannot understand her father, Bechdel suggests, without placing him as precisely as possible within the community he inhabited.

Taken together, these works exemplify comics' ability to investigate the profound connections among people, events, and places. It is perhaps not surprising that all of these examples are the long-form comics usually categorized as *graphic novels* or *graphic narratives*.[4] As cartoonist and comics theorist Scott McCloud (2006) has pointed out, longer works give creators the chance to explore place more fully: "As 300-page graphic novels have become more common, some North American cartoonists are also starting to explore the potential of multi-panel and even multi-page scene-setters in hopes of creating more powerful and memorable worlds" (167). Artists and writers should regard these worlds not as simple backdrops, he argues, but as "environments" that play an essential role in the development of characters and events (178).

We might go a step further and say that every comics panel is itself an immersive environment. Consider, for example, how carefully Eisner has thought about the place of readers in his portrait of the pensive teenager in *A Contract with God*. Because we see Willie from behind, we do not have access to his facial expression, though we gaze at the same view that he sees. Just as Willie feels both connected to his community and estranged from it, so do we simultaneously share his perspective and wonder about his emotional state.

That comics help readers imaginatively engage with space and place is a foundational idea within comics studies.[5] In her analysis of comics depicting the suburbs, Hillary Chute (2017) writes, "Comics—a medium whose panels enclose and juxtapose space—is perfectly suited to reveal how the suburbs fence out the undesirable, and how geographical and social spaces are linked" (156). Less well-explored are the ways that specific regional contexts have fostered the creation of comics. One explanation for this is that the production and distribution of comics rapidly evolved into a national and international industry during the twentieth century. Syndication, or the distribution of comic strips to newspapers nationwide, came to comics by the 1890s. Jeremy Dauber (2022) points out, "By 1908, 75 percent of American Sunday papers were publishing comics, and 75 percent of that market was served by three syndicates" (10). Moreover, many cartoonists worked remotely. The much-touted bullpens of Marvel and DC during the mid-twentieth century exaggerated the extent to which creators rubbed shoulders in New York City locations.[6] In *Al Jaffee's MAD Life: A Biography*, for example, Mary-Lou Weisman (2010) describes how the annual trips taken by the magazine's freelancers were necessary because in general, *Mad*'s "gang of idiots" didn't regularly share space with each other (187).[7] Bearing this in mind, it makes sense that histories of comics, when attending to questions of place, have tended to use broad categories. The second volume of *The Comic Book History of Comics*, for example, focuses on comics' evolution within the national contexts of Japan, France, Mexico, Brazil, and other countries.

To the extent that specific sites have factored into the analysis of comics production, experts in the field have primarily focused on urban locations. There are good reasons for this: From the vibrant newspaper culture of the early twentieth century to the excitement of contemporary comics conventions, cities have served as centralized locations for comics culture. Scott McCloud recounts in *Making Comics* that he only needed to walk "two and a half blocks" from his workplace at DC Comics to the entirely different offerings at the Kinokuniya bookstore in midtown Manhattan, which carried a strong selection of manga (216).

Densely packed with people, goods, and buildings, cities have also offered comics creators a rich array of possibilities for visual storytelling. As explored by Benjamin Fraser in *Visible Cities, Global Comics* and the contributors to the anthology *Comics and the City: Urban Space in Print, Picture and Sequence*, in many ways comics replicate urban architecture and topography. Panels and page designs often resemble the rectangular high-rises, boxy windows, and grid-like street plans of many modern cities.[8] These urban influences affect comics studies as well. *Gutter*, a key term in the field used to describe the white space between panels, evokes an unglamorous but necessary feature of city life.[9]

Smaller cities, towns, and rural locations have played a lesser role in analyses of comics production thus far. Chute's analysis of comics and the suburbs demonstrates the benefits of this approach.[10] At the local level, news outlets, public libraries, and arts organizations play important roles in drawing readers' attention to the artists working in their midst.[11] One book-length study that explores a specific region outside of city limits is Cullen Murphy's *Cartoon County: My Father and His Friends in the Golden Age of Make-Believe*, which describes the dense concentration of cartoonists living in Fairfield County, Connecticut, in the second half of the twentieth century. Murphy's account of creative exchange among these artists is very much in the spirit of this book. In fact, his fascinating reminiscences about Connecticut-based figures (such as Mort Walker, Bob Fujitani, and his own father, John Cullen Murphy) have led me to regard the Nutmeg State as a bit of a cross-region rival to the Hudson River valley in terms of comics achievement. Perhaps this book will tempt comics creators who live in Connecticut to reconsider their life choices and settle down in the valley instead.

Murphy's reminiscences and interviews make clear that it was a combination of social, cultural, financial, and transportation-related factors that drew his father and other cartoonists to southern Connecticut. The same thing is true of the Hudson River valley. Accordingly, we will think about the region not just as a place but also as an ecosystem. Different factors leading to comics art and production coexist in a mutually reinforcing relationship.

Lines of Connection

Ecosystems involve both human and nonhuman participants. *The Oxford English Dictionary* defines *ecosystem* both as "a biological system composed of all the organisms found in a particular physical environment, interacting with it and with each other" and as any other "complex system." The latter, more general sense of the term has gained currency in many different fields, including law, fashion, economics, and information science.

Thinking about comics as ecosystems has proven useful to discussions of the medium. Nicolle Lamerichs uses the term when considering the interactions between digital comics and their fandoms.[12] In "Critics and Creators: The LGBTQ+ Comic Ecosystem," Justin Hall explains how his work as a curator, editor, and cartoonist has provided a supportive environment for queer creators and readers.[13] Kenneth Oravetz (2021) describes the spatial, social, and commercial aspects of comic-book shops, and even individual store shelves, as "micro-ecolog[ies]" of ideas and artistic work. While differing in their subject matter, all these investigations demonstrate the benefits of thinking about comics not just as printed or pixelated products but as multiple, overlapping processes of interaction.

As we apply this idea to the Hudson River valley, we will explore a wide variety of contributors to this environment. Our studies will encompass not just comic strips, graphic narratives, and comics magazines but also book and magazine illustrations, single-panel cartoons, animated cartoons, and lithographs. To be sure, these are distinct forms, and audiences bring different expectations and analytical practices to each one. But we encounter them in overlapping spaces and times, and many artists discussed in this book have moved fluently among them.[14] An "interpictorial approach," to use Rachel Harris's useful phrase (259), can generate new ways of thinking about all participants in the ecosystem. Indeed, Ramzi Fawaz has argued that instead of trying to draw strict boundaries around or within comics, we should follow the medium's "lines of cultural flight across audiences, styles, genres, and contexts" ("A Queer Sequence" 591).

That will be our method here. We will look carefully at moments in which artistic practices, technologies, and businesses associated with comics converge with other media. This will help us acknowledge not just the complexity of comics but also the richness of other cultural products associated with the Hudson River valley. Our methodology follows the lead of the river itself, with its breadth, depth, shifting currents, and confluence with many tributaries.

How Green Is Our Valley?

In addition to informing our sense of comics in relation to other regional art, our investigations will emphasize the *eco-* part of the equation—that is, biological and environmental factors—and their interaction with human-made systems. During twenty-plus years living in the city of Poughkeepsie, I have found that the Hudson River provides regular reminders of our place in larger ecosystems. Your neighborhood's proximity to the river might determine whether you receive four or ten inches of snow. Driving along Route 9 on a chilly October morning, you might notice that a ribbon of fog hovers over the river, even after the skies overhead have cleared. The sight of currents occasionally flowing northward reminds you that from Manhattan to Hyde Park (or thereabouts), the river is actually an estuary that includes salty waters from the Atlantic Ocean via the upper New York Bay. And the horns and clattering wheels from Amtrak and Metro-North trains make it sound as if snippets of city noise have migrated north along with the ocean currents.

While digital debates periodically erupt over where "Upstate New York" truly begins, it is not terribly difficult to define the valley as a region.[15] Our explorations will generally follow the definition established by the Hudson River Valley National Heritage area, which spans from Yonkers to the upper limits of Rensselaer County, north of Albany (see figure I.3).

Figure I.3. Subregions of the Hudson River valley as defined by the Maurice D. Hinchey Hudson River Valley Heritage Area. *Source:* Kris Fitzgerald, 2K Design, for the Maurice D. Hinchey Hudson River Valley Heritage Area. Used with permission.

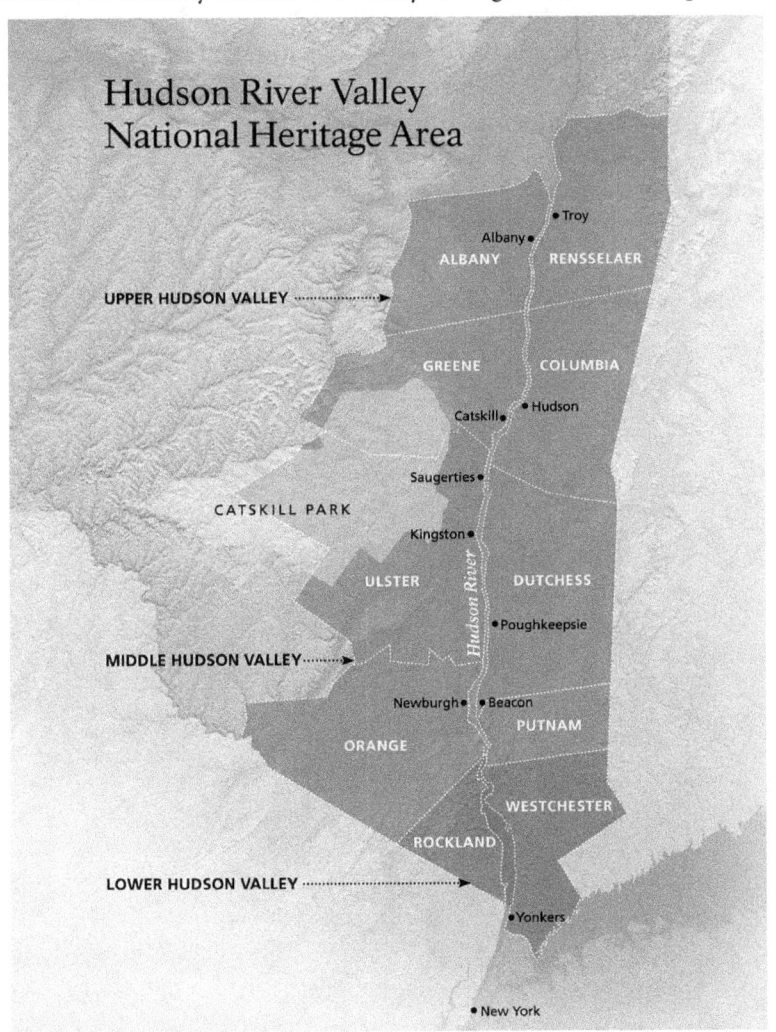

We will primarily focus on the middle Hudson valley, but we will stop at many points to the north and south as well.[16]

While defining the region is relatively straightforward, the situation on the ground is a complicated one. Waterways, vegetation, geology, and other natural factors coexist with densely connected residential and transportation networks. For us comics readers, it will come as no surprise that a mix of verbal and visual elements is the best way to convey this complexity. As seen in figure I.4, a graphic from the Science Collaborative of the National Estuarine Research Reserve System (NERRS) uses shading, texture, streamlined shapes, and a mix of words and images to convey the Hudson River's ecosystem as both a natural and constructed space.

NERRS's mission, "Helping Communities Thrive and Adapt to a Changing Coast," points to an important dimension of ecosystems as a concept: We often use the term to refer to areas that are vulnerable to exploitation or depletion. This is certainly a crucial element of the Hudson

Figure I.4. *Source:* Image courtesy of the NERRS Science Collaborative.

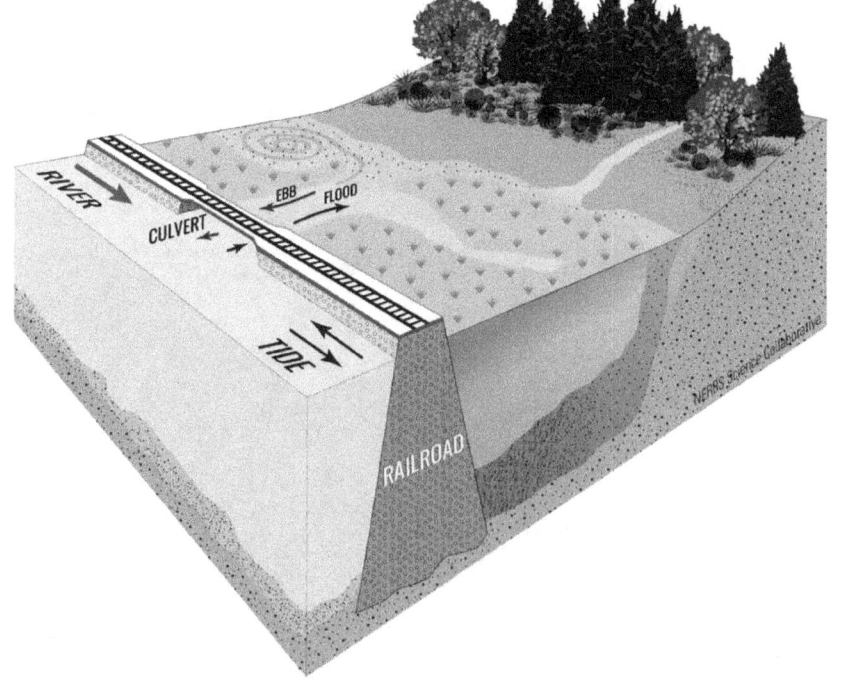

River valley's story. As the region became more populated and industrialized in the eighteenth and nineteenth centuries, the river functioned all too literally as a "gutter." George L. Lankevich (2006) has pointed out that the region's vibrant tradition of entrepreneurialism gradually became a threat rather than an asset: "Since the 1820s, the accomplishments of Hudson valley entrepreneurs had created business legends . . . [but] for over a century, the refuse of an industrial age was dumped into the Hudson, and by the mid-1900s the environmental cost of past achievements was becoming evident . . . the river was filled with the pollution of civilization, and its 'dead spots' were gradually increasing in size" (110). Environmental activism, litigation, and legislation have greatly improved the situation, though pollutants still threaten those who swim and fish in the waterway.[17]

Artists' visualizations of the river and region have played a key part in efforts to restore its health as an ecosystem. As we shall see in chapter 1, in the nineteenth century, artists such as Thomas Cole and Frederic Edwin Church produced landscape paintings that helped to build distinctively American artistic traditions and to define the Hudson River valley as a region worth visiting and valuing.[18] While the Hudson River school of art became less prominent after the Civil War, it persisted in the national consciousness and continued to make the area an important tourist destination in the nineteenth and twentieth centuries.[19] By the 1960s, this cultural legacy factored into a watershed moment in American environmentalism. After decades of litigation, the Scenic Hudson decision acknowledged that the beauty of the river and its environs was an asset that the government had a duty to protect on behalf of its citizens.[20] The Hudson River valley helped Americans understand how cultural, political, and natural ecosystems are inextricably intertwined.

By the end of this book, I hope you will agree that comics as art, community, and industry deserve to be considered within these interlocking systems. In part 1, we will place comics and related art into dialogue with traditions of Hudson River valley landscape art. Chapter 1 will explore how Washington Irving's "sketches" of the region influenced nineteenth- and early twentieth-century depictions of the valley by John Frederick Kensett, Thomas Nast, Fanny Palmer, and Arthur Rackham. Small in scale but wide ranging in their influence, these works provided artistic and technological precedents for comics' emergence as a medium. Chapter 2 will show how twentieth- and twenty-first-century creators have built upon earlier artists' legacies and combined them with strategies used in contemporary comics.

Whereas part 1 shines a light on comics as artistic products, part 2 focuses on the processes by which comics have been created in the Hudson River valley. Chapter 3 tells of the Western Printing site, a parcel of land in Poughkeepsie that fostered two innovative business ventures before becoming a massive industrial facility that, in the middle of the twentieth century, churned out millions of comic books each month. Along the way, it became an important employer and a nexus of community interaction and artistic activity in the mid-Hudson valley. Adjacent to the Western Printing site geographically and temporally, chapter 4 recounts the saga of Wendy Pini and Richard Pini, the Poughkeepsie-based creators behind the stunningly inventive comics series *ElfQuest*. The region provided the Pinis with the support needed to function both as pioneering "indie" creators and as engaged community members who drew inspiration from the people and nature they encountered in the Hudson River valley. The breadth of the artistic creation produced within the region is detailed in chapter 5. Providing portraits of artists past and present, the chapter highlights the many different factors that generate a comics ecosystem: the teaching strategies of open-minded educators; conversations in local comics shops; displays at comics conventions and county fairs; and social events such as Friday-night happy hours and coffee-shop chats. A conclusion will allow us to consider potential future developments for comics in the region.

It is important not just to celebrate the past and present but also to look forward. That an ecosystem is dynamic and diverse does not necessarily mean that it is also egalitarian. Our travels in the valley will reveal that labor struggles, gender bias, racial prejudice, and social stereotypes play as large a role in comics creation as they do in other industries and artistic communities. Not everything grows and thrives within this ecosystem. This is not a natural or inevitable state of affairs but a result of human decision making and institutional norms.

Comics' ability to depict simultaneous events, contradictory feelings, and multiple perspectives will prove very useful as we come to terms with complex narratives of the valley's history and future. In the museum world, the Metropolitan Museum of Art took an important step forward when it placed written responses from Indigenous artists and thinkers next to Hudson River valley landscapes in its American Art wing. Visitors to the gallery now gaze at walls in which the paintings' assertion of a distinctive American identity and majestic landscapes are accompanied by critical reminders of how those territories were acquired and at what cost. The Thomas Cole National Historic Site went a step further with its

2024 exhibit, *Native Prospects: Indigeneity and Landscape,* which placed artwork by Indigenous creators alongside works by Cole and other artists associated with the Hudson River school. A similarly forward-thinking exhibit mounted at this location will frame our investigations in chapter 1.

Comics can do the same thing as these museum initiatives on a scale that is smaller but easier to reproduce and distribute. There is no better space than the comics page for visualizing and communicating how more than one thing can be true at the same time.

Our own explorations will consider multiple perspectives and histories. Even the placename *the Hudson River valley* makes something tidy and seemingly inevitable about a process of colonization, war, disease, and forced removal. For the Munsee and Mahican people who have lived here, the area constitutes part of Lenapehoking, a broader region defined by the Delaware River as well as the Mahicannituck, the river with water that flows both ways.[21]

The Mahican name for the river evokes a model of fluid, dynamic thinking and representation. Building on these conceptions, Potawatomi botanist and author Robin Wall Kimmerer (2015) challenges readers to resist the impersonal language often used for bodies of water and other natural features:

> A bay is a noun only if water is *dead.* When *bay* is a noun, it is defined by humans, trapped between its shores and contained by the word. But the verb *wiikwegamaa*—to *be* a bay—releases the water from bondage and lets it live. . . . To be a hill, to be a sandy beach, to be a Saturday, all are possible verbs in a world where everything is alive. Water, land, and even a day, the language a mirror for seeing the animacy of the world, the life that pulses through all things, through pines and nuthatches and mushrooms. (55)

Within Kimmerer's "braided" way of knowing the world, the Hudson River emerges not just as an object for art but also as a living being with the agency to speak and to teach.[22] Her approach is shared by Indigenous people living in, or associated with, the region. Joe Baker writes, "Lenape culture bears a sophisticated understanding that put nothing beyond or outside the obvious web of life that is present on Earth" (Baker, Coumans, and Whitney 26). Engaging artistically and respectfully with our environment is just one step in the process. Art is important; so are policymaking, environmental protection, and the development of new roles for Indigenous nations in defining land use and resource protection. All these initiatives benefit from careful attention to the natural features that define our environment. Comics will not solve everything, but they are a great way to practice and to generate this attentiveness.

In this spirit, my students and I recently applied Kimmerer's ideas by trying to draw the Hudson River—which flowed within easy view of our classroom's building—as a verb. Students depicted the waterway speaking, laughing, and splashing around their drawing pads. One student, Isaiah Rettig, developed these ideas more fully for a later sketch and brief analysis. "While many people think of the river as flowing, the river itself is helping the world flow around it," Rettig noted. "In a way we are all rivering near the river." Flowing freely across college-ruled notebook paper, Rettig's lines help us think about the river as a dynamic actor in the ecosystem (see figure I.5). As we explore all the evidence of comics creativity in the valley, let's keep Rettig's insight in the back of our minds. Perhaps we are not the only ones shaping the creative ecosystem in the area. How have cartooning and "rivering" blended? And how does the river draw *us*?

Figure I.5. *Source:* Image courtesy of Isaiah Rettig.

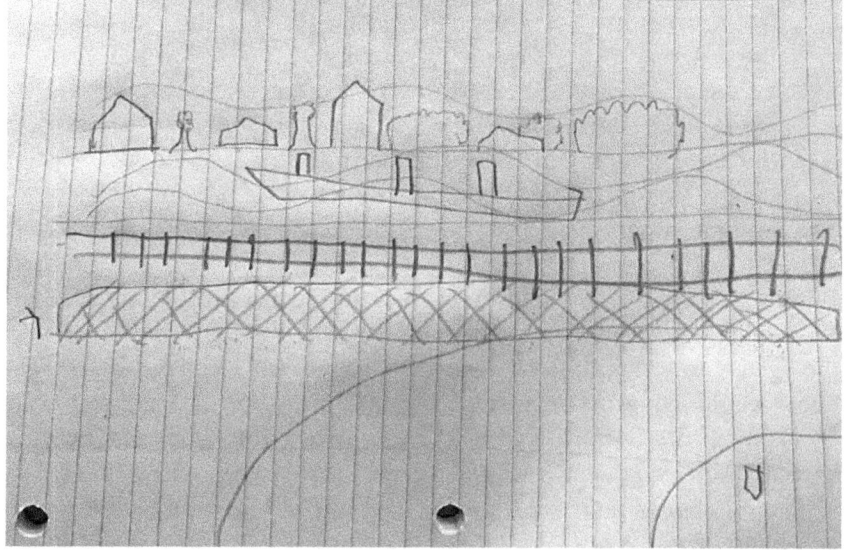

Part I

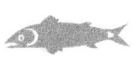

Landscape Art and Comics

CHAPTER 1

Framing the Region in Nineteenth- and Twentieth-Century Pages, Prints, and Panels

June is a splendid month in the Hudson River valley. The river sparkles. The leaves rustle. The Catskills loom, indigo blue, in the distance. Taking advantage of a lovely day in mid-June 2023, I went with my daughter Tara to see *Women Reframe American Landscape: Susie Barstow & Her Circle/ Contemporary Practices*, an exhibit at the Thomas Cole National Historic Site in Catskill, New York (see figure 1.1).[1] By presenting the first-ever sustained exploration of Susie Barstow's art and life (1836–1923), the exhibit positioned a woman artist squarely within the canon of Hudson River school painters. At the same time, the show placed the work of contemporary artists into a critical, sometimes contentious dialogue with the Hudson River school and with the Cole homestead itself.

It was an exhilarating exhibition. Located in a separate studio, the Barstow works amply justified the prominence she enjoyed during her own lifetime and rectified the "art-historical amnesia" surrounding her work in the century since her death.[2] Within the Cole residence, twenty-first-century women's artworks offered inventive approaches to landscape art as well as new ways to perceive Cole's paintings and the physical features of the house, which was built primarily by enslaved men and women in the early nineteenth century. As we visitors moved throughout these spaces, we began to talk to each other and to our guides about the interplay between the artworks and the rooms in which they were installed.

Figure 1.1. Entrance to Cedar Grove, the main residence at the Thomas Cole National Historic Site. *Source:* Photo by the author.

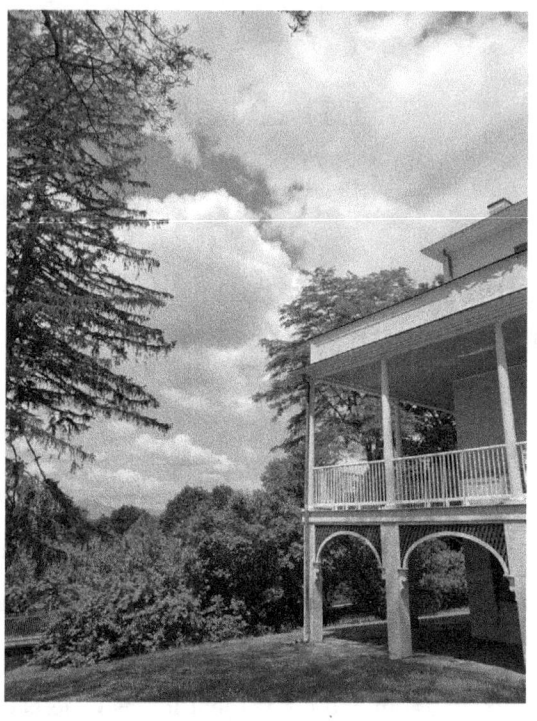

When we were finished at the exhibit, Tara and I took the ten-minute drive over the Rip Van Winkle Bridge to Olana, the estate of renowned Hudson River school artist Frederic Edwin Church. We picnicked on the grounds and snapped photos of the views. It was a great way to cap off our day trip. Olana's view of the river is unparalleled at any time of year.

We might regard the little story I just told as a "peak Hudson River valley experience." For over two centuries, this kind of anecdote—"Here is a beautiful place I just visited near the river; here is a visual record of the experience; here are the reasons that you should take a trip there, too!"—has been told and retold about sites in the region. Every recollection, every sketch, and every photo both participate in longstanding traditions related to the Hudson River valley and offer potentially new perspectives. I hope that chapters 1 and 2 of this book can do the same thing. Specifically, we will explore how comics and related forms depict the Hudson River valley's natural features and cultural traditions. Across different times and contexts, patterns emerge in artists' practices. Many works invoke and interpret Washington Irving's tales; satirize tourism and travelers; propose new ways to engage with nature; and describe the region as a portal that is benevolent, dangerous, or both.

In this chapter, we will take our own excursion back to the nineteenth century and the early decades of the twentieth century. Using a broad definition of comics history that encompasses illustration and engraving as well as cartooning, we will explore how these practices intersected with the creation of landscape art in this period. To begin our inquiry, we will consider how Washington Irving (1783–1859) not only defined the region through his written works but also described drawing as an important way to experience the area. We will then examine works by four artists who built on Irving's ideas about the valley: John Frederick Kensett, Thomas Nast, Fanny Palmer, and Arthur Rackham. None of these artists used the Hudson River valley as a home base, but each of them contributed to the development of landscape art, valley lore, and comics.

Kensett (1816–1872), a well-known landscape painter associated with the Hudson River school, played with page design and blurred the distinction between letters and images in his illustrations for a book about scenic destinations in the valley and beyond. Nast (1840–1902), now remembered primarily for his political cartoons, created a montage of panels that interspersed landscapes with tourists' adventures and misadventures. Palmer (1812–1876) was a painter, lithographer, and sometime cartoonist who produced some of the best-known and most widely distributed prints sold by Currier & Ives. Both Palmer's career and the activities of the firm who employed her bring to light new dimensions in the history of American cartooning. The work of Rackham (1867–1939) also deserves a larger place in our understanding of the comics medium. Produced across the Atlantic Ocean, Rackham's illustrations of Irving's "The Legend of Sleepy Hollow" take visual storytelling in stunning new directions.

Richly varied in their responses to the Hudson River valley, these artists' works demonstrate the benefits of placing comics, cartooning, and illustration in conversation with other artistic media and historical movements. As argued in the recent scholarly volume *Seeing Comics through Art History* and within the *Art History Teaching Resources* digital platform, comic studies has much to offer to art history as a discipline, as well as to literary studies, history, journalism, and other fields. The case studies explored in this chapter suggest that oil paintings are only part of the story of Hudson River valley art in the nineteenth century. Magazine cartoons, book illustrations, and lithographs did not carry the same prestige as large painted landscapes, but they still played an influential role in the visual culture of the period and allowed for the expression of complex ideas.[3]

In addition to affecting our notions of art history, putting comics in dialogue with landscape art can also enrich how we understand the evolution of comics. What Henry Pratt (2023) has called "the standard history" (3) of the medium typically traces its development through the invention of the printing press; the illustrations of nineteenth-century satirists such as Rodolphe Töpffer; the flourishing of newspaper journalism and comic strips; the development of superheroes and comic books in the 1930s; and the emergence of alternative comics and literary graphic novels in the late twentieth century. This one-sentence summary is, obviously, a simplified version of the story. For those wanting to delve deeper, Pratt offers readers a helpful three-page overview, while Jeremy Dauber's *American Comics: A History* provides an expansive and thorough book-length study.[4] From David Kunzle's groundbreaking *The Early Comic Strip* through topics-based studies such as Hilary Chute's *Why Comics?*, scholars have acknowledged the wide range of influences, technologies, and practices involved in the development of the medium. The history of comics is as surprising, complex, and weird as comics themselves. As we will see, landscape artists and the Hudson River Valley have played intriguing parts in that story.

In the broadest sense, placing landscapes and comics in dialogue might also help us create more thoughtful and accurate representations of American history. The awe-inspiring depictions of the Hudson River valley and other sites painted by Cole, Church, and others can be read and understood in many ways. Some aspects of their work supported a story of American nationhood that was destructive, then and now. As Teresita Fernández (2023), featured in the *Women Reframe Landscape* exhibit, puts it, "When we think of the sublime and the supposedly beautiful representations of the 'Hudson River Valley,' we must contextualize them against the brutal drive for westward expansion, the massacres of Indigenous peoples, and the enslavement of African people, all of which were intricately woven into these warped ideas of beauty" (91). In place of an uncritical celebration of these works, Fernández calls for a more layered approach to nature, history, and art: "Anywhere we are, we are actually in many places at once—a concept I refer to as the idea of 'stacked landscapes.' Anywhere I am in the world, the matter that surrounds me—the mountains, rocks, trees, and streams—all hold a great deal of information and knowledge. . . . We live on haunted land, just as Cole's home sits on haunted land that remembers everything that has happened there" (91). The Guerrilla Girls' *Reality Check* on the Hudson River school (see figure 1.2), which appeared at the same exhibit, demonstrates how this "stacking" works in practice.

Figure 1.2. *Source:* Image courtesy of Guerrilla Girls.

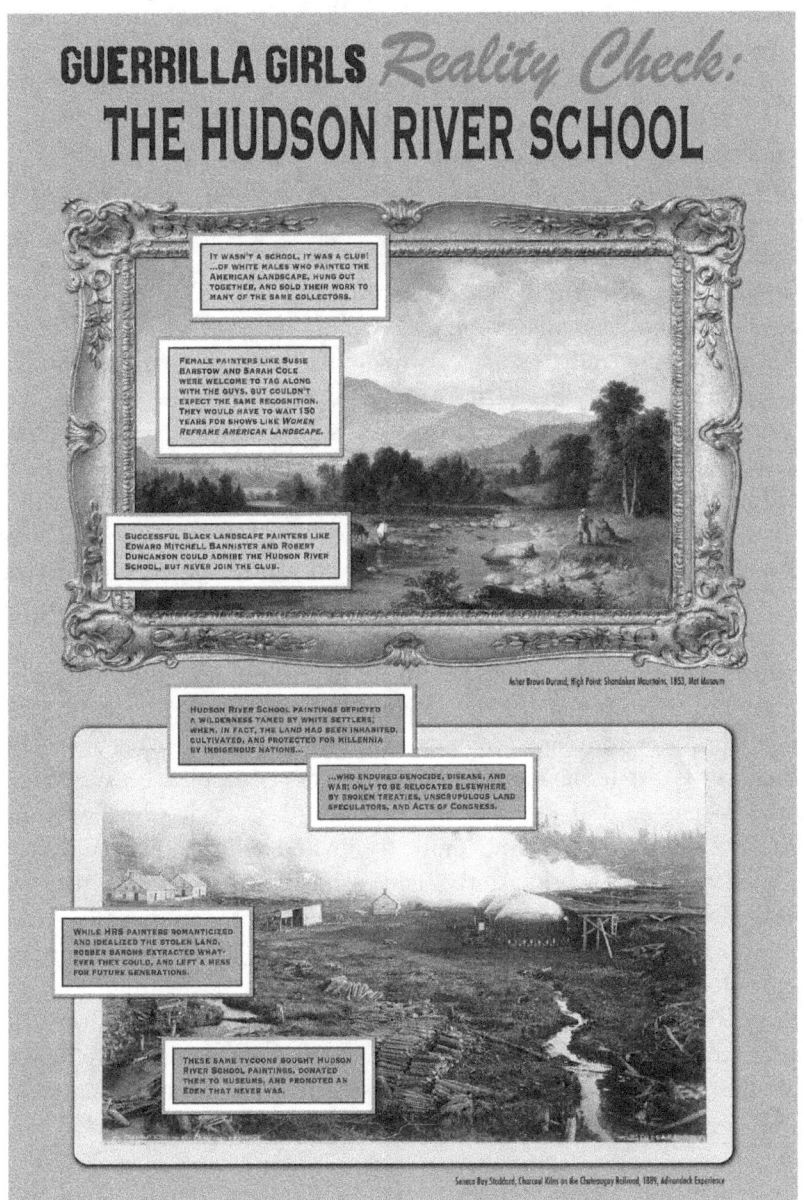

Reality Check places Asher Brown Durand's painting *High Point: Shandaken Mountains* (1853) atop Seneca Ray Stoddard's photograph *Charcoal Kilns on the Chateaugay Railroad* (1889). The charred earth and piled-up logs in the latter work reveal the industrial devastation taking place in New York state while patrons were eagerly viewing, and buying, idealized Hudson River valley landscapes. The Guerilla Girls' prominently framed text boxes add another layer to the mix; they inform viewers about the forced removal of Indigenous people from the region and about the exclusion of women and Black artists from the Hudson River school's commercial and artistic activities.

Like *Reality Check*, comics can use framing, color, and spatial arrangement to engage audiences in reconsidering simplistic narratives. In fact, the panels-in-a-page setup characteristic of the medium provides an ideal opportunity to create "stacked landscapes." Instead of a single sweeping view, many comics combine multiple visual elements to acknowledge contradictory stories and differing experiences. Unbound by the demands of linear or realistic representation, comics provide contexts in which characters can access new stories about the past, test out new identities, and imagine new ways of interacting with the environment.

As we will see in this chapter, Kensett, Nast, Palmer, and Rackham show that these practices were well under way in nineteenth-century cartooning, illustration, and lithography. To understand the cultural context of their work, we will first consider how the Hudson River valley was defined as a uniquely American space by that indefatigable framer of the region, Washington Irving. Exquisitely attuned to his artistic, social, and natural environments, Irving's own work created a vocabulary and set of tropes for understanding the valley as a complex ecosystem. His stories contained both positive and harmful ideas. Irving celebrated new forms of American lore and implicitly invited other writers and artists to build upon his work. At the same time, his visions of artistic and social ecosystems in the new nation provided only circumscribed roles for nonwhite people. Adapting Rebecca Wanzo's ideas about American cartooning and race (2020) to a regional context, we might say that racist caricature is "not a side note" but "central" to Hudson River valley artistic traditions (7). Cultural ecosystems are not intrinsically benevolent: they contain and disseminate destructive ideas as well as fruitful ones.

Washington Irving:
Sketching a Region and Nation

Like the Hudson River itself, Irving's life contained shifting currents. This quintessential American writer was the child of immigrants from Scotland and England who spent long spells of his life in Europe.[5] Perhaps as a result, his writerly voice was fluid and agile, and he drew from a wide variety of sources for his stories. One example of his cross-cultural translations will be extremely familiar to most comics fans. When Irving drew upon English folklore to give New York City the nickname *Gotham* in 1807, he provided twentieth-century writers for DC Comics with a useful placename for the urban home of Batman and other characters.

Irving played around with authorial names, too. Perhaps taking his cue from another groundbreaking and influential taleteller, Geoffrey Chaucer, Irving wrote many of his stories in the voices of alter egos.[6] He attributed several of his most famous stories about America to a fictional Dutch American New Yorker, Diedrich Knickerbocker, a figure later commemorated in the name of New York City's basketball franchise. Among the stories told in Knickerbocker's voice is "The Legend of Sleepy Hollow," a tale that has had long staying power in American culture and that demonstrates both the flexibility and the limitations of Irving's imagination.

"The Legend of Sleepy Hollow" appeared in Irving's *The Sketches of Geoffrey Crayon, Gent.* (1819–1820), a collection of stories set in both Europe and America that established his renown on both sides of the Atlantic. The *Sketches'* fictional narrator, Geoffrey Crayon, introduces the collection by comparing his work to that of a visual artist:

> As it is the fashion for modern tourists to travel pencil in hand, and bring home their portfolios filled with sketches, I am disposed to get up a few for the entertainment of my friends. . . . I fear I shall give equal disappointment with an unlucky landscape painter, who had travelled on the continent, but, following the bent of his vagrant inclination, had sketched in nooks, and corners, and by-places. His sketch-book was accordingly crowded with cottages, and landscapes and obscure ruins . . . [but he left out places like St. Peter's and the Coliseum], and had not a single glacier or volcano in his whole collection. (745)

Comparing writing to drawing is a fitting strategy for a speaker whose name denotes the French term for *pencil*, which can be used for both tasks. At the same time, Crayon's first name and initials seem to connect him to the author of the *Canterbury Tales*. Just as Irving moves between tapping into European and American stories in the *Sketch-Book*, so does Crayon blend verbal and visual artistry.

Although Crayon describes himself as a wayward and poorly focused artist,[7] Irving's stories show that "nooks" and "by-places" offer rich possibilities for storytelling. In fact, "The Legend of Sleepy Hollow" contends that spending time in a secluded spot in the Hudson River valley can actually change a person's relation to reality. Residents of the area "are given to all kinds of marvellous beliefs; are subject to trances and visions, and frequently see strange sights, and hear music and voices in the air. The whole neighborhood abounds with local tales, haunted spots, and twilight superstitions; stars shoot and meteors glare oftener across the valley than in any other part of the country, and the night mare, with her whole nine fold, seems to make it the favourite scene of her gambols" (1059). Irving describes the valley as a kind of portal through which alternate realities can emerge. The area functions as a cultural ecosystem as well as a natural one. Stories related to its natural features are circulated among Dutch farmers, old women, enslaved Black Americans, and Indigenous people who have resided in the valley. As J. Woodrow McCree (2021) has argued, Irving attends carefully to those who have a "strong sense of place" (50) and more longstanding connections to the region than British Americans do. A key component of this connectedness is the permeability between past and present events. Ichabod Crane cannot put scary Hessian ghost soldiers out of his head, no matter how much Cotton Mather he reads. The rest of the country might have left the past behind to focus on capitalist hustle and bustle, but Sleepy Hollow retains the lore and slower pace of an earlier time.

The complexity of the tale's storytelling structure provides an additional temporal blending for us to sort through. Irving's book as a whole is attributed to Crayon, but "The Legend of Sleepy Hollow" is described as a story found among Knickerbocker's papers after his death. To borrow Teresita Fernández's term, Irving is more than willing to show how the land can be "haunted" by the traces of previous inhabitants, whether in the form of written documents or spoken stories.

Some aspects of "The Legend of Sleepy Hollow" show Irving working through the implications of this natural and cultural ecosystem in open-minded ways. Irving's narrator points out that people experience the region's supernatural influences even if they hail from other locations: "However wide awake they may have been before they entered that sleepy region, they are sure, in a little time, to inhale the witching influence of the air, and begin to grow imaginative—to dream dreams, and to see apparitions" (1060). In this passage, Irving extends all the possibility of a fluid identity to his readers and potentially to anyone who comes to America. Your experience of the Hudson River valley will not be defined by where you were born, he suggests to his readers. How will this new place affect you? What might you dream in this place?

But it would be inaccurate to say that Irving's "you" encompasses all potential readers. At several key moments, sketching gives way to racist caricature in "The Legend of Sleepy Hollow." When a Black messenger—presumably enslaved, given that the story is set in the late eighteenth century—enters Ichabod Crane's classroom to inform him about a party at the Van Tassels' house, Irving describes the man as wearing a "round crowned fragment of a hat" and riding a "ragged, wild, half-broken colt" (1072). Irving highlights the contrast between the man's shabby appearance and his speech and behavior: "Having delivered his message with that air of importance, and effort at fine language, which a negro is apt to display on petty embassies of that kind, he dashed over the brook, and was seen scampering away up the hollow, full of the importance and hurry of his mission" (1072). Irving invites readers to chuckle about the messenger's efforts to step outside his linguistic and social sphere. Unlike Ichabod Crane, with his idiosyncratic vanities and insecurities, the unnamed messenger exemplifies the truth about an entire group of people ("a negro").

Similarly, later in the story, Irving deploys a veritable catalogue of racist tropes to describe Black people's reactions to Crane's dancing at the party: "He was the admiration of all the negroes, who, having gathered, of all ages and sizes, from the farm and the neighbourhood, stood forming a pyramid of shining black faces at every door and window, gazing with delight at the scene, rolling their white eye balls, and showing grinning rows of ivory from ear to ear" (1077). Crane becomes ludicrous through his association with people who observe the party while standing outside the Van Tassels' house. Irving includes Black Americans in the climactic social event of the tale, but only as a grotesquely rendered set of outsiders.[8]

These moments coincide with Irving's depictions of Indigenous people. Many recent studies note that within Irving's works, Indigenous culture typically emerges as an appealing, conveniently exiled relic of the past. As Laura Murray (1996) has put it, Irving "dwelt with romantic fascination on the Native Americans' loss of land and life and lifeways, removing Native Americans from history and positioning them in the realm of romance" (212). This strategy serves Irving's broader goals; he seems bent on puzzling out a new way to be white. He acknowledges that Americans will be different from Europeans and will need to engage with the Indigenous and Black people around them, but only in ways that back up the "claim of ownership" that he and other whites make on the land (Hannah Lauren Murray [2021] 54). For Irving, matters are, in all senses of the term, settled.

Defining the land became central to Irving's work during the later decades of his long career. Even as he celebrated Sleepy Hollow's separateness from the hustle and bustle of other American locales, Irving spent the later years of his life firmly connecting the Hudson River valley to commercial propositions. Using his own estate, Sunnyside, as a model, he championed the region as a picturesque destination where people should indulge their own "vagrant inclinations" by visiting, sketching, writing, and spending their money. Several visitors to Sunnyside made sketches of Irving's study, a space that itself celebrated the art of drawing: Two of George Cruikshank's illustrations of Irving's work occupied a prominent place above the mantelpiece.[9]

Irving's writings were not the only factor that made the Hudson River valley a defining location within the American cultural ecosystem. Thomas Cole exhibited paintings of Catskill locations to great acclaim in the mid-1820s, giving the area new prominence as a subject for art; Andrew Jackson Downing published groundbreaking treatises on landscape design; and steamboat transportation was becoming more well established and accessible.[10] But the vividness of Irving's ideas—binding together unforgettable stories, evocative musings on place, and narrow-minded portraits of some of his fellow Americans—still makes them a force in our culture today. Within the world of comics, "Rip Van Winkle" and "The Legend of Sleepy Hollow" have appeared in graphic adaptations of literary works, such as the *Classics Illustrated* and *Classic Comics* series. As we shall see, freer interpretations emerge in Arthur Rackham's illustrated, book-length version of the tale (see the end of this chapter), the graphic novel *Hollow*, and the animated cartoon *The Legend of Smurfy Hollow* (discussed in chapter 2). We will also explore comics that do not directly invoke Irving or his characters but that share his characterization of the region as a portal to alternate worlds.

Before attending to these developments, though, let's remain in the nineteenth century a bit longer. During Irving's lifetime and in the decades afterward, many creators "grew imaginative" in response to Hudson River valley landscapes. One of these artists, John Frederick Kensett, also followed Irving in exploring the interplay between verbal and visual forms of communication.

John Frederick Kensett's Vistas and Vignettes

On the face of it, John Frederick Kensett seems like an unlikely figure to appear in a book about comics. His paintings of the valley and other locations made him a well-known member of the Hudson River school. Fifteen of his landscapes are currently visible to visitors to the Metropolitan Museum of Art, an institution that he helped to found (see figure 1.3).[11] Kensett brought a distinctive sensibility to landscape painting. In the first decade or so of his professional life, Kensett worked alongside his father as an engraver. He turned to painting landscapes in 1840,

Figure 1.3. John Frederick Kensett (1816–1872), *Hudson River Scene*, 1857. *Source:* The Metropolitan Museum of Art, bequest of Maria DeWitt Jesup, from the collection of her husband, Morris K. Jesup, 1914. Public domain.

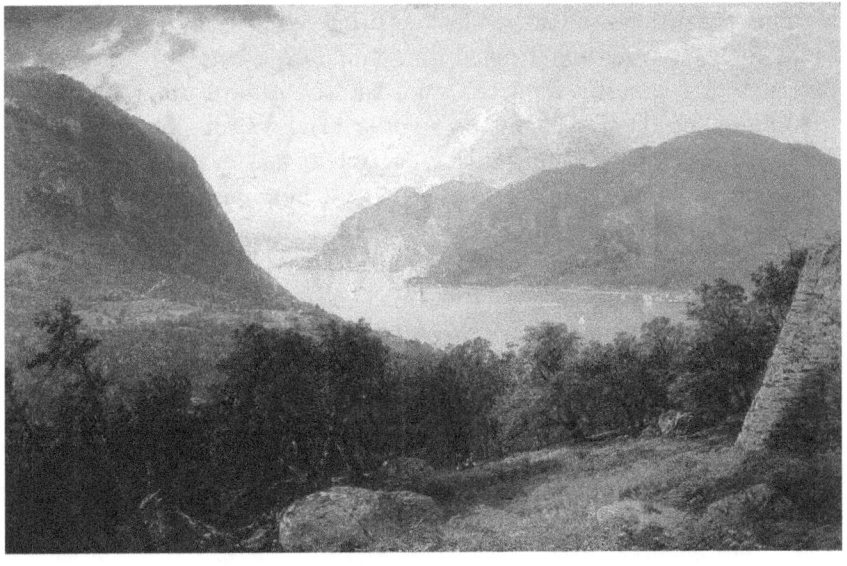

traveled to Europe, and gained success as a painter upon his return to the United States.[12] Kevin J. Avery (2009) has described him as part of a "second-generation" group of artists associated with the Hudson River school; as Kensett's career progressed, he increasingly favored "a more tranquil and simplified" style in his paintings.[13]

Our attention to Kensett will focus on a moment when he briefly returned to the practice of mass-produced art. In 1852, he drew pencil sketches that formed the basis for engraved-wood illustrations to *Lotus-Eating: A Summer Book*, an odd little volume written by Kensett's friend George William Curtis. Invoking in its title both *The Odyssey* and Alfred Tennyson's 1833 poem about seafarers lured into a pleasurable daze, the book takes readers up the Hudson River, comparing it to the Rhine, then moves on to the Catskills, Niagara Falls, Trenton, and Newport. As Melissa Geisler Trafton (2011) has noted, Kensett's illustrations of these travels are an anomaly in his career: "It was unusual for a painter to design the illustrations for an entire book. Kensett never again did anything like this; other prints associated with his work are either single illustrations or engravings copied after his paintings" (104). The scale of his work is strikingly different from his painting, too: All the sketches are under five inches tall.[14] Unlike his sizable landscape paintings, Kensett's drawings in *Lotus-Eating* are portable, small, and funny.

Within the context of nineteenth-century art, these drawings function as vignettes—decorated capital letters or other designs used to fill the margins in currency, books, and other printed material.[15] Kensett's work as an engraver would have given him ample experience with this form. Incorporating expertly rendered mini-landscapes and other innovative techniques, his illustrations in *Lotus-Eating* make a strong case for regarding vignettes as part of the artistic ecosystem that eventually produced comics as we know them.[16] Kensett blurs the boundaries between letters and images; exploits page design as a form of communication with readers; and attends carefully to the relationship between a drawing and its frame. Into all this, he integrates evocative, small-scale vistas that resemble many of the landscapes within panels that we will explore in chapter 2's analysis of twentieth- and twenty-first-century comics.

The text of *Lotus-Eating* invites these creative approaches. Kensett's collaborator, Curtis, both evokes Irving's depictions of the valley and energetically breaks new ground. Curtis points out that his experiences of sailing up the river are influenced by "Hudson tales of the Sketch-Book and Knickerbocker's History," as well as by Felix Darley's skillful illustrations of Irving's work.[17] Compared to the Rhine, Curtis writes, the Hudson is "larger and grander:" "Its spacious and stately character, its varied and magnificent outline, from the Palisades to Catskill, are as epical as the loveliness of the Rhine is lyrical. . . . Here everything is boldly touched. What lucid and penetrant heights, what broad and sober shadows! The river moistens the feet, and the clouds anoint the head, of regal hills . . . [N]o European river is as lordly in its bearing, none flows in such state to the sea" (22–23). The kind of double lens used here, in which the Hudson wends its way alongside the Rhine in Curtis's mind, recalls the interplay between American and European subject matter found in Irving's work.

Nevertheless, Curtis's treatment of Hudson River valley destinations suggests that by the middle of the nineteenth century, rhapsodic descriptions of the region had begun to go a little stale. Once Curtis begins to describe conditions on the actual steamboat taking him up the river, he becomes much less lyrical: As Trafton has said, his "text and sardonic tone explicitly parody tourists, the purported audience for the book" (107).[18] Possibly drawing on his experience as a journalist, he offers Dickensian details of mealtimes: "What an appalling ordeal an American table d'hôte is! What a chaos of pickles, puddings, and meats! And each man plunging through everything as if he and the steamer were racing for victory. The waiters, usually one third the necessary number, rush up and down the rear of the benches, and cascades of gravies and sauces drip ominously along their wake" (30). Dashing from penetrant heights to chaotic pickles, Curtis's prose suggests that he, like Kensett, sees himself as part of a "second-generation" approach to the Hudson River valley that will replace well-worn tropes and practices with irreverent new perspectives.

Accordingly, Kensett's art establishes a humorous tone from the book's very first page, as seen in figure 1.4. Framed by lushly detailed vegetation and rocks, the Hudson River does, in fact, look majestic and "lordly." But integrated into this landscape is a decorative capital *W* formed by the trunks of the trees—perhaps eastern white pines—featured in the illustration. Trafton points out that both the orientation and the shape of the image are unusual for books of the period: Whereas most illustrations were boxy in shape, in *Lotus-Eating* "the undulating edges of words and images fit together as mirror contours" (111). Similarly, the book's third chapter begins with a drawing that hugs the text on the page (see figure 1.5).

While the illustration's foreground features realistically detailed trees, it also contains a barely visible capital *I* that connects directly to Curtis's text rather than to the landscape itself. Silhouetted, apparently euphoric people

Figure 1.4. George William Curtis, *Lotus-Eating* (1852), illustrated by John Frederick Kensett, p. 1. *Source:* Public domain.

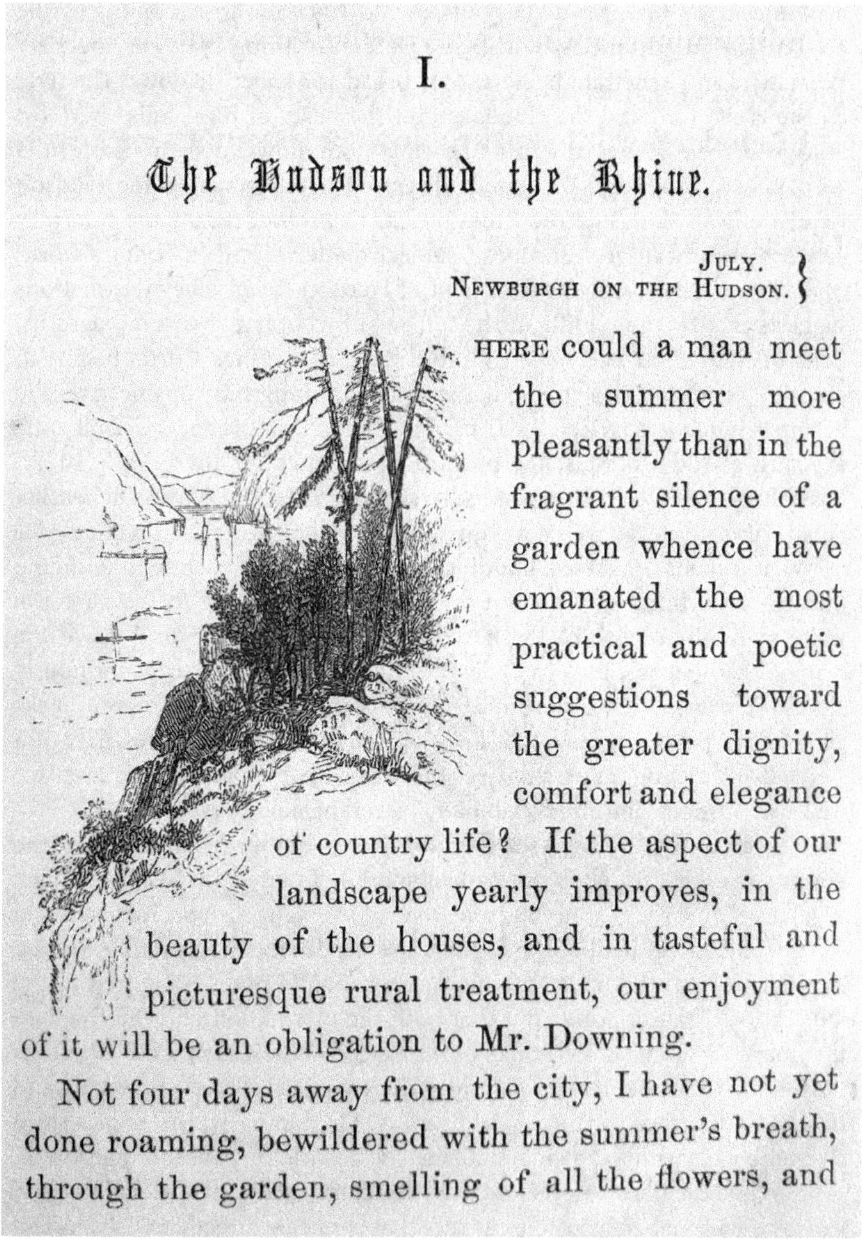

I.

The Hudson and the Rhine.

HERE could a man meet the summer more pleasantly than in the fragrant silence of a garden whence have emanated the most practical and poetic suggestions toward the greater dignity, comfort and elegance of country life? If the aspect of our landscape yearly improves, in the beauty of the houses, and in tasteful and picturesque rural treatment, our enjoyment of it will be an obligation to Mr. Downing.

Not four days away from the city, I have not yet done roaming, bewildered with the summer's breath, through the garden, smelling of all the flowers, and

Figure 1.5. *Lotus-Eating*, p. 43. *Source:* Public domain.

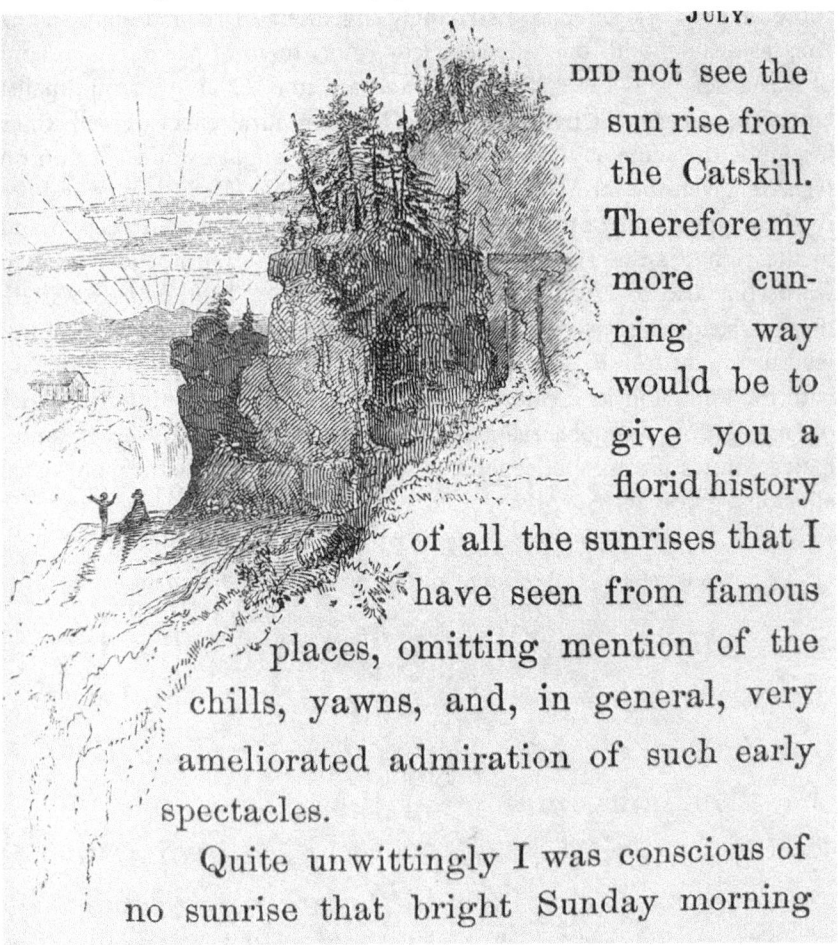

JULY.

DID not see the sun rise from the Catskill. Therefore my more cunning way would be to give you a florid history of all the sunrises that I have seen from famous places, omitting mention of the chills, yawns, and, in general, very ameliorated admiration of such early spectacles.

Quite unwittingly I was conscious of no sunrise that bright Sunday morning

greeting the dawn provide a funny counterpoint to Curtis's description of his failure to get out of bed. In the background, Kensett presents the sunrise and mountains with the skillful economy that became a defining characteristic of his landscape paintings. Relying on white space and simple linework to convey radiant light, the vignette's background would also not be out of place in a comics panel.

Not every chapter of *Lotus-Eating* begins with a landscape; some are merely decorated initials or simpler drawings of plants shaped in the forms of letters. While this strategy is seen in other printed works of the time, some of Kensett's letters are strikingly ingenious in their design. In the chapter dealing with the Massachusetts resort town of Nahant, a garland of leaves serves as both a capital *O* and a frame for another minimalist landscape, as seen in figure 1.6. The *O* has an aural effect as well, since it sounds the same as the whole word *Oh!* We might even see a pun on *vignette*, given the term's derivation from the Italian for *little vine* and the ivy-like appearance of the leaves that make up the letter. With this *O* and in the vignettes described above, Kensett uses lettering not just to form words but also to create intricate visual texts. As Trafton has asserted, these strategies also close the gap between "the act of reading text and of reading an illustration" and place the reader in a collaborative relationship with the book and its creators (113). By implicitly positioning the reader of *Lotus-Eating* as an observant and knowledgeable partner, Kensett anticipates comics creators' engagement with their audiences through visual allusions, jokes, and surprises.

Figure 1.6. *Lotus-Eating*, p. 145. *Source:* Public domain.

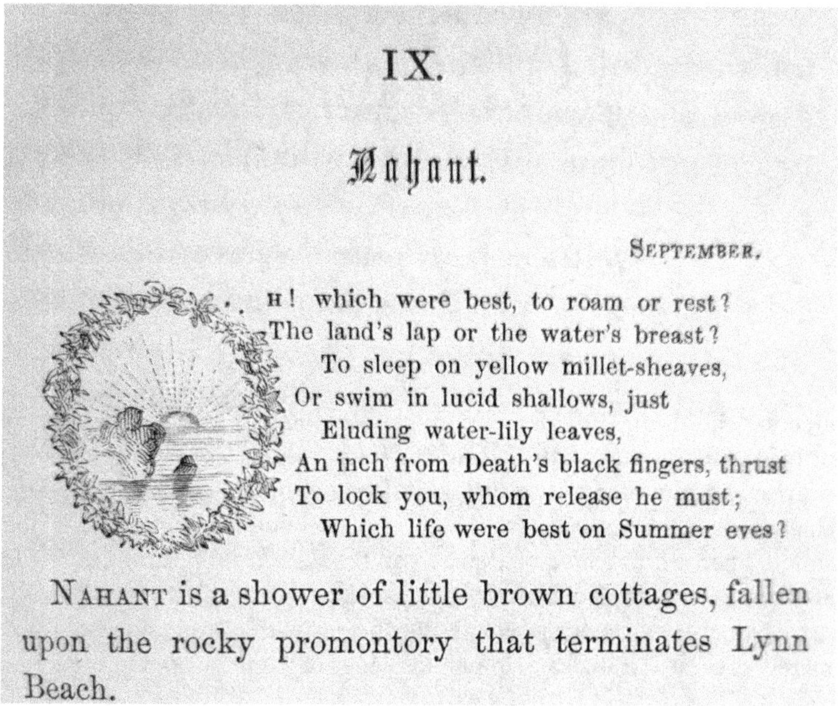

IX.

𝔑𝔞𝔥𝔞𝔫𝔱.

SEPTEMBER.

H! which were best, to roam or rest?
The land's lap or the water's breast?
To sleep on yellow millet-sheaves,
Or swim in lucid shallows, just
Eluding water-lily leaves,
An inch from Death's black fingers, thrust
To lock you, whom release he must;
Which life were best on Summer eves?

NAHANT is a shower of little brown cottages, fallen upon the rocky promontory that terminates Lynn Beach.

Kensett's playfulness may reflect an effort to distract as well as to entertain. Perhaps reflecting the heated climate of the 1850s, Curtis and Kensett have even less to say about social and political struggle than Irving did.[19] Focused primarily on comparing tourist destinations in the United States to their European counterparts, Curtis says little about interactions among different groups of Americans. A fleeting reference to historical struggle emerges when Curtis takes readers to Niagara Falls. Recalling the "hopeless and heartless Indian wars" that took place in the region, Curtis describes military leaders such as Montgomery and Montcalm as "heroes where heroism little availed, for the Indian element mingled in the story, and where the Indian is, there nobility and chivalry are not" (94). The passage's casual dismissiveness is significant. Like Irving's reference to the presumptuous habits that "a negro is apt to display," Curtis's comment summarily excludes a huge swath of people from honorable behavior. For his part, Kensett does not visually stereotype Indigenous people or any other ethnic group in his vignettes.[20] But sidestepping questions of who owns and inhabits the land is a choice in and of itself, with its own impact. Kensett's drawings present American destinations as serene pleasure grounds. Colonization has taken place so fully that it does not need to be acknowledged. As amusing and inventive as they are, his vignettes engage readers' imaginations while also steering them away from thinking too deeply about questions of ownership, exclusion, and exploitation.[21]

Kensett's tendency toward simplification grew more pronounced in subsequent years. In the last decade or so of his career, he painted increasingly austere studies of light, water, and distant mountains. It was Curtis who would become intensely involved in the arts of engraving, illustration, and cartooning itself. He was named editor of *Harper's Weekly* in 1863 and served in that role for almost thirty years.[22] One of the most influential artists with whom Curtis worked was Thomas Nast, who gained fame for his political cartoons. Disputes over appropriateness of Nast's caricatures became a subject of heated contention between the two men.[23] As explored below, though, Nast shared Curtis and Kensett's interest in the Hudson River valley and in combining different artistic modes to depict it. In some ways, Nast's engagement with the valley is a mirror image of Kensett's. Kensett was a landscape artist whose illustrations employ strategies found in comics and cartooning; Nast was a cartoonist whose illustrations show his interest and expertise in landscape art.

Thomas Nast's Satirical Scenery

People and controversy were the lifeblood of Nast's work. An immigrant from Germany who grew up in New York City, Nast's career reflected the heyday of American illustrated periodicals in the second half of the nineteenth century. Nast worked for *Frank Leslie's Illustrated Newspaper* at the outset of his career and held a staff position at *Harper's Weekly* for twenty-four years. In an 1874 *Harper's* cartoon (see figure 1.7), he humorously depicts the media-saturated environment of his day.

While the gentle satire of this cartoon would not be out of place in a twenty-first-century *New Yorker* magazine, Nast fearlessly participated

Figure 1.7. *Source:* Thomas Nast, *Harper's Weekly*, March 1874. Public domain.

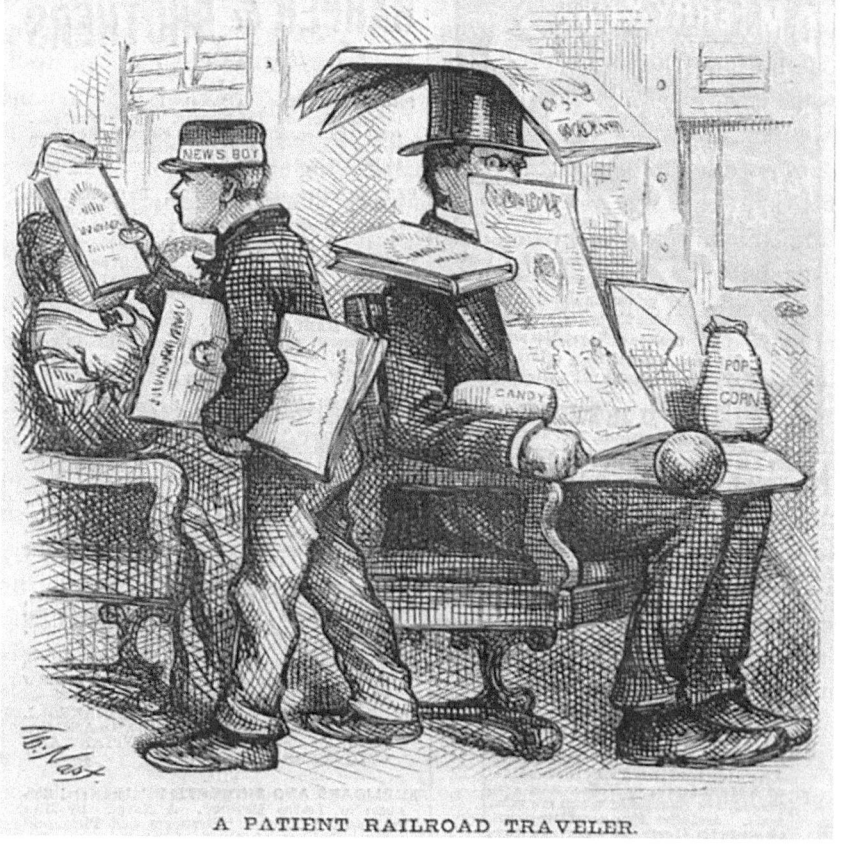

A PATIENT RAILROAD TRAVELER.

in social and political debates. His depictions of Boss Tweed and Uncle Sam became indelibly imprinted in American visual culture (see figure 1.8). Nast's personification of America as a top-hatted older man and use of labels and symbols to support one side of an argument (in this case, debates about a national income tax) popularized artistic practices that editorial cartoonists still use today. Throughout much of his career, Nast used forceful caricature to support rights for Black Americans, Indigenous people, Chinese immigrants, and other groups. His grosser representations often expressed a targeted form of anger: As Morton Keller explains, in Nast's work "the Confederates, the anti-Reconstruction, pro-Johnson Democrats, and the Tweed Ring and the Catholic church were parts of a collective whole. It stirred in Nast the peak of his distinctive mix of artistic inventiveness and political passion." Particularly toward the end of his career, however, Nast joined other whites (including Curtis) in turning away from the cause of Black empowerment, and he proved willing to include racist caricature in his work.[24]

As with many other cartoonists described in this book, Nast combined his activities as a cartoonist with other forays in publishing and art. He

Figure 1.8. *Source:* Thomas Nast, *Harper's Weekly*, March 1878. Public domain.

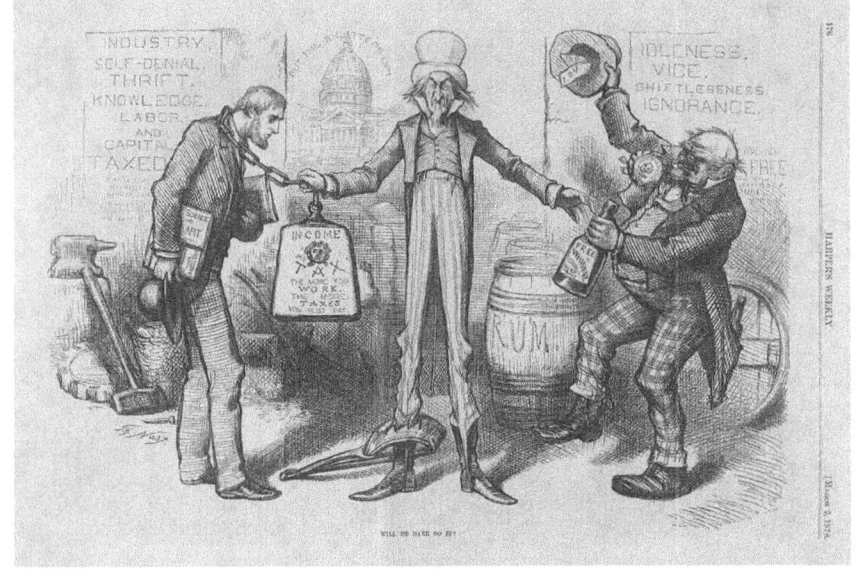

worked extensively as a book illustrator, drawing images for 110 books in his lifetime.[25] Like Kensett, he experimented with new technologies for visual storytelling and engaged with Hudson River valley lore in the process. In 1875, he produced *Uncle Sam's Panorama of Rip Van Winkle and Yankee Doodle*, a series of twelve color images pasted onto wood.[26] By turning a hand crank, children could watch the images unfold before them. The panorama might not quite count as animation, but it does demonstrate Nast's interest in creating sequential art, not just one-panel works. In this format as well as in his cartooning career, Nast both resists and indulges in caricature. He includes a Black woman in the center of a community reacting with surprise at Rip Van Winkle's post-nap predicament. The portrait is a respectful one. As shown in figure 1.9, she stands

Figure 1.9. *Source:* Thomas Nast, *Uncle Sam's Panorama of Rip Van Winkle and Yankee Doodle* (1875). Courtesy of Yale Library Digital Collections. Public domain.

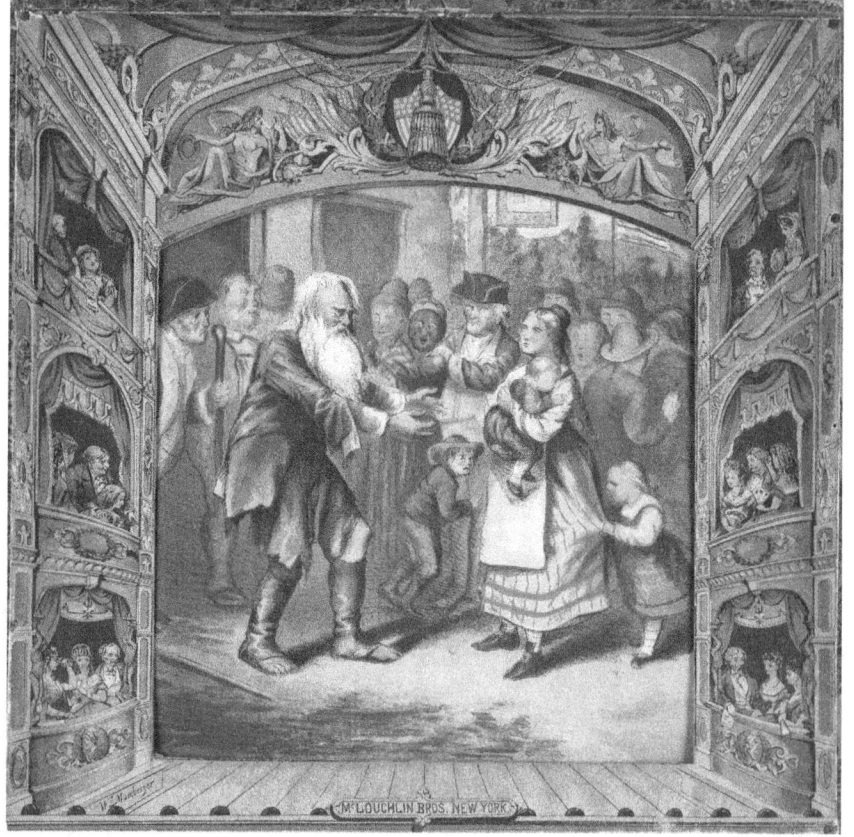

in the center of the group; her expression is no more exaggerated than the faces of the white townspeople; and she wears a beautifully striped headscarf and dress. In the very next panel, however, Nast resorts to careless caricature: When depicting Yankee Doodle's settlement of America, he portrays small and childlike "Indians" fleeing in terror.

Both the capaciousness and the limits of Nast's imagination are on full display in another example of his engagement with Irving's work, as well as with the broader natural and cultural ecosystem of the Hudson River valley. Appearing as a two-page spread in the July 21, 1866, issue of *Harper's Weekly*, Nast's *Sketches among the Catskill Mountains* offer readers the chance to think satirically, pragmatically, and romantically about the Hudson River valley landscape (see figure 1.10).

Like *Uncle Sam's Panorama*, *Sketches* shows Nast's interest in sequential art, not just single-panel work: It is a carefully designed montage of twenty-seven images. At the center of the sequence—and in the seam of the magazine's two pages—flies the American flag in front of the Catskill Mountain House, a nineteenth-century tourist destination painted by Cole and other Hudson River school artists.[27] Above the Mountain House are two carefully framed views of the river and valley from North Mountain

Figure 1.10. *Source:* Thomas Nast, *Harper's Weekly*, July 1866. Archives and Special Collections, Vassar College Library. Public domain.

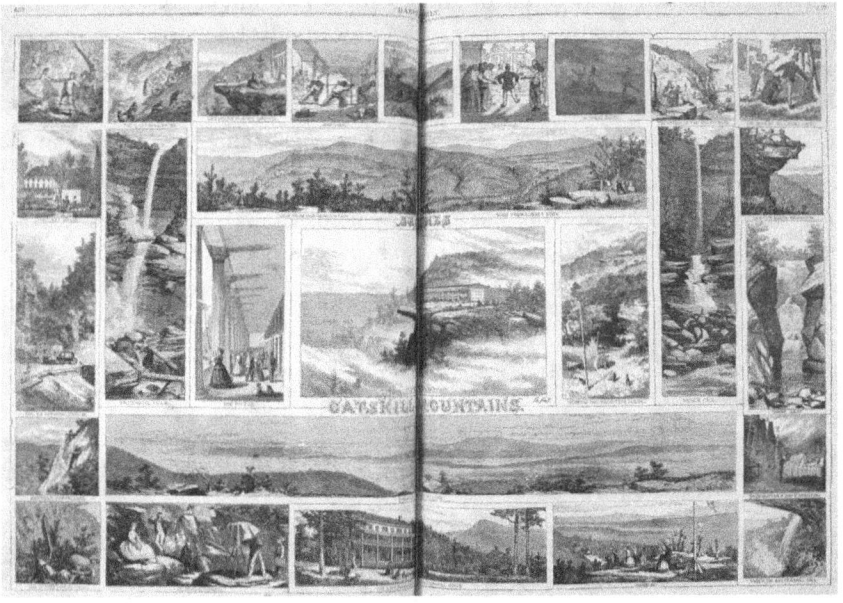

and from Sunset Rock. The panel immediately below the Mountain House has an even broader horizontal span and offers a panoramic view of a Catskills sunrise from the hotel. A smaller panel at the center bottom depicts another lodging, the Laurel House. Meanwhile, symmetrically arranged side panels depict tourist attractions: Kaaterskill Falls, a "Half-Way House," and the Rip Van Winkle House on the left; Haine's Falls and Fawns Leap on the right. In the left- and right-hand bottom corners of the spread, Nast depicts, respectively, the stairs leading to Kaaterskill Falls and the view when standing underneath them.

These twelve images function as beautifully rendered conventional landscapes. In the remaining fifteen drawings, though, Nast focuses on the people traveling to and exploring these picture-perfect sights. The larger vertical panels on either side of the Mountain House suggest a pleasant experience. On the left, visitors take in the views and socialize on the piazza; on the left, a coach approaching the hotel moves on a picturesque path. In a similar vein, Nast's depiction of life "on the road" in the top center of the pages shows people moving through a serenely majestic landscape.

All the other panels, however, indicate—sometimes subtly, sometimes bluntly—that the reality on the ground is far from ideal. With Fernández's ideas in mind, we might say that Nast has "stacked" his landscapes to indicate the complexity of tourism as an experience: It can include both sublime views and unpredictable encounters with nature and other people. Moving from arrival to departure in a top-to-bottom fashion, these panels depict tourists struggling to journey up mountains, becoming disoriented in cliffside clouds, and enduring the embrace of a hungry (or affectionate) bear, among other predicaments (see figure 1.11). Two panels reflect on artistic practices themselves. *The Artist in the Mountains* depicts male

Figure 1.11. Three panels from the upper right corner of Thomas Nast's *Sketches among the Catskill Mountains. Source:* Archives and Special Collections, Vassar College Library. Public domain.

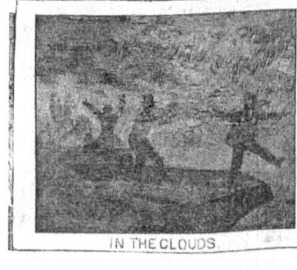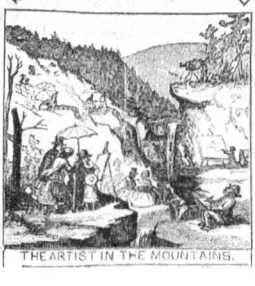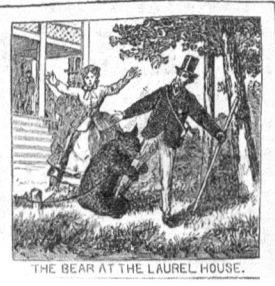

artists and their companions competing for precious easel space, while *The Photographer* presents a more sedate process that attracts the admiring attention of spectators.

While the spread does not, to my knowledge, include an image of a cartoonist, Nast makes use of strategies that are today common within the medium. Deadpan captions such as "In the clouds" heighten the humor of the hapless tourists' wanderings. White gutters between drawings interact in fascinating ways with elements within the panels, such as the vertical white waterfalls that flank the sequence's central images of the Mountain House. Nast also gives viewers a wide degree of latitude in choosing how to proceed through the narrative on the two-page spread. Depending on their own inclinations and reading practices, they might admire the view from Sunset Rock, smirk at the painters crowded on a cliff, or shiver at the prospect of a bear hug.

Like Kensett, Nast uses the scenery, lore, and tourist industry of the Hudson River valley as an opportunity to explore new possibilities for verbal and visual art on the page. In contrast to the idealized, unpopulated scenery in Kensett's vignettes, however, Nast directly addresses the social and political aspects of tourism. He lays bare that a tourist experience is essentially an economic transaction and recognizes the hard work contributed by Black people to that process under unfair conditions. But he cannot tear himself away from stereotype in telling that part of the story. In a two-panel sequence at the very top of the spread labeled *Arriving* and *Departing*, respectively, he notes the racial and economic interactions taking place at the hotel. *Arriving* depicts several Black porters struggling to move a massive trunk into the hotel under the eyes of a frantically gesturing white guest. *Departing* depicts that same guest claiming empty pockets to the nine or ten staff members, mostly Black and presented using elements of racist caricature, who have extended their hands for tips. This cartoon is not as mean spirited as Irving's stereotypical depictions in the "Legend of Sleepy Hollow." The main target of the two panels seems to be the guest's miserliness (or overspending on the trip) and the transactional nature of tourism in general. Nevertheless, Nast's exaggeration makes the porters look ridiculous, too. The presence of these tropes in the work of a cartoonist who often challenged anti-Black attitudes demonstrates that, as Qiana Whitted has asserted, "the lens of racial stereotype has a wide scope in the comics industry" (190).[28]

The combination of caricature, scenery, and social critique in *Sketches among the Catskill Mountains* adds new layers to our understanding of Nast's career. If we remember him today as the "father of political cartoons" and "the prince of caricaturists," we should also acknowledge his engagement with landscapes, illustration, and sequential art.[29] By bringing together multiple "sketches" of the Hudson River valley region, Nast contributed to a cultural ecosystem defined by Irving and fed by Kensett and many other artists and writers. As mass culture and the publishing industry expanded in the nineteenth century, Nast was far from the only artist to put landscape traditions into new and readily accessible forms. As Richard C. Wiles (2009) has put it, American culture after the Civil War featured "a whole panoply of popular journals, profusely illustrated throughout the nineteenth century with engravings of the fantastic and the tragic as well as with beckoning glimpses of watering holes, mountain retreats, and peaceful vistas to be sought out and enjoyed on the spot" (216). Nast encapsulates all these elements in his two-page spread for *Harper's*.

Periodicals were not, however, the only means of disseminating landscape art to a broad range of Americans. Another influential participant in this process was the production of prints by Currier & Ives and the work of their most prolific employee.

The Lithographed Landscapes of Fanny Palmer

Have you ever heard of Frances Flora Bond "Fanny" Palmer? Many of her works are owned by major museums, though they are rarely displayed in their permanent collections.[30] The nature of Palmer's art, along with her gender, might explain her low profile. An immigrant from England who settled in New York in 1844 and lived there for the rest of her life, Palmer served as an in-house artist for Currier & Ives for over thirty years. As we shall see, her talents also extended to cartooning, though she seems to have abandoned this practice relatively early in her career. Landscapes became her specialty, and lithography, her area of technical expertise. We tend to have a less reverent attitude toward art created for mass production than toward individual paintings encountered in museums or galleries. As Walter Benjamin (1935) pointed out in his essay "The Work of Art in the Age of Mechanical Reproduction," "That which withers in the age of mechanical reproduction is the aura of the work of art" (221). While Benjamin's essay focuses primarily on photography and film, he also describes lithography as another important development in the commercial production and distribution of art. Given that Palmer never branched out into oil painting (as did Kensett) or achieved fame as a controversial and idiosyncratic cartoonist (as did Nast), her career might strike some viewers as insignificant. How can art have great value when it is commissioned by a commercial enterprise and designed for popular consumption and inexpensive distribution?

Comics readers know how. We understand that the accessibility and portability of mass-produced art can make it a familiar and much-loved companion in our home. Even as pictorial newspapers were piling up on end tables throughout nineteenth-century America, printed landscapes featuring the Hudson River valley also appeared in domestic spaces. David Schuyler (2012) has pointed out that "many a parlor or simple kitchen far from eastern shores or cities was decorated with prints of the Hudson Valley from *American Scenery* (1840) or colored lithographs distributed by Nathaniel Currier and James Ives. Ideas hatched or nurtured in the Hudson Valley spread across the continent" (174–75). Palmer's work played an essential role in this process, as Nancy Siegel (2011) has noted: "Palmer became the most important lithographer for Currier & Ives, producing both original and copied art for the firm. She was undoubtedly responsible for decorating more American parlors than any other artist at mid-century" (163).[31] In addition to popularizing many of the tropes of Hudson River school art, Palmer advanced lithography in ways that eventually fostered the industrial production of comic books.

The scope and influence of Palmer's work received its due in 2018 with the publication of Charlotte Streifer Rubinstein's *Fanny Palmer: The Life and Works of a Currier & Ives Artist*, which offers a lively account of Palmer's life as well as outstanding reproductions of all the prints attributed to her. Rubinstein traces Palmer's professional trajectory from work as a lithographer in Leicester, England, to the independent firm she cofounded with her husband in New York City. Under the auspices of this business, Palmer created two issues of *The New York Drawing Book* (1847). Designed for aspiring artists to copy, these booklets offered six drawings apiece; their subject matter included landscapes and portraits of people in pastoral settings.[32] The first image of the second booklet offers a view of the Hudson River from Fort Lee that, with its looming mountain and lively sailboat, resembles perspectives found in oil paintings of the period.

Whereas Kensett began as an engraver and then moved into the more rarefied region of "high" art, Palmer remained a lithographer. Supporting the Guerrilla Girls' representation of the Hudson River school, Rubinstein (2018) notes that women not only confronted bias but also had few opportunities to connect with colleagues and patrons: "The Sketch Club and the Century Club, for example, where artists mingled with prominent collectors and community leaders, were all-male enclaves" (25). Even given these obstacles, Palmer's art met with success. In an indication of her talent for caricature, her work was featured on the cover of *Yankee Doodle* magazine in 1846 (see figure 1.12).

Figure 1.12. *Source:* American Antiquarian Society. Public domain.

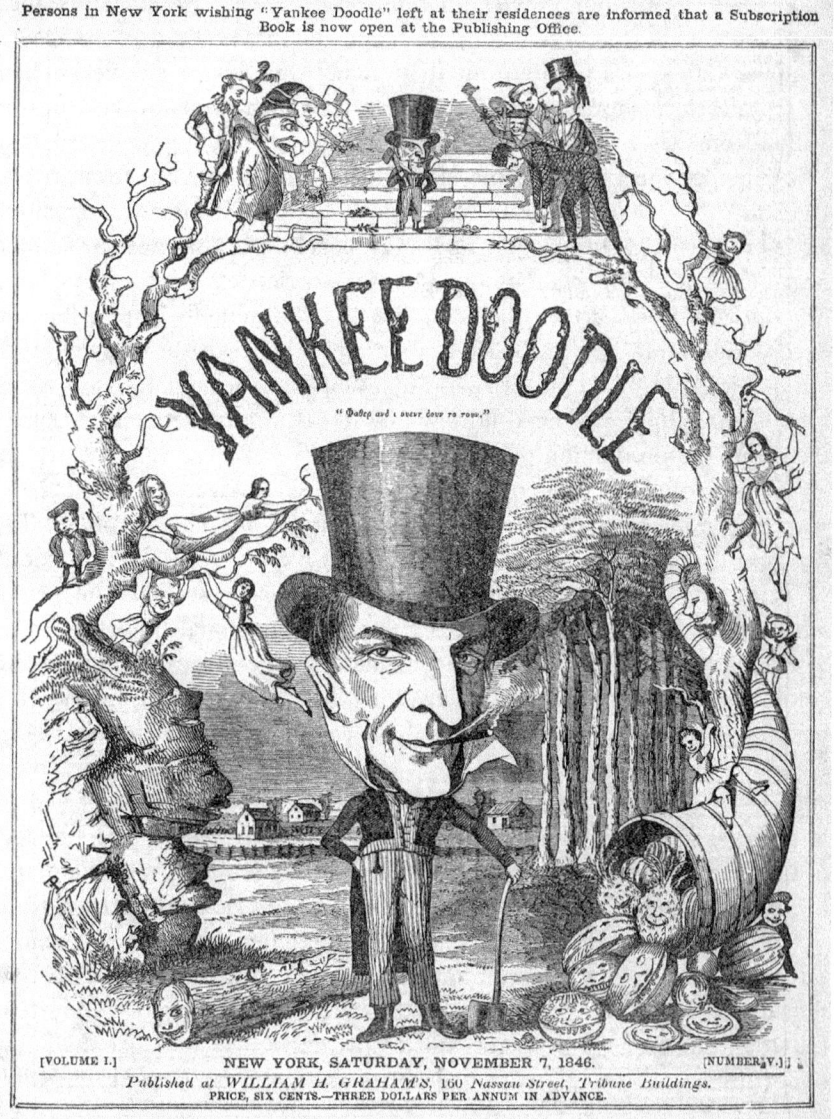

While the smirking titular figure occupies the most space on the cover, Palmer carefully renders the farmland and woods he has mastered in the background. This idealized scenery coexists with anthropomorphized logs that seem perfectly happy to have been severed from trees. Smiling men—potentially appreciative readers, perhaps?—blend seamlessly into the shading and contours of the rocks, offering another merging of cartooning with landscape art. Given this and Palmer's other prominent publications, it stands to reason that Nathaniel Currier took her on as a full-time artist in 1849. As Rubinstein notes, "She was now an award-winning artist whose shop was located right around the corner from his store, and her prints were being shown in the windows of local print dealers" (50). She closed her business, moved to Brooklyn, and eventually became "the firm's most versatile staff artist" (54).

It is at this point that Palmer's work in cartooning seems to have ceased—even though, as we shall see, other Currier & Ives artists created a great deal of work in that medium, particularly after the Civil War. An unpublished and undated cartoon (see figure 1.13) provides a tantalizing glimpse of her talents for it. Organizing her sequential art around a simple and effective staircase design, *Love, Marriage, and Separation* takes a highly skeptical view of matrimony. Recalling Nast's combination of idyllic mountain vistas with tourism-related absurdities, Palmer depicts conjugal bliss as just one step in a much more challenging journey. By the penultimate step in the process, the couple prepares to separate: "No more Love's pleasing toils their minds engage/But scornful words, reproach, and jealous rage." We can only imagine what her full-length graphic novel on the subject might have said. While we cannot be sure precisely why Palmer never published or further developed this work, it

Figure 1.13. *Source:* Museum of the City of New York. Public domain.

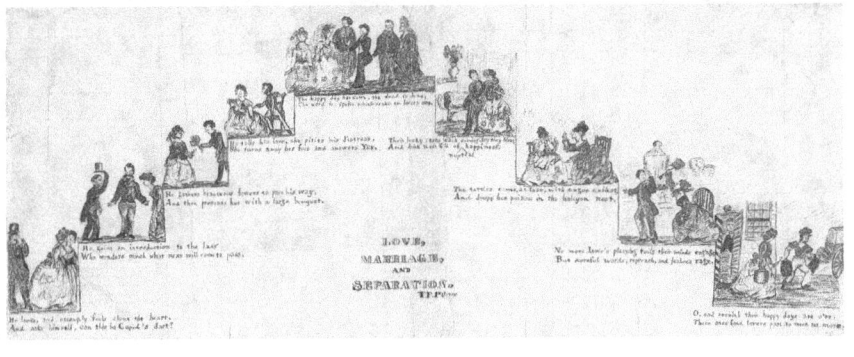

seems highly likely that it struck her as too risky. The social and cultural ecosystem of nineteenth-century America would not support a woman artist's questioning of marriage and gender roles.

The Hudson River valley, on the other hand, provided perfectly acceptable subject matter during Palmer's career with Currier & Ives. Fifteen prints depicting the region have been identified as Palmer's, and Rubinstein finds evidence that she traveled to the region for plein air work. In tribute to Washington Irving, she created a landscape of the "Sleepy Hollow" church immediately following the writer's death in 1867; her work also featured the beauties of the Catskills and surrounding mountains.[33] Like the Hudson River–school painters, she celebrated the Catskills and Irving's stories about them. As the decades went by, Palmer's prints offer reflections on the country's turmoil and change. *West Point Foundry, Cold Spring: Hudson River N.Y.* (1862) shows a river that feels minimized and domesticated in relation to surrounding tree-covered mountains and the sailboats, steamboat, and train moving upon it. A plume of smoke coming from the foundry looks as if it will, as it rises, block the view of the river altogether.[34]

Similarly, the steamboats edging past one another in Palmer's composition *A Night on the Hudson: "Through at Daylight"* (see figure 1.14) allow

Figure 1.14. *Source:* Albany Institute of History and Art. Public domain.

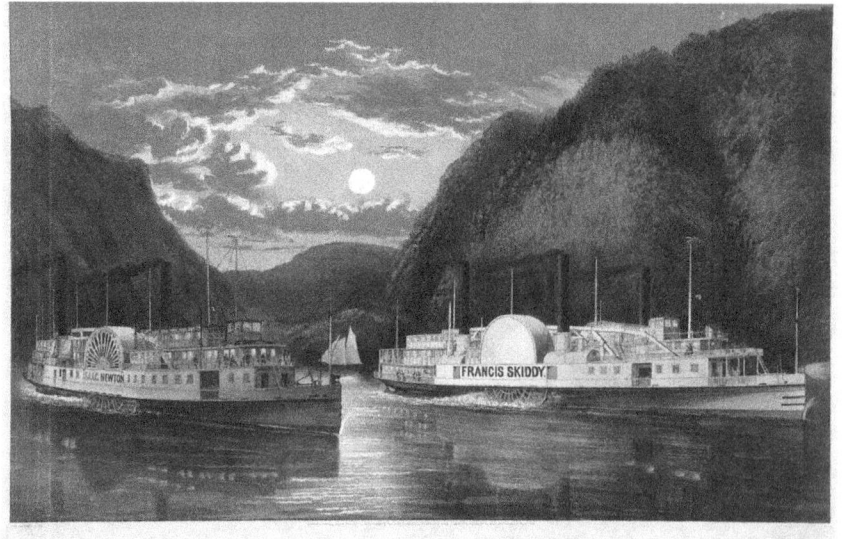

only a small sliver through which the viewer can observe a picturesque sailboat and moonlight gleaming on the water. Rubinstein regards this work as an example of "the bold massing of light and dark" seen elsewhere in Palmer's work (184). Given that she created the work in 1864, perhaps the print's depiction of a moonlit path upriver hints at a positive postwar future for the country. While her landscapes do not offer the humorous tone found in Kensett's illustrations to *Lotus-Eating* or Nast's *Sketches*, Palmer invited viewers to reflect on the relationship between scenic and industrial elements in the Hudson River valley and beyond.

Palmer's forward-thinking approach also extended to the technology of lithography itself. She was a skilled technician who could carve designs directly onto lithographic stones and other surfaces.[35] While affording only faint praise to the quality of Palmer's work, early Currier & Ives historian Harry T. Peters acknowledges that she worked with Nathaniel Currier's brother, Charles, to develop a more pliable crayon for the firm's lithographers. He also describes Palmer as one of the artists who provided models for the women, many of them immigrants from Germany, who served as Currier & Ives's colorists.[36] This aspect of Palmer's work represents another point of continuity between her work in lithography and later practices in the comics industry. When women colorists worked on comics at Western Printing in the 1940s and 1950s (see chapter 3), they were participating in a sphere of women's art carved out by Palmer and her colleagues in the previous century. Appropriately, Western Printing played a role in the extension of the legacy of Currier & Ives; during the 1950s, it printed Travelers Insurance calendars that featured Currier & Ives's landscapes.[37]

As with Irving, Kensett, and Nast, Palmer's work advanced restrictive ideas as well as expansive ones. Palmer's tenure at Currier & Ives overlapped with the firm's production of racist cartoons in the years after the Civil War. During the 1850s and 1860s, the firm's leaders advocated for abolition and supported the Union cause. Afterwards, however, they capitalized on anti-Black sentiment. Most notably, the bestselling Darktown Comics series of cartoon prints, primarily created by Thomas Worth, offered hateful, putatively funny put-downs of Black people supposedly reaching beyond their station.[38] These were enormously successful—one print sold seventy-three thousand copies, and one anecdote told of the Duke of Newcastle buying a one-hundred-print set.[39] Although Palmer apparently did not participate in the creation of this series, her work demonstrates its own willingness to countenance racial stereotypes. One of her early pastoral scenes depicted a Black domestic worker cheerfully enduring rude behavior from a white child, and her Western landscapes regularly depicted Indigenous people as passive or potentially dangerous.[40] Like Kensett's illustrations for *Lotus-Eating*, Palmer's prints avoid caricature but offer reassurance and self-justification to white viewers. Behind the snowy scenes and jingling sleighbells conventionally associated with Currier & Ives is a more complicated reality for the firm, for Palmer, and for the people who bought their products. Palmer's complicity with racist ideas coexisted with her artistic talent and professional tenacity. American landscapes, like comics, can conceal and misrepresent just as powerfully as they show and tell.

Arthur Rackham's Tumultuous *Legend*

Given this history, perhaps the most true-to-life artistic representations of the Hudson River valley are the turbulent images produced by an outsider: the British artist Arthur Rackham. By all accounts a mild-mannered person, Rackham's illustrations are anything but placid. His art often veers from the fantastical to the purely raw: his illustrations of Edgar Allan Poe's short stories "The Pit and the Pendulum" and "The Tell-Tale Heart," for example, would run well afoul of the comics code developed in the middle of the twentieth century (see chapter 3).[41] As we shall see, his interpretation of "The Legend of Sleepy Hollow" involves stark silhouettes, jagged linework, and ruptured frames. Recalling the rock-embedded faces in Palmer's *Yankee Doodle* cover, many of his illustrations fuse natural and human elements. Rackham goes a step further, however, to suggest that humans are not quite the masters of their natural environments that we might like to imagine we are. While fantastical in many respects, Rackham's images point to aspects of the American story that are all too realistic. He does not allow viewers to ignore that the beauties of the Hudson River valley have their brutal side.

By the time Rackham published his illustrated, book-length version of "The Legend of Sleepy Hollow" in 1928, he had worked closely with Irving's stories for decades. His work for editions of Irving's *Tales of a Traveller* and *Bracebridge Hall* helped launch his career in 1895. Ten years later, a lavishly rendered edition of "Rip Van Winkle" and accompanying public exhibition made him one of the most celebrated artists in England. The increasing enthusiasm of American audiences for his work led Rackham to travel to New York City and, briefly, Boston in 1927.[42] Rackham published

The Legend of Sleepy Hollow just a few months after returning from this trip.[43] One of his biographers, Derek Hudson (1960), has suggested that Rackham illustrated *Sleepy Hollow* with "the American market in mind" (126). A limited number of deluxe editions were produced, but the wider run was produced less expensively, containing only eight color plates, with the remaining thirty illustrations composed in black and white.[44]

Like the other artists in this chapter, Rackham had extensive experience with landscape art; a wide range of drawings and paintings offer realistic depictions of specific sites in his native England. Eventually, however, his success as an illustrator led him to set landscape painting aside in favor of full-time illustration.[45] Remarks Rackham made to a January 1910 meeting of the Authors' Club in London suggest that he made the choice with a realistic sense of its implications.[46] Modestly requesting that his listeners regard his speech as "the random thoughts of an illustrator," Rackham noted the difference in prestige between painting and illustrating: "The work of the picture painter and the illustrator are so closely related, and the honors of the profession are given so almost exclusively to the former, that the men of greater gifts feel no encouragement to devote their powers to a minor branch except as a stepping stone to the major." Moreover, the painting on the wall functions as a "permanent companion," while engagement with illustrations is often more fleeting. But this very limitation also provides the artist with opportunities: Because illustrations might only be looked at "for a fraction of time, now and then, the page being turned next," they allow for "bizarre and unusual effects of arrangement, violent actions, exaggerations and other matters of spasmodic interest [that] may find a place almost forbidden on the walls of a room."

Proposing ideas shared by many of us comics enthusiasts in the twenty-first century, Rackham describes the page as a place where fantastic things can happen, in all senses of the term. The very aspects of the page that function as limitations—proximity to viewers, limited image size, and so on—can also carve out a space for strangeness and intensity. His images in *Sleepy Hollow* show just how powerful the effects can be and how closely Rackham's techniques connect to those of later comics artists.

The edition's first color plate (see figure 1.15) sets the tone for what will follow. The most prominent figure in the image is not the horseman himself, or Ichabod Crane, but the jet-black horse whose jagged limbs are completely unmoored from land and are barely distinguishable from dark-blue ruptures in the sky. Human figures are crowded into the bottom margin with terrified expressions like that of the Hessian's head, which

Figure 1.15. *Source:* Wikimedia Commons. Public domain.

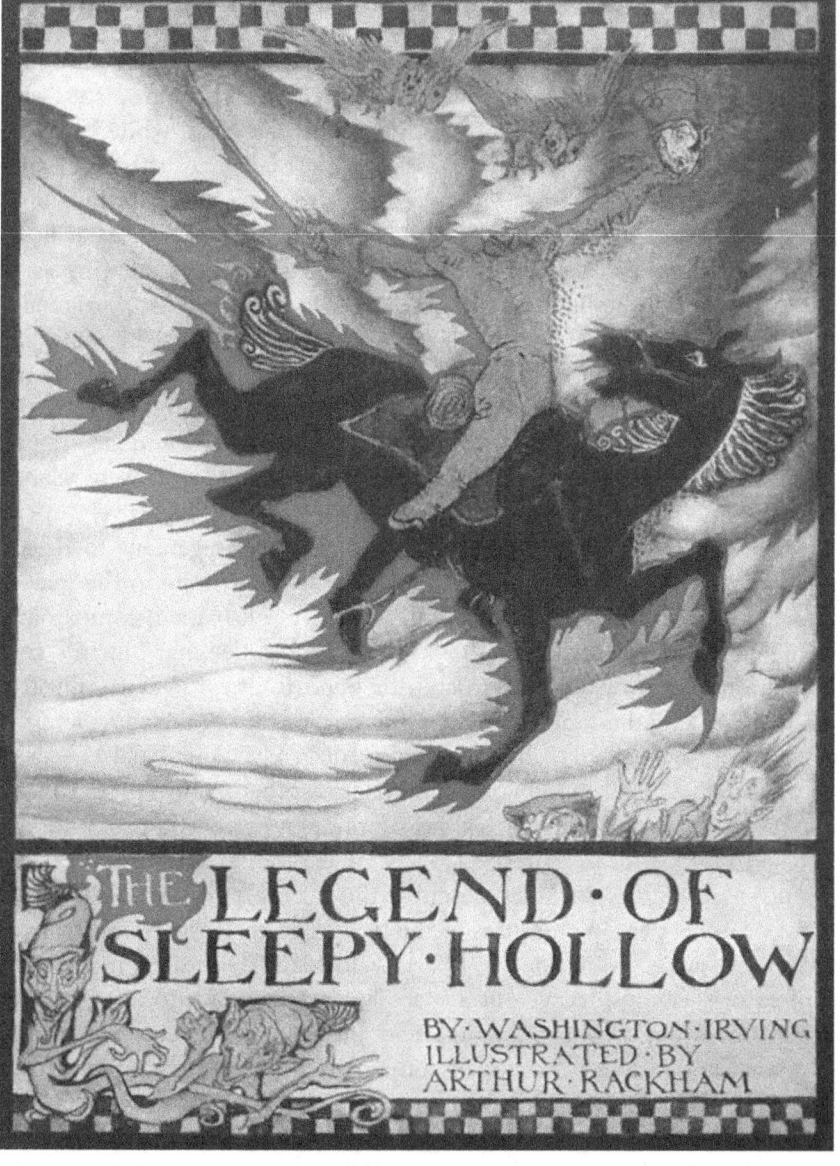

clearly is not in control of the situation. Much more confident are the malevolently smiling elves who lounge in the bottom left corner and encroach on *The* in the title. Neither these elves nor the owls flying in have the slightest respect for the tidy black-and-white tiles that Rackham has fixed to the top and bottom of the page. Within the written legend, Irving couches the horror of his tale in two layers of fictional personae (Diedrich Knickerbocker and Geoffrey Crayon) and hedges his bets about whether Crane has been driven away by Brom Bones or an actual ghost. By contrast, Rackham's frontispiece unambiguously foregrounds the big, bad horse coming after all of us.

Rackham reinforces this impression with an illustration of the horseman after his first reference in the text proper (see figure 1.16).[47] Here, the torso of the silhouetted, decapitated human rider closely resembles the neck of the horse, which does have a head. The image depicts not a horseman per se, but a horse/man hybrid. As in the frontispiece, the sky looks ruptured, and the horse/man seems to have come through a kind of portal. Other forces appear on the ground: a ghastly pursuer prods the horse/man from behind, while a smiling tree gleefully beckons. Unable to stabilize the image, the panel's frame merges with tree roots in the lower left-hand side and then breaks apart altogether in the lower center and right-hand parts of the panel. In Rackham's hands, "sketchy" artwork conveys chaos and danger, not the whimsical details proposed by Irving or the satirical incongruity depicted by Nast.

Rackham's landscapes indicate that natural features of the environment are at least as important as, and possibly more powerful than, humans. A color plate shows Crane interacting with the young ladies of Sleepy Hollow, as Irving describes. The next illustration, however (see figure 1.17), is less conventional. Rackham adds a black-and-white image

Figure 1.16. *Source:* Wikimedia Commons. Public domain.

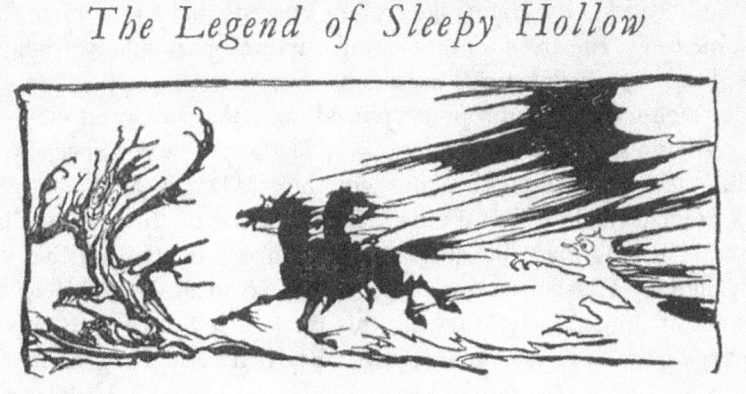

The Legend of Sleepy Hollow

Figure 1.17. *Source:* Wikimedia Commons. Public domain.

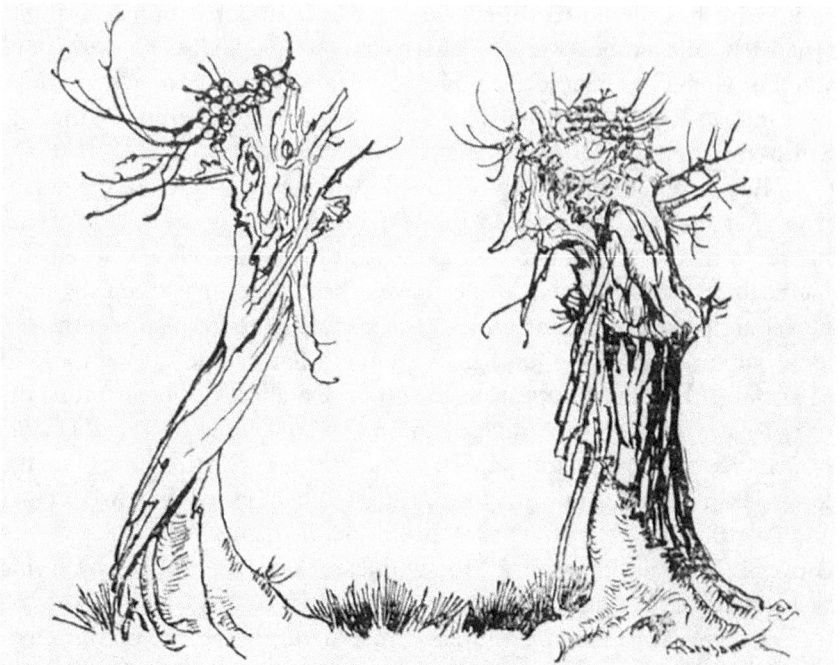

of two flirting trees. The tree on the left actively takes the initiative, while the one on the right reacts receptively, smiling and seeming to gather its skirts coquettishly.[48] Rackham here suggests a new way to regard Crane's intensely anxious response to nature in the tale. While Irving invites our ridicule—he notes that Crane fears not just hooting owls but also fire-flies and beetles—Rackham's illustration suggests that Crane might be on to something. The trees are not doing anything particularly frightening here, but they mock Crane's pretensions, and they occupy an uncertain space—neither fully anthropomorphized nor safely botanical.

The noise of the trees is also part of the problem. Especially after trading stories of haunted locations with the "old Dutch wives" of the town (35), Crane is made almost frantic: "How often was he thrown into dismay by some rushing blast, howling among the trees, in the idea that it was the Galloping Hessian on one of his nightly scourings?" (38). Rackham's illustration immediately following this passage reinforces the uncertain identity of the trees (see figure 1.18). They bend and sway, their trunks

Figure 1.18. *Source:* Wikimedia Commons. Public domain.

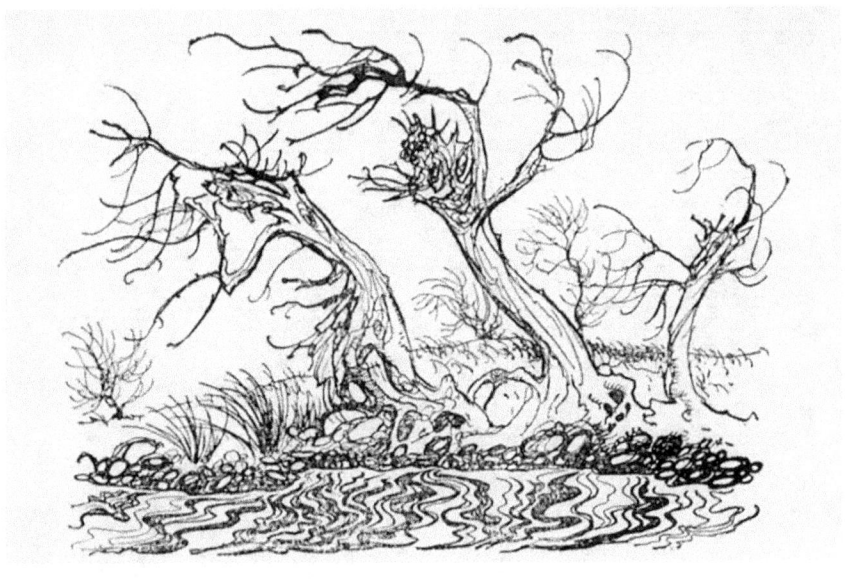

variously displaying a leering grin, vaguely defined features, or no face at all. Complementing these figures are the swaying grass, the agitated pond, and the rocks that seem to vibrate at the water's edge.

In this and other drawings of trees in this section, Rackham supplies visual evidence that the Dutch wives and Crane both have a relatively accurate sense of their surroundings, not an unreasonably fearful one. Crane is distinct from the wives, though, in the predatory attitude that accompanies his anxiety. In addition to desiring Katrina, he has visions of voraciously consuming the domestic animals at the farm: "In his devouring mind's eye he pictured to himself every roasting-pig running about with a pudding in his belly, and an apple in his mouth; the pigeons were snugly put to bed in a comfortable pie, and tucked in with a coverlet of crust" (43). Even more so than Irving, Rackham demonstrates the foolishness of these visions and the vulnerability of Crane in comparison to his environment. Irving characterizes Sleepy Hollow as alluring and weird; Rackham goes a step further and highlights that it is willful and wild.

One illustration (figure 1.19) does offer a peaceful pastoral view, depicting the lovely scenery that accompanies Crane as he travels to the Van Tassels' party.[49] Given everything that has come before, however,

Figure 1.19. *Source:* Wikimedia Commons. Public domain.

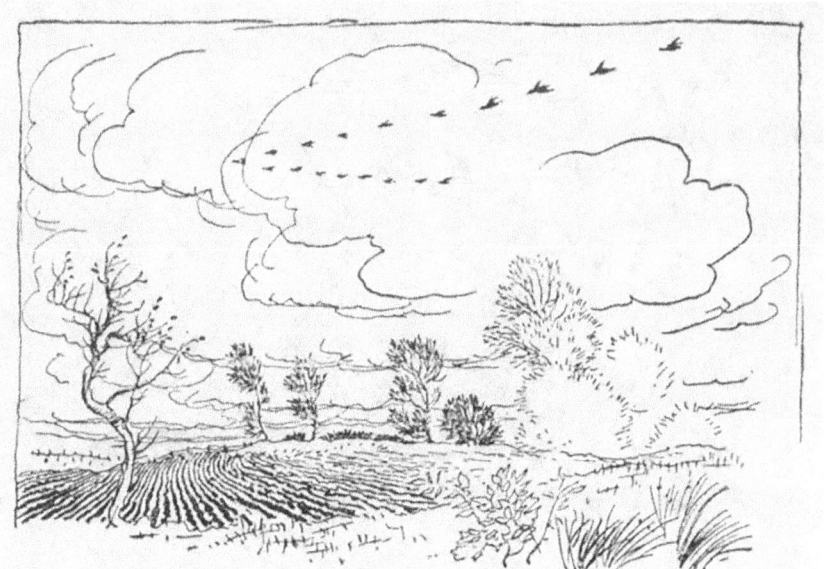

Rackham may trust his readers to notice the broken frame at the bottom of the panel, which suggests the fleeting nature of this lull in the action. Irving's text functions in a similar way: As he travels, Crane "moves through the goodliest scenes of the mighty Hudson" anticipating "the treasures of jolly autumn" and anticipates slapjacks prepared "by the delicate little dimpled hand of Katrina van Tassel" (68). But Irving adds an ominous hint or two. A bluejay "*pretend[s]* to be on good terms with every songster of the grove" (66; my emphasis); a sloop on the quiet river seems to be "suspended in the air" (69). Here, Rackham's subtle landscape reinforces the foreshadowing provided by Irving himself.

For the end of the tale, Rackham keeps his focus on environmental horrors. Not a single color plate or illustration in the 1928 volume depicts the action-packed sequence in which a terrified Crane flees his pursuer, never to be seen again. Instead, the final view we get of a horse/man depicts a story Crane hears before he leaves Van Tassel's house: "The tale was told of old Brouwer, a most heretical disbeliever in ghosts, how he met the horseman returning from his foray into Sleepy Hollow, and was obliged to get up behind him; how they galloped over bush and brake, over hill and swamp, until they reached the bridge; when the horseman suddenly turned into a skeleton, threw old Brouwer into the brook, and sprang away over the tree-tops with a clap of thunder" (80). Rackham's image (figure 1.20) electrifies this story.[50] Taking Irving's image of a skeletonized horseman a step further, Rackham turns both horse and man into bones barely distinguishable from the silhouetted tree trunks and branches surrounding them. The man's threatening, spreading arms echo the movements of the trees, and nothing attaches the figure to the ground. With this image (which brings to mind the transformation of Jon Osterman into Dr. Manhattan in *Watchmen*), Rackham gives terrifying shape to Irving's coy evasions regarding the tale. The specter of death is not just connected to the landscape—it IS the landscape, whether we want to puzzle it out or not. We can attempt to determine which parts of the image belong to the horse/man, and which to the trees—but in any case, this is a much grimmer game than Irving's teasing uncertainty, or Kensett's embedded letters.

Figure 1.20. *Source:* Wikimedia Commons. Public domain.

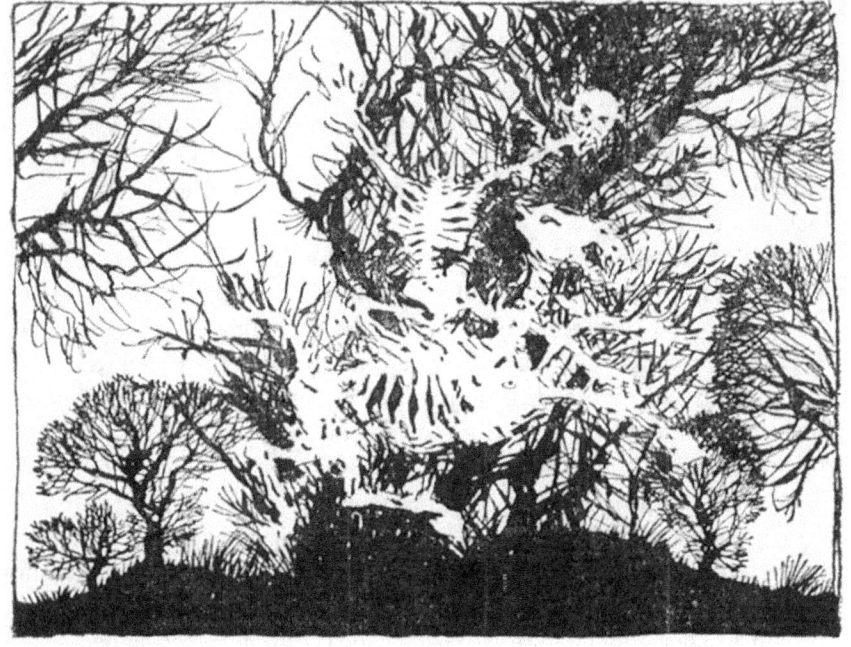

The image brings to mind lynching, another situation in which victims become inseparable from the trees around them. In 1927, the year Rackham visited America, at least sixteen Black people were lynched.[51] While his *Sleepy Hollow* illustrations do not directly address white supremacist violence, he vividly evokes the horror in American landscapes and lore. Recalling Fernández's description of American lands as "haunted" by the past, Rackham indicates in his *Sleepy Hollow* illustrations that the Hudson River valley landscape is not simply alive; it has a consciousness and agency all its own and can be malevolent as well as beautiful.

As explored in chapter 5, it would fall to Black cartoonists such as E. Simms Campbell and Melvin Tapley to depict and resist racism overtly in the first half of the twentieth century through their art. Rackham's sweeping lines and dynamic approach to nature influenced many artists, including Disney animators. Hamilton notes, "Family tradition has it that [Rackham] was invited to California by Walt Disney to work with him on *Snow White* [*and the Seven Dwarfs*]" (140). Although Hamilton did not lend credence to this claim, significant connections have been established by other scholars in the decades since. Rachel Harris has noted close similarities between Snow White's flight from the witch and Rackham's forest illustrations in his tale of Undine (265), while Robin Allan (1999) describes early Disney animator Gustaf Tenggren as a known appreciator of Rackham's work (79).[52] We may have Rackham to thank, at least partially, for what Harris calls the "multisensory and mysterious" depictions of nature in the best Disney-animated films (266). Certainly, Disney's own version of "The Legend of Sleepy Hollow" (in the 1949 cartoon *The Adventures of Ichabod and Mr. Toad*) makes effective use of threatening, Rackham-esque trees.

In exploring how Kensett, Nast, Palmer, and Rackham have engaged with the Hudson River valley and with comics-adjacent artistic strategies, we have focused on a relatively narrow corner of nineteenth-century art. Trafton has pointed out that there were many layers to the "preoccupation with text and image" in the period: "Signs on the street, banknotes, illustrated handwriting manuals, periodicals, and the plentiful printed ephemera such as trade cards, printed advertisements, and billheads, all involved the simultaneous reading of words and pictures" (114). As comics studies moves forward, we should investigate even more fully the connections between these media and the visual vocabulary of comics and cartoons in the twentieth and twenty-first centuries. In doing so, we might develop a richer understanding of landscape art itself. As Siegel (2011) has pointed out, the genre encompasses a wider range of practices than is often acknowledged: "Women created exquisite landscape drawings, paintings, and embroideries, often to embellish the home. That these works were never intended to grace an academy wall or garner large commissions should not take away from their value as aesthetic objects. A painting by Cole or Durand in a private collection likely would have shared space in a library or drawing room with framed engravings, hand-painted porcelain, and embroidered needlework" (160). As comics readers, we know to focus our attention not just on items framed on the walls, but also periodicals piled on tables or sitting, well-thumbed, on nightstands. Produced by a wide range of creators, these small-scale landscapes warrant a place in discussions of Hudson River valley art, along with the grand paintings associated with the Hudson River school. With this in mind, we will turn to more recent history in the next chapter. What new ways of thinking about landscapes do we find in the panels and pages of twentieth- and twenty-first-century comics?

CHAPTER 2

Envisioning the Valley in Twentieth-
and Twenty-First-Century Comics and Cartoons

As Rackham's talk in 1910 made clear, drawings within books affect us differently than framed artwork on the walls of a museum or home. But does that mean that comics should not be considered in discussions of landscape art? I will use the case studies in this chapter to suggest that they should. Often embedded within a larger narrative and involving a more intimate encounter between reader and artist, landscapes within comics have the potential to generate meaningful reflections about places and people. Many of the works we will explore tap into strategies deployed in the nineteenth century by Kensett, Nast, Palmer, and Rackham. As we shall see, the depictions of the Hudson River valley in these selections also often challenge the limited, and limiting, views of American identity at times advanced by these artists and by Irving before them. But that represents a point of continuity, too. It remains as true in the twentieth and twenty-first centuries as it was in the nineteenth: If you want to reflect on American history or imagine a new future for the nation, engaging with the Hudson River valley is a good way to do it. Socially, aesthetically, and environmentally, the region's ecosystem can serve as a portal through which creators can tap into the past to invent new ways of living for the future.

A 1968 *New Yorker* cartoon by Rick Oldden provides us with a helpful transition from earlier years to the present day (see figure 2.1). Oldden's

57

Figure 2.1. *Source:* Richard Oldden/*The New Yorker* Collection/The Cartoon Bank. Used with permission.

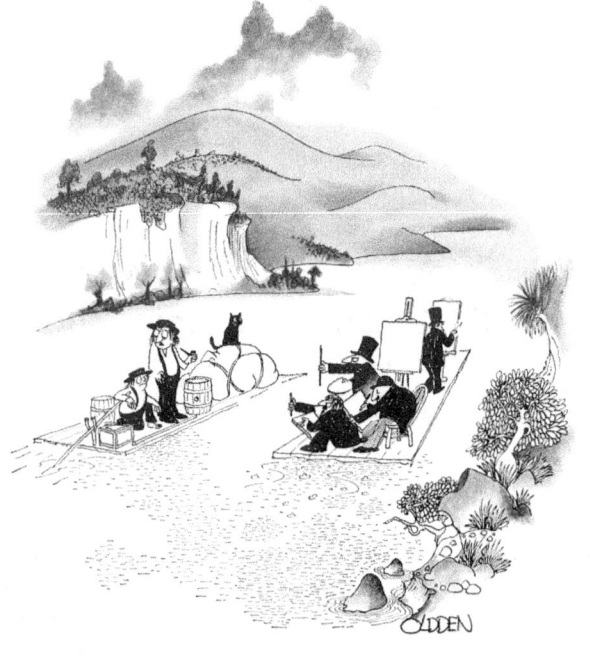

"That's the Hudson River School, son."

one-panel cartoon invokes multiple layers of river-related American lore. On the left are two figures, presumably father and son, who resemble the protagonists of a nineteenth-century Mark Twain story. They wear rustic clothes and share their space with barrels of provisions, steering equipment, and a cat who clearly regards herself as the raft's superior officer. The son looks dismayed about the behavior of the passengers on the other raft, who reflect a different reality altogether. Formally dressed, these men travel on a fully equipped, open-air art studio. Three of the artists peer intently at the son, having apparently decided to render him as a picturesque rural figure; another passenger focuses exclusively on the landscape ahead of him. The father's laconic comment brings home the gag and highlights the gap between two influential approaches to American rivers—Twain's folksy, funny stories of life on the Mississippi and the Hudson River school's awe-inspiring vistas.

As we have already learned, Oldden is not the first artist to depict artists dramatically plying their craft in the valley. We can connect the artists on the right not just to the Hudson River school itself, but to the satirical depictions of tourism and artmaking associated with the valley found in *Lotus-Eating* and, even more closely, in Nast's panel *The Artist in the Mountains* in his *Sketches* sequence. In crowding his raft with top-hatted, self-important artists, Oldden treads much the same ground as Nast's depiction of the overpopulated scenic overlook in the Catskills. Both cartoonists seem to suggest that the valley encourages creativity not just as an individual pursuit, but as a showy and social activity.

We should attend, too, to the decisions of another artist on the scene: Oldden himself, who has taken great care with the landscape surrounding both rafts. Recalling Rackham's sentient trees, the plants, earth, rocks, and water currents in the cartoon interact with one another in an even livelier way than the human figures do. Some of the grass looks ready to launch itself into the water, while a shrub leans comfortably against the riverbank. In the background, trees spill over the Palisades-like cliff. Watercolor washes provide depth to the mountain and texture to the sky. These techniques make the Hudson River ecosystem a living, breathing presence.

Unlike Rackham's *Sleepy Hollow* illustrations, the cartoon presents these features as nonthreatening. It is possible, though, that Oldden regarded them as threatened. In the late 1960s, the Hudson River valley—particularly the Storm King Mountain, site of a proposed Con Edison electrical facility—formed a central locus of the burgeoning environmentalist movement. In a landmark decision in 1965, the Second Circuit Court of Appeals determined that the valley's viewshed was a "scenic, historical and recreational" asset deserving of protection.[1] Oldden's combination of scenery, humor, and lore may well have struck a political note in the awareness of many *New Yorker* readers of the period.

We might even see a semiautobiographical element to the cartoon. Although Oldden lived in Southern California rather than the Hudson River valley, he engaged with a lively community of cartoonists in Laguna Beach.[2] He would have had many opportunities to observe the collegiality, and perhaps the absurdities, that can flourish within a community of artists.

Oldden's cartoon deftly places the history and art of the Hudson River school in dialogue with other lore and contemporary concerns. With this in mind, let's turn to cartoons and comics that invoke the valley in their engagement with American policies, politics, and history. Each demonstrates that small panels can vividly convey the big picture.

Confronting History in *The Essence of Democracy,* *Maus,* and *Loyalty Betrayed*

Like Oldden's cartoon, Fred O. Seibel's *The Essence of Democracy* uses the Hudson River valley landscape to invoke multiple stories in a single panel. Published on the editorial page of the June 11, 1939, *Richmond Times-Dispatch*, the cartoon depicts an event that generated worldwide interest (see figure 2.2). As part of their diplomatic journey to the United States on the eve of World War II, King George VI and Queen Elizabeth spent three days at Springwood, the Roosevelt family estate on the Hudson River in Hyde Park. Among the many memorable events of the trip was an outdoor luncheon held at Top Cottage (then called Dutchess Hill), the president's small getaway about a mile uphill from Eleanor Roosevelt's personal house, Val-Kill. In addition to other foods, the menu included hot dogs, an apparently new experience for the king and queen.[3] The luncheon as a whole was quite elaborate, involving more than 160 guests, a full catered lunch, and musical performances by Indigenous musicians.[4]

Focusing on the event's most famous participants, Seibel depicts the president and king cordially enjoying their lunch despite significant differences between them. Much more formally dressed than his counterpart, George VI rests securely on a tree stump, his crown ensconced on a nearby cushion. FDR mans the grill while perched precariously on a log. (This position would have been impossible for him, given his disability; interestingly, Seibel may reflect FDR's real-life practices by having him anchor himself to the log with a strong left hand.) In a show of friendly solidarity, the two leaders are eating their all-American lunches with (metaphorical) relish.

The foreground alone would have made a point about democratic allies in the face of imminent war in Europe. Seibel chooses, however, to provide a wealth of additional information. A detailed rendering of the cottage provides Seibel with an opportunity to put the First Lady and the queen in secondary, domestic places; they are friendly with one another but occupy a much less significant place in the scene. In reality, the *Poughkeepsie Eagle-News* reported, "Mrs. Roosevelt did not sit at any of the tables, making it a point to circulate around and see that everyone was taken care of" (2). Placing the women alongside their husbands and putting hot dogs in their hands was apparently something Seibel was not prepared to do.

Seibel was, however, certainly keen to give his readers a full sense of the significance of the Hudson River valley as a venue. While editorial

Figure 2.2. *Source:* Lee Enterprises. Used with permission.

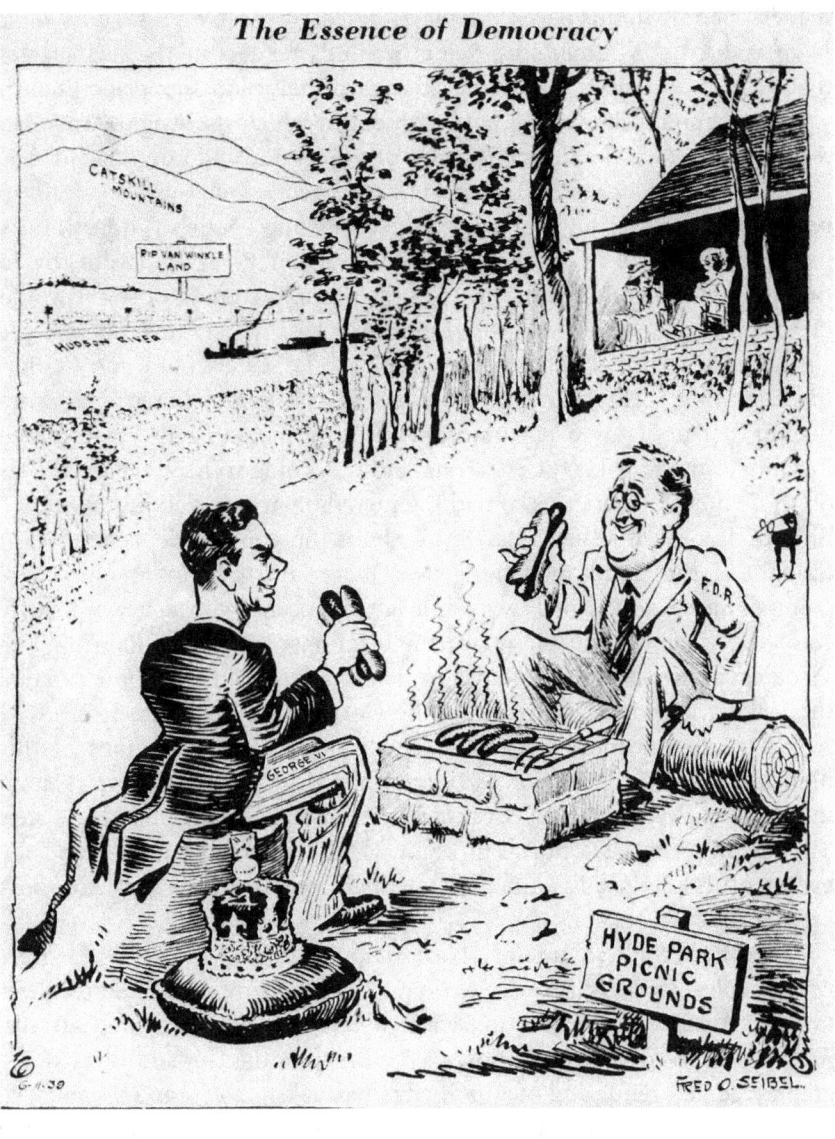

cartoons of the period usually provide little in terms of background detail, Seibel renders the landscape carefully and provides labels for important locations. He presumably knew the area well, given that he was born in central New York State and began his career with several years of work in Albany before moving south.[5] For his *Times-Dispatch*'s Virginian readership,

Seibel emphasizes the broader cultural and historical resonance of this picnic's happening in this particular place. In clearly marking *Rip Van Winkle Land* and *Catskill Mountains*, Seibel reminds readers of the Irving tales that defined American literature and earned their place alongside English works. Geopolitically, 1939 was a moment in which the Anglo-American relationship would develop new forms of connection and interdependence.

In fact, Seibel seems to indicate an element of that new relationship in the darkly inked tugboat and barges chugging south so industriously in the background of the cartoon. The Hudson River leads directly to the Atlantic Ocean, of course, and in the years to come, Roosevelt would do everything he could to send resources across the sea, even before the United States formally entered the war.[6] While Seibel could not see into the future, his inclusion of these boats seems to hint at the grim realities that in fact underlay everything on this trip, including the determined joviality of the four key players. England was going to need whatever was on those boats. "There was something incredibly moving about the scene," Eleanor Roosevelt would later write about the couple's departure. "One thought of the clouds that hung over them and the worries they were going to face, and turned away and left the scene with a heavy heart."[7] Knowing what was to follow, we might almost wish that, like Rip Van Winkle, the whole world could have fallen asleep and somehow avoided the waking nightmare wrought by the Nazis and their supporters.

One of the most wrenching and well-wrought depictions of this nightmare, Art Spiegelman's *Maus* (completed in 1991), also draws upon the Hudson River valley to connect European and American experiences. The region serves as a portal through which readers can understand the events of the Holocaust and connect them to warnings about America's present and future.

In the second volume of *Maus*, *Maus II: A Survivor's Tale: And Here My Troubles Began*, Vladek Spiegelman shares his most terrible recollections of Auschwitz with his son while they visit a resort in the Catskills. *Maus II*'s back cover superimposes a road map of the Hudson River valley atop a detailed rendering of Auschwitz's barracks, offices, and crematoria. Intensifying the contrast between everyday American road trips and the horrors of the camps, the valley map highlights locations that invoke iconic national stories, such as Monticello, Woodstock, and Liberty. Dwarfing the vertical paths of the river and thruway are the rows of barracks and the stylized smoke coming out of the crematorium. The back cover is a "stacked" landscape representing history not as a linear timeline but as overlapping layers of time and experience.

The figure uniting the two maps is a portrait of Vladek—not the elderly man speaking to his son, but the Holocaust-era prisoner in his concentration-camp uniform. Vladek's position on the cover fits the story told within the comic, which defies straightforward boundaries. Far from a linear narrative of persecution and survival, *Maus II* reveals the painful recursion involved in memory, history, and storytelling. As Spiegelman's depictions of the Catskills region indicate, this back-and-forth process is mentally and emotionally taxing. Accordingly, the landscape around his characters does not provide visual respite to them or to readers. Instead of experiencing a pastoral American idyll, Art and Vladek walk through a dense thicket of trees, signs, furniture, and other people. Even their speech bubbles overlap. Although this crowded community represents a triumph of Jewish survivorship, it places additional pressure on the father and son as they retrace Vladek's hellish journey.

Several images within *Maus II* recall the overlapping maps on the book's back cover. It is not just that Vladek faces challenges as he confronts the past; it is that there is no firm separation between the past and present. Time and again, Spiegelman visually connects Vladek's European past with the forests, roads, and hills of New York. Given the anti-Semitic rhetoric and violence that continue to erupt within Hudson River valley communities well into the twenty-first century, these images remain all too accurate. Moreover, Vladek's own harsh reaction to a Black hitchhiker they pick up during their travels demonstrates the pervasiveness of racist thought, even among those who have been the victims of it.

In its depiction of the Catskills as a crowded summer retreat, its collapsing of the distance between the present and the past, and its refusal to look away from devastating truths, *Maus II* provides a corrective to romanticized depictions of the valley and of America as a whole. As shown in chapter 1, nineteenth-century artists expressed skepticism about idealized landscapes, too: Nast's *Sketches among the Catskill Mountains* depicts sites just as jam-packed with vacationers as the one in *Maus II*. In depicting Vladek and Art making their way through well-trodden paths and poolside bingo games, *Maus II* also emphasizes ordinary sights in a way that recalls Irving's *Sketch-Book*. Like the "unlucky landscape painter" described by Geoffrey Crayon, *Maus II* focuses on "nooks, and corners, and by-places" in describing important interactions between Vladek and

Art. A landscape "crowded with cottages" may not be the most scenic vista, but perhaps it provides father and son with a reassuringly mundane backdrop for their talks about the horrors of Auschwitz.

While *Maus II*'s panels connect the Catskills to a global catastrophe, the comic *Loyalty Betrayed* by Lee Francis IV and Weshoyot Alvitre depicts atrocities that took place in the Hudson River valley itself. As with *Maus II*, the broader story emerges through attention to a father and son—in this case, Daniel and Abraham Nimham, leaders of the Wappinger people who joined other Indigenous soldiers in a group known as the "Stockbridge Militia" that supported the American side during the Revolutionary War.[8] On August 31, 1778, the militia was ambushed by British and Hessian soldiers near the site of Van Cortlandt park in the northern reaches of the Bronx, leading to the deaths of Daniel, Abraham, and many of their comrades. As seen in figure 2.3, Alvitre's panel starkly depicts the destruction. Leafless tree trunks provide a visual echo for the fallen and wounded warriors scattered across the battlefield, which Alvitre renders in a bleak palette of pale tan and green.

The losses did not end there: Instead of acknowledging the militia's contributions, the postwar American government forced the Stockbridge Mohicans to move west. Survivance and commemoration, however, are also part of the story. The comic concludes with present-day Indigenous veterans visiting the memorial to the militia that was built in 1906 and still resides within Van Cortlandt Park today (see figure 2.4).

Alvitre foregrounds the veterans, ensuring that they loom as large in the panel as does the memorial itself. In this way, she ensures that readers attend to the present-day Indigenous people reacting to the events, not

Figure 2.3. *Source:* Smithsonian Institution, National Museum of the American Indian. Used with permission.

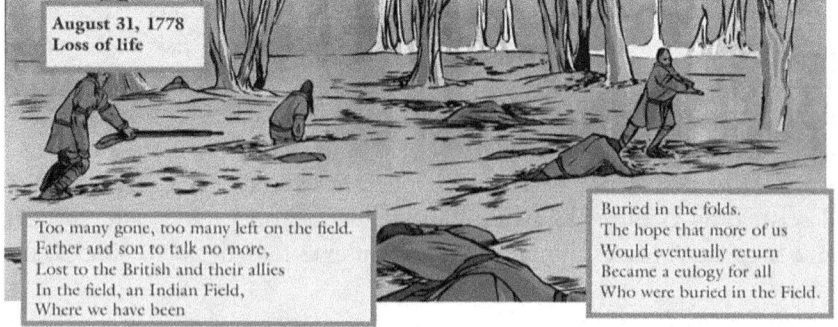

Figure 2.4. *Source:* Smithsonian Institution, National Museum of the American Indian. Used with permission.

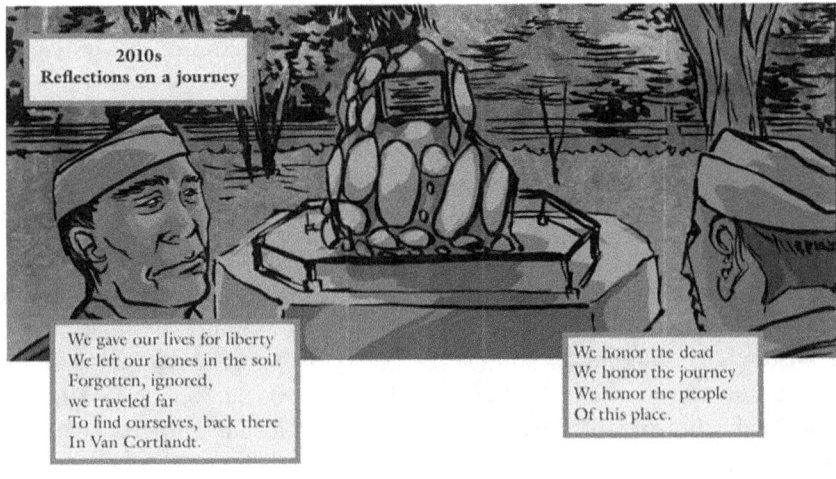

just to the historical events marked by the memorial. Colors intensify this message; the final panel of the comic is colored with rich browns and greens, not with the pallid washes seen in the battlefield scene. Unlike the Indians depicted symbolically or decoratively in the landscapes created by Palmer and so many other American artists, Alvitre's veterans take the lead in framing how we think about the region and its history.

This message is further supported by the comic's place within a larger conversation. *Loyalty Betrayed* is one comic in *Telling Stories with Pictures: Collected Comics from "Native New York,"* an anthology created as a companion to the exhibit *Native New York* launched in 2021 at the National Museum of the American Indian in New York City. As of this writing, the exhibit is still on display, and the entire anthology is offered in open-access format online. Designed for a wide variety of readers, *Telling Stories with Pictures* not only corrects omissions and obfuscations in American history but also offers ways for us to envision the Hudson River valley's history in relationship to other regions. Instead of depicting settlement as a fait accompli, Francis and Alvitre present history as a recursive process of departure and return, devastation and renewal. We might apply this insight to comics culture itself. *Telling Stories with Pictures* demonstrates how Indigenous comics creators can shape accessible and powerful stories despite the medium's often-harmful depictions of native people.[9] Creative and critical engagement with the past can generate forward-thinking narratives.

Fantasy genres can play an important role in this process as well, as demonstrated by the next three works we will explore. By weaving the region's history into richly detailed fictional worlds, these works bring to light new ways of interacting with our natural and cultural ecosystems.

Immersive and Inventive Environments in
Sailor Twain, The Legend of Smurfy Hollow, and *Spill Zone*

Set in the nineteenth century and featuring exactly the kinds of visual ephemera of the period described in chapter 1—signs, maps, books, and so on—Mark Siegel's graphic novel *Sailor Twain: Or, the Mermaid in the Hudson* (2012) offers an unnerving blend of history and fantasy. The plot focuses on a steamboat's crew and passengers, as well as an alluring mermaid who finds her way onto the watercraft and into the hearts of several nearby humans.

Recalling Rettig's idea of "rivering," Siegel's art presents the Hudson River as a living, breathing presence. It dominates *Sailor Twain*'s story and the visual space of its pages. The comic's grayscale palette, with subtle pencil shading, allows Siegel to blur the distinctions among the river, the land, and the atmosphere surrounding it. At times, Siegel depicts this environment with panels evocative of landscapes produced by Palmer, Kensett, and other nineteenth-century landscape artists, as in figure 2.5.

Figure 2.5. *Source:* From *Sailor Twain: Or: The Mermaid in the Hudson*, by Mark Siegel. Copyright © 2012 by Mark Siegel. Reprinted by permission of First Second, an imprint of Roaring Brook Press, a division of Holtzbrinck Publishing Holdings Limited Partnership. All Rights Reserved.

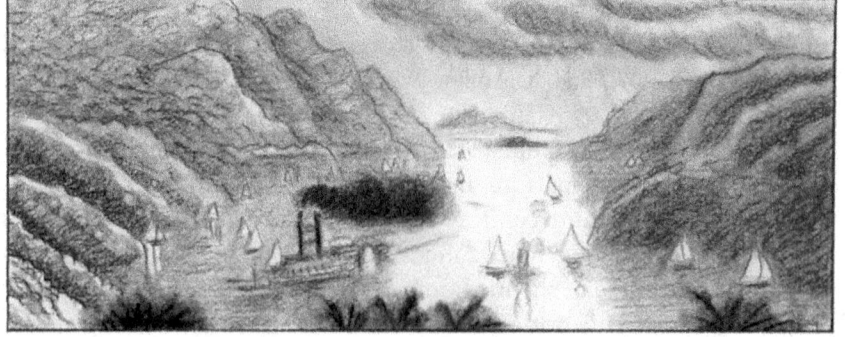

Even in this relatively idyllic scene, the dark smudge of smoke coming from the steamboat hints at more ominous realities. Other panels, such as figure 2.6, make clear that the threat comes not just from human-made transportation but also from the natural environment itself. Massive storms are only part of the problem: Several characters give way to ardent and even destructive desires conjured up in the Hudson's roiling waters. As in Rackham's *Sleepy Hollow*, Siegel creates landscapes that pointedly challenge humans' ability to navigate the natural world and their own emotions.

Sailor Twain also evokes another aspect of the *Sleepy Hollow* story. As depicted by Irving, Ichabod Crane quivers with avarice as well as lust: He finds the plenitude of the Van Tassels' farm just as alluring as Katrina's appearance. Similarly, Siegel's tale depicts greed as a driving force in the region. The steamboat and even the river itself function as money-driven workspaces: Readers get close-up views of the filthy, exhausting work done by crewmen who shovel coal into the steamboat's boiler. Ornate dress and

Figure 2.6. *Source:* From *Sailor Twain: Or: The Mermaid in The Hudson,* by Mark Siegel. Copyright © 2012 by Mark Siegel. Reprinted by permission of First Second, an imprint of Roaring Brook Press, a division of Holtzbrinck Publishing Holdings Limited Partnership. All Rights Reserved.

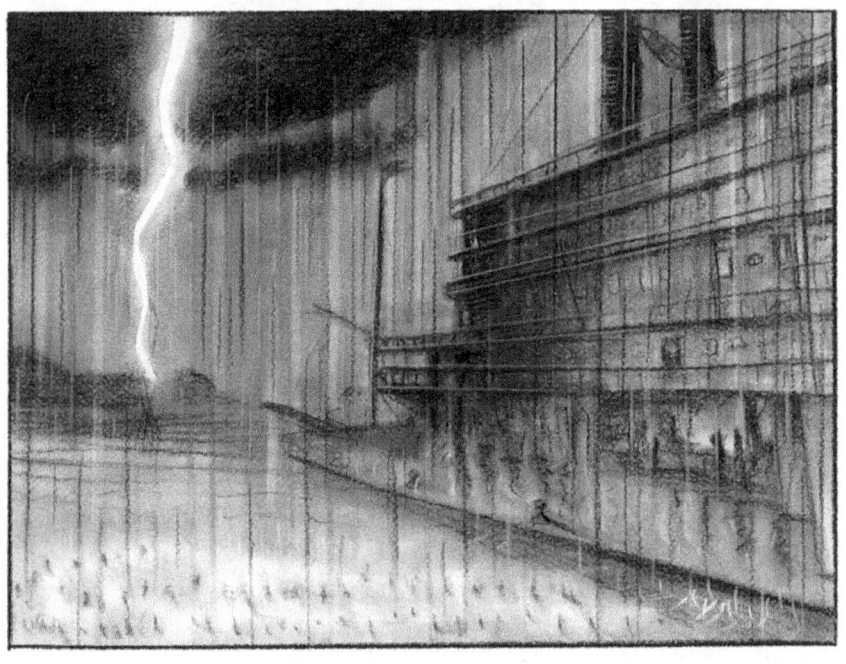

décor separate full-freight tourists from servants and crew, while floridly written ads lure potential tourists. When one character calls the whole scenario a "prison," the accuracy of her description is borne out by ample visual and narrative evidence. Like a view seen through clouds of smog, the comic's landscapes offer beauty without a lot of breathing room. Intertwined with *Sailor Twain*'s fantasy elements is a realistic rendering of nineteenth-century industrial pollution. Siegel's use of black-and-white charcoal for his art seems particularly apt for portraying the coal-generated fumes enveloping most of the story's action.

A simultaneously sublime and polluted landscape also emerges in *Spill Zone*, a work in two volumes (2017 and 2018) created by writer Scott Westerfeld, artist Alex Puvilland, and colorist Hilary Sycamore (see figure 2.7).[10] Visually, the comic could not be more different from *Sailor*

Figure 2.7. *Source:* Excerpt from *Spill Zone Book 2: The Broken Vow*, by Scott Westerfeld, illustrated by Alex Puvilland. Copyright © 2018 by Scott Westerfeld. Reprinted by permission of First Second, an imprint of Roaring Brook Press, a division of Holtzbrinck Publishing Holdings Limited Partnership. All Rights Reserved.

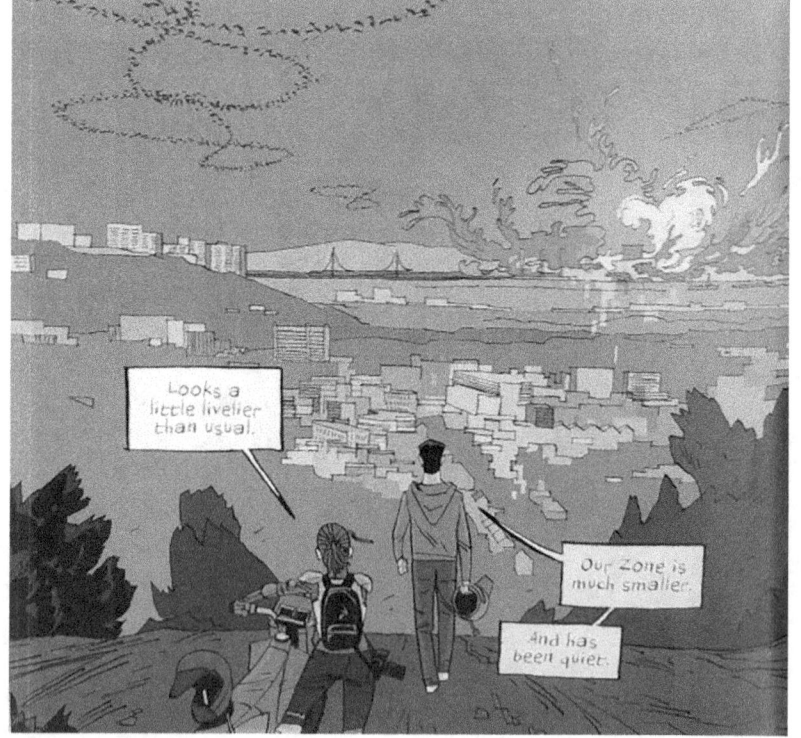

Twain. Instead of moody grays and blacks, *Spill Zone* confronts readers with day-glo pinks, yellows, purples, and oranges—most spectacularly in the eponymous disaster area, which covers the heart of the city of Poughkeepsie. But like *Sailor Twain*, *Spill Zone* presents the Hudson River valley as a beautiful and dangerous space that can function as a portal to alternative realities. Instead of the mermaid-controlled depths of the river, Westerfeld connects the region to a mysterious space-time disruption. An initial eruption in Poughkeepsie kills many residents; three years after the event, the "spill zone" remains cordoned off and filled with toxic dust. Centered around orphaned survivors Addie Merritt and her younger sister, Lexa, *Spill Zone* combines fantastical elements with realism, satire, and climate fiction tropes. Westerfeld is a graduate of Vassar College, and *Spill Zone* captures the greater Poughkeepsie area's scenic vistas and quirky landmarks, such as the iconic Hoe Bowl bowling alley pictured at a climactic moment in Book 2.

Like *Sailor Twain*, *Spill Zone* combines elements of fantasy with factors that are all too real, such as the evisceration of Poughkeepsie's once-thriving downtown with arterial highways, the economic challenges confronted by many residents of the city, and the environmental toll of the factories that formerly populated the area (including, as we will see, Western Printing).

Especially given the intensity of Sycamore's colors, *Spill Zone* suggests that there is something excessive about the sense of place in the Hudson River valley—too many industries; too dense an artistic legacy; too poignant a contrast between the prosperous past and the challenging present. But Westerfeld cuts through this potentially stultifying set of circumstances with a splendid main character. Resilient and unsentimental, Addie capitalizes on her friendships and artistic talent to uncover key truths about what happened and to quash threats to her community. She also remains open to new relationships; she allies with Don Jae, a survivor of a similar disruption in North Korea, to address the root causes of the disaster. Confronting reality and forging new partnerships, rather than succumbing to anxiety or nostalgia, are useful practices for characters within *Spill Zone*, as well as for modern-day citizens of the Hudson River valley and beyond.

Lessons in community engagement also crop up in a seemingly unlikely place: *The Legend of Smurfy Hollow* (2013), a twenty-two-minute, direct-to-video animated film directed by Stephan Franck and written by Todd Berger. Although generally more lighthearted in tone than either *Sailor Twain* or *Spill Zone*, *Smurfy Hollow* offers younger audiences a fantasy story with real-world lessons.

Berger's script connects to Irving's work both by retelling the Headless Horseman story and by placing an extra narrative frame around the tale. Whereas Irving told the story through the persona of Diedrich Knickerbocker, *Smurfy Hollow* opens with stop-motion Smurfs telling scary stories around a campfire. One of those tales, which involves an encounter with the Headless Horseman, unfolds as an animated cartoon told in flashback.

Within this story, the Smurfs learn that the natural world around them is not a playground or consumer paradise. Hoping to best Brainy Smurf (voiced by Fred Armisen) in the annual Smurfberry-gathering contest, Gutsy Smurf (Alan Cumming) follows him into the hollow despite having heard stories about the area's dangers. Recalling the rapaciousness of Ichabod Crane amid the abundance of the Van Tassels' farm, Gutsy Smurf scares off Brainy with a jerry-rigged horseman, pounces upon Brainy's trove of Smurfberries, and considers his victory assured. Soon, however, unexpected challenges arise in the form of bats, looming trees, and the Smurfs' nemesis, Gargamel. Lured into one of Gargamel's traps, three Smurfs find themselves suspended in a lovely but threatening landscape. They fall silent, and the film's motion and sound come to a halt. The Smurfs usually appear in close-up, but at this moment they appear as small and vulnerable bits of blue within a much larger vista (see figure 2.8). The scene evokes the glowing colors and carefully rendered vegetation

Figure 2.8. As in other versions of Irving's tale, the Smurfs face a dangerous predicament in a pastoral setting. *Source: The Smurfs: The Legend of Smurfy Hollow* © 2013 Sony Pictures Animation Inc. All Rights Reserved. Courtesy of Sony Pictures Animation.

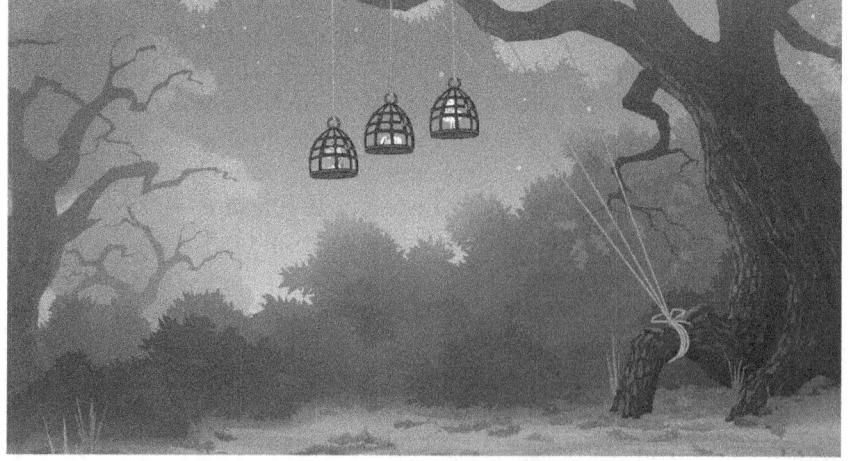

of a Hudson River school painting. As seen in figure 2.9, Asher Brown Durand's 1845 painting *The Beeches* also features diminutive people, dark trees, and radiant light on the horizon. Whereas Durand's trees slant away from the path, however, those in *Smurfy Hollow* lean menacingly toward the cages and their occupants. They would not be out of place in one of Rackham's illustrations of the story.

The Smurfs' situation rapidly improves. They escape by means of cooperation and pluck; the horseman turns out to be one of Papa Smurf's teaching strategies; and the competitors show that they have learned to support one another instead of always competing. The cartoon does,

Figure 2.9. Asher Brown Durand (1796–1886), *The Beeches* (1845). *Source:* The Metropolitan Museum of Art, Bequest of Maria DeWitt Jesup, from the collection of her husband, Morris K. Jesup, 1914. Public domain.

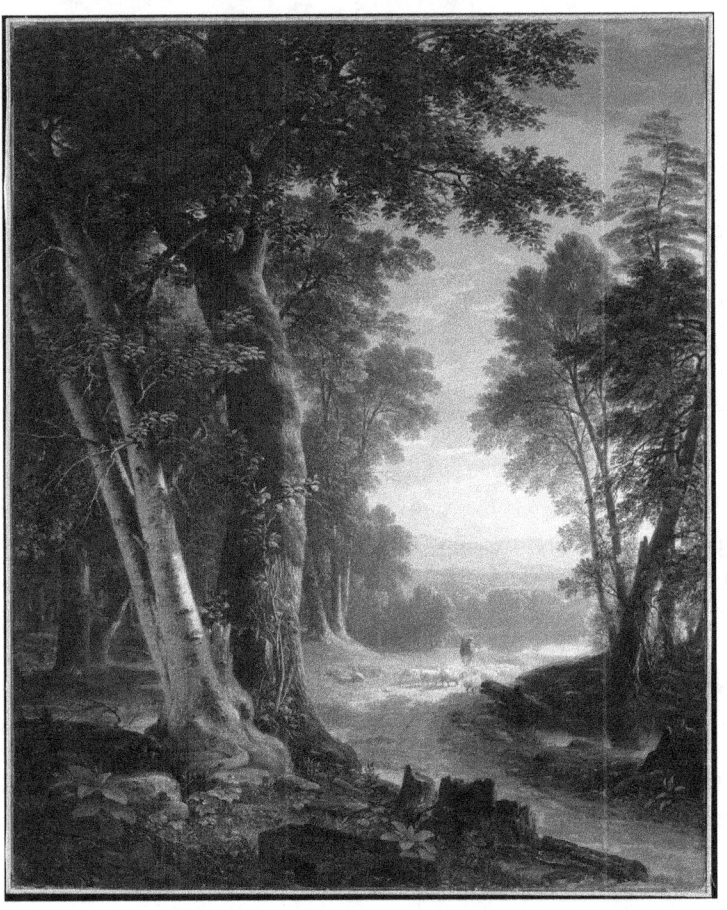

however, end with a Rackham-esque reminder that nature is not easily controlled: As soon as they have finished talking about the story, the stop-motion Smurfs in the frame narrative are chased out of their campsite by a swarm of bats. In *Smurfy Hollow* as in *Sailor Twain* and *Spill Zone*, the Hudson River valley functions not simply as a scenic backdrop, but as a living presence that actively shapes the experiences of humans (and small humanoids). While *Sailor Twain* comes down on the side of pessimism, both *Spill Zone* and *Smurfy Hollow* imagine ways for protagonists to engage respectfully with their environments and to gain maturity and a stronger sense of community in the process. Other works focus even more closely on the psychological effects of encounters with the Hudson River valley. In the next section, we will examine two comics and an animated cartoon that present the region as an opportunity to rest, learn, and grow.

Forward Motion in "Cookalein," *Spider-Man: Into the Spider-Verse*, and *Hollow*

In all three of these works, the Hudson River valley evokes powerful feelings of freedom and change. As explored in the introduction, Will Eisner's groundbreaking work *A Contract with God* carefully attends to the importance of place in people's lives: He depicts Dropsie Avenue in the Bronx as a fractious and close-knit community. The final story in the collection, "Cookalein," explains that the arrival of warm weather in the spring brings a sense of release to the neighborhood: "When at last winter relaxed its imprisoning grip, summer arrived and life oozed from inside the tenements onto the streets. The new freedom of movement gave the tenant's lifestyle a new cadence" (125). Particularly fortunate are "the vacationers" whose penny-pinching throughout the year enables them to head to the country. Cookalein, the resort visited by many in the neighborhood, offers a relatively spartan resort experience: Families sleep in one room, and women cook meals in a shared kitchen. Recalling both Nast's *Sketches among the Catskills* and Spiegelman's *Maus II*, the Catskills in "Cookalein" are less a place for solitary reflection than for crowds, parties, and quarrels.

Even so, Eisner makes clear on a three-panel page (see figure 2.10) that the train ride north offers a sense of freedom and invigoration. For the first time in the entire graphic novel, the reader looks at New York

Figure 2.10. *Source:* From *A Contract with God and Other Tenement Stories*, Will Eisner Centennial Edition, by Will Eisner. Copyright ©2006 by Will Eisner Studios, Inc. Copyright (c) 1978, 1985, 1989, 1995, 1996 by Will Eisner Studios, Inc. Used by permission of W. W. Norton & Company, Inc.

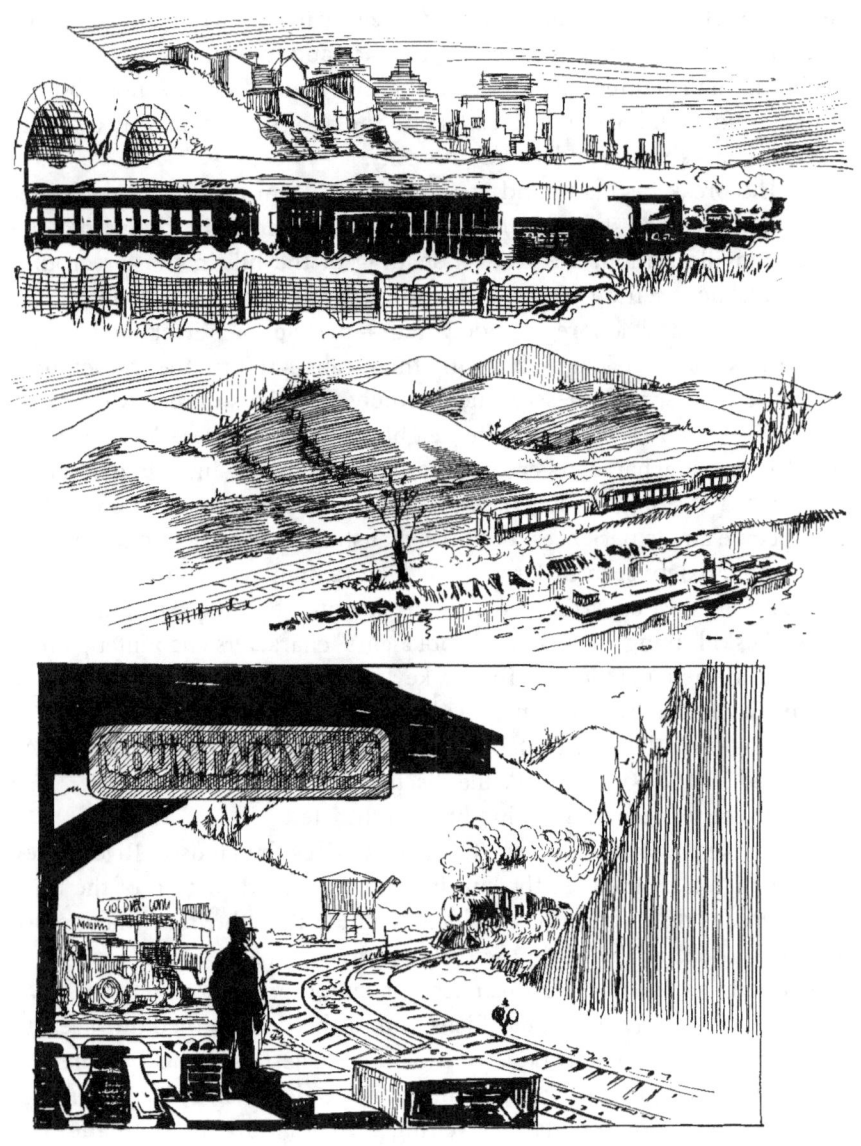

City from the outside. In contrast to the jumbled density of Dropsie Avenue, the city provides a placid backdrop as the train heads north. In the page's middle image, the change in perspective is even more striking. Mountains replace buildings, and the dark ink spots and vertical shading seen throughout A Contract with God give way to thinner, mostly diagonal lines that evoke an expansive feeling of space and movement. Without any visible human figures in the scene, the eye focuses on the northbound train, tugboat, and barge. The reader and the book's characters get a respite from the city's visual and verbal intensity.

The break begins to end in the page's bottom panel. Although scenic mountains are still seen in the distance as the train chugs into the Mountainville station, the vertical shading of the hill in the foreground links this new setting back to Dropsie Avenue. The solid black of the station's roof and a foregrounded man—perhaps a porter since there are others in the background with their cabs—return the viewer to a circumscribed space. These elements imply that the summer will not, in fact, serve as an escape from the neighborhood's realities. As they settle into Cookalein, characters enjoy a loosening of rules—including, notably, improvised sleeping arrangements—as well as the chance to encounter new people and experiences. But the exhausting scrutiny, exploitation, and economic anxiety seen in Dropsie Avenue remain very much in force in the Catskills. Just as Art and Vladek are haunted by the past as they walk amid Catskills bungalows, so do "Cookalein's" characters encounter painful realities in their new locale. In one key storyline, fifteen-year-old Willie, whom Eisner has said was modeled on himself, has a sexual experience that ends with the abuse of his partner and his own humiliation.[11] As suggested by the portrait of Willie discussed in the introduction (I.2), his summer memories are anything but lighthearted.

Unlike Maus II, however, "Cookalein" gives the Hudson River valley a wide-angled moment in the sun in its three-part depiction of the train ride. Perhaps this is because Willie's difficulties, though wrenching, do not approach those of Vladek in the scale or intensity of the trauma involved. The train trip's feeling of joyous release is temporary, but nonetheless real.

In A Contract with God, Eisner takes the comics medium itself to new destinations; the work is one of the earliest and most influential examples of the graphic novel form. Four decades later, Spider-Man: Into the Spider-Verse represents an exciting leap forward for both the Spider-Man character and for animated films themselves. With its diverse and appealing characters, its well-crafted story, and its brilliant incorporation of print-comics tropes into animated cartooning, *Into the Spider-Verse* offers a particularly striking use of the Hudson River valley landscape. As with "Cookalein," the journey upstate opens up new possibilities.

About a third of the way into the movie, Miles Morales and his reluctant mentor, Peter Parker, travel by bus out of New York City to the headquarters of sinister businessman Wilson Fisk. The switch to a new environment for Miles is perhaps foreshadowed by the scene immediately before their departure; as Peter wolfs down hamburgers, Miles sits against a mural of a Mediterranean landscape of the sort seen in many tristate-area diners. Despite Peter's resistance, the two find themselves on the road, with the Hudson River valley indicated not just by the signage on the bus but also by the glowing autumnal foliage they pass through (see figure 2.11). The area is less specifically defined than in *Spill Zone*, though alert viewers have noted that the topography resembles that of Route 32, an actual highway connecting New York City with the Catskills region.[12]

Into the Spider-Verse's directors and animators offer a somewhat surprising take on conventional depictions of the region's scenery. A substantial snowfall on the ground accompanies the autumn leaves, suggesting that a late-October storm has blown through. None of the characters comment on this. But as Miles begins to learn more about how to swing on his webs, and Peter slowly begins to embrace his role as instructor,

Figure 2.11. *Source: Spider-Man: Into the Spider-Verse* © 2018 Sony Pictures Animation Inc. All Rights Reserved. Courtesy of Sony Pictures Animation.

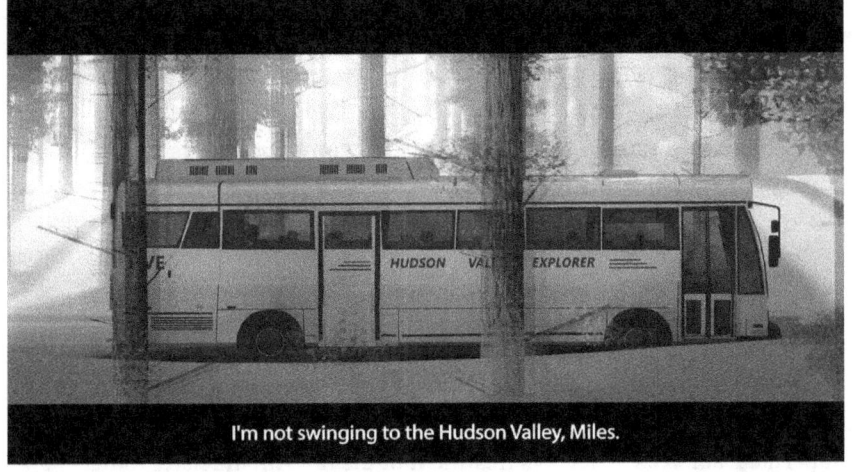

I'm not swinging to the Hudson Valley, Miles.

their paths through the colorful leaves and pristine snow suggest the benefits of strange and surprising combinations. Miles and Peter are not perfectly in sync, but the two begin to forge a bond. Soon, amid their tree-to-tree battles with another villain at the facility, Doc Ock, Miles and Peter find themselves collaborating with a new hero, Gwen Stacy. In many ways, then, the trip to the Hudson River valley serves as a proto-portal for experiences later in the film. Miles eventually encounters multiverses that are much more colorful and chaotic.

Like many a real-life New Yorker before him, Miles returns to Brooklyn from the Hudson River valley strengthened and sustained for the challenges awaiting him in the city. Similarly, the film's creators and performers (particularly Shameik Moore, who voices Miles) offer audiences a smart, humane respite from thoughtless cinematic mayhem and from racist tropes pervasive in comics, literature, and art, including a significant number of the works we have covered so far. While Washington Irving was not willing to imagine characters such as Miles and his family and friends, there are some parallels between his tales and *Into the Spider-Verse*. Just as Irving grounded distinctly American literary traditions in the valley's dreamlike landscape, so does *Into the Spider-Verse* connect its innovative approach to comics storytelling to a strangely beautiful place beyond city limits. To rephrase a point made earlier in this chapter: If you want to imagine new possibilities for superheroes, the Hudson River valley is a good place to do it.

Even more sustained engagement with valley locations and lore emerges in *Hollow*, the 2022 young adult graphic novel written by Shannon Watters and Branden Boyer-White, illustrated by Berenice Nelle, and infused with jewel tones by colorists Kaitlyn Musto, Kieran Quigley, and Gonçalo Lopes. Izzy Crane is a bright nerd whose family has just moved to Sleepy Hollow, New York. At first she is taken aback by the town's wholehearted embrace of Irving's legacy, which manifests itself through the high school's mascot, a full calendar of town festivals, and the local pizza place's logo of a pie-hurling horseman.[13] Eventually, she finds new friends, falls in love with the cute Van Tassel girl in her classes, and comes to appreciate the community spirit in her new hometown.

The plot weaves itself in and out of Irving's original tale. When Izzy has the courage to confront the horseman, she finds out that this seemingly dangerous phenomenon has the best of intentions: They were originally a Hessian soldier who swore to protect the Van Tassel family against hostile supernatural forces.[14] *Hollow*'s treatment of the horseman relates to Rackham's in interesting ways. Whereas Rackham, as we have seen, presented the horseman as an animal-human amalgam, this comic presents the horse, headless body, and pumpkin as a trio of separate personalities. All three partner with Izzy and her friends to expel the true threat to the town, a malignant figure who has long been harming Van Tassels.

Even as it consciously revises Irving's work, *Hollow* recalls its progenitor in blending horror, history, humor, and horses to envision a new American story. Watters, Boyer-White, Nelle, and the team of colorists present readers with a community in which same-sex relationships are accepted as a matter of course; in which longstanding traditions evolve in response to individuals' aspirations; and in which an interest in the occult coexists with expertise in science, mathematics, history, and literature.

In both Irving's tale and *Hollow*, the glories of the region serve as a kind of defense mechanism against potentially hostile readers, whether they are Eurocentric nineteenth-century audiences or modern-day opponents of LGBTQ+ graphic novels. Irving deftly sidesteps skepticism about the merit of American literature by evoking, in meticulous detail, the natural and cultural riches of the Hudson River valley. Similarly, *Hollow*'s splendidly illustrated and colored landscapes provide visual support for the comic's implicit argument about the importance of respect, collaboration, and flexibility in communities. A little open-mindedness, *Hollow* suggests, will only enhance that Hudson River valley glow.

The Once and Future Landscape

Building on the combination of old and new in *Hollow*, we will conclude our exploration of landscapes in comics by considering how future creators might continue to reframe the Hudson River valley in years to come. Two intriguing examples are provided here by Kait Dugan and Amanda Nessel, two emerging artists who have spent a good deal of time on the banks of the Hudson River during their undergraduate years at Marist University. Each powerful in its own right, Dugan's and Nessel's comics offer perspectives that we might place in dialogue with one another. Dugan emphasizes the integral role the region's landscape and culture have played in her own life and celebrates her rootedness in the valley (see figure 2.12). Inspired by a local cultural institution and by the scenery she has seen all her life, Dugan grounds her authority as an artist in ties to her community.

Figure 2.12. *Source:* Kait Dugan. Used with permission.

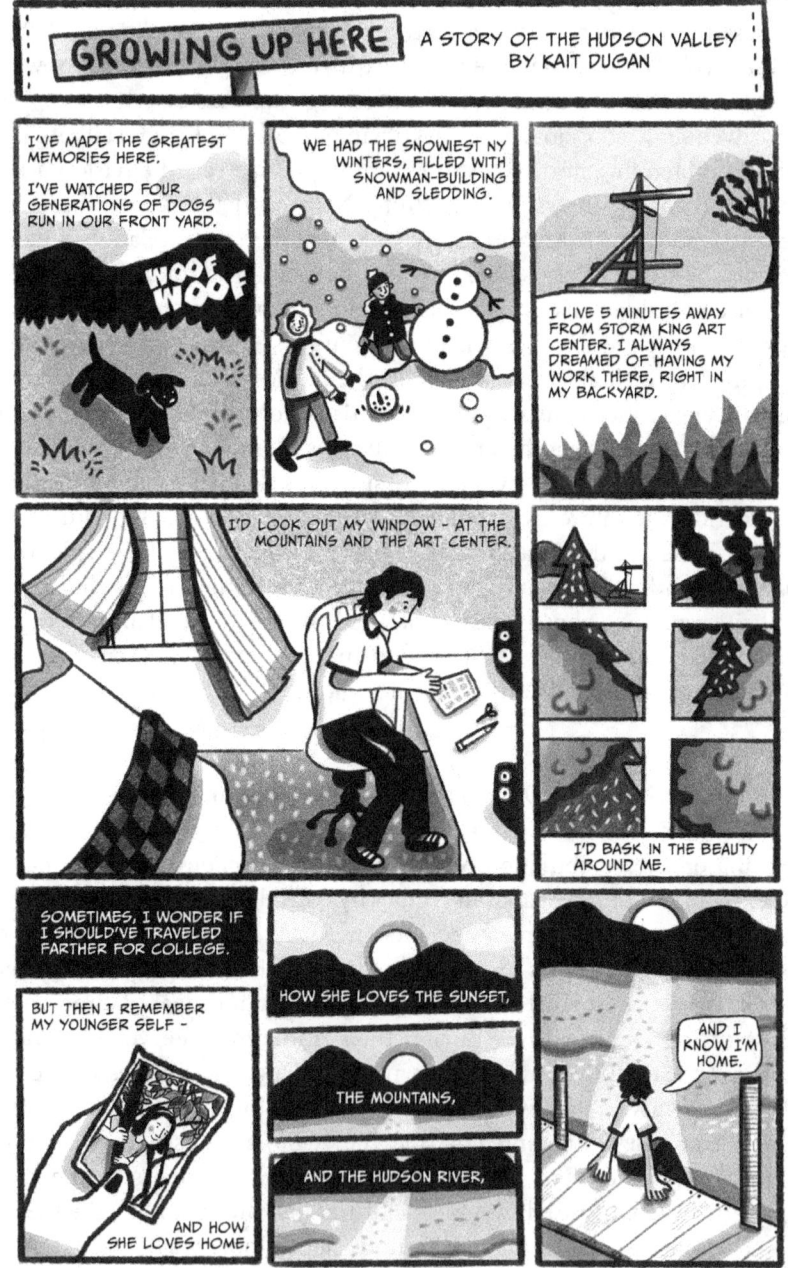

Nessel also experiences a sense of connection with the river and with other artists. In her case, however, the common bond includes both pleasure and anger at the intrusions of industry, transportation, and pollution on her encounters with nature (see figure 2.13). The abandoned canvas in Nessel's final panel serves as a potent warning that the region's scenery and the air itself remain vulnerable to industrial exploitation and pollution. The valley's cultural and natural legacies are by no means assured.

Figure 2.13. *Source:* Amanda Nessel. Used with permission.

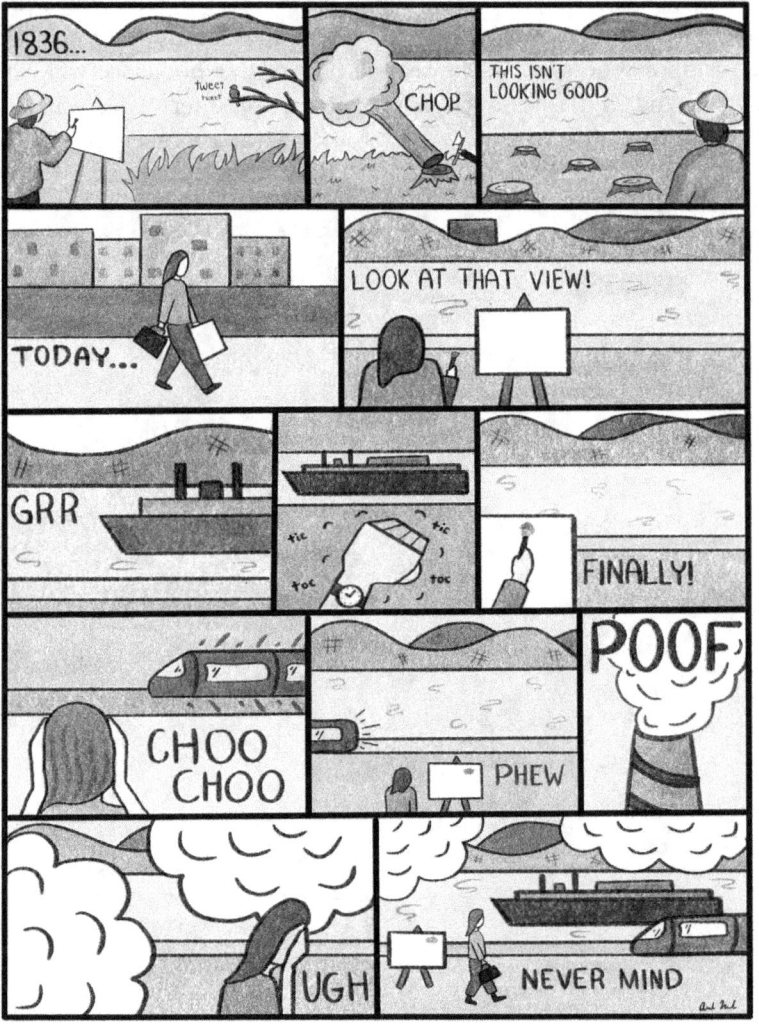

As our environment changes in rapid and often alarming ways, both Dugan's and Nessel's reactions are worth keeping in mind. The complex comics explored in this chapter remind us that multiple, even contradictory emotions can share space with one another. An ideal medium for portraying multiple frames of reference, comics can help us manage the uncertainty, dangers, and opportunities for our landscapes in the future.

We are limiting ourselves, however, if we think about comics only in terms of the meanings they convey on the page. Many comics are themselves industrial products, and all are generated by people who form networks through physical and virtual events, discussions, and communities. The Hudson River valley has played, and continues to play, a vital role in these processes. In the second half of this book, we will explore the valley and comics production as dynamic and intertwined ecosystems.

Part II

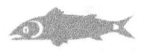

Local Creators and Production

CHAPTER 3

Imaginative Industry at the Western Printing Site

In chapter 1, we traveled to the Thomas Cole National Historic Site and to Olana, two beloved and well-known tourist destinations in the valley. Now, our studies will take us to a spot that is less picturesque but equally significant. If you go to the Mid-Hudson Plaza on Route 9 in Poughkeepsie and look just south of several big-box stores there, you will find a low-slung industrial building that has seen better days. As you walk close to it, a large concrete pad comes into view, which covers a good-sized patch of land in front of the building. Encroaching on the concrete is a vacant lot that animals and plants have reclaimed. On a recent visit, I spotted milkweed, chicory, and mugwort, as well as a healthy-looking groundhog and two kildeer calling to each other anxiously as I walked around (see figure 3.1).

About two hundred feet east of the site, a new branch of the Dutchess Rail Trail system opened in December 2023. When other branches are completed, this new route, the Northside Line, will connect the city of Poughkeepsie with destinations such as Marist University and the Hudson Heritage mixed-use commercial development.[1] In its current state, the new branch provides pedestrians and cyclists with an opportunity to travel right past the one-story building described above.

This structure serves as the last physical remnant of the Western Printing and Lithographing Company's Poughkeepsie outpost—a massive

Figure 3.1. The only remaining structure from the Western Printing facility in June 2023. *Source:* Photo by the author.

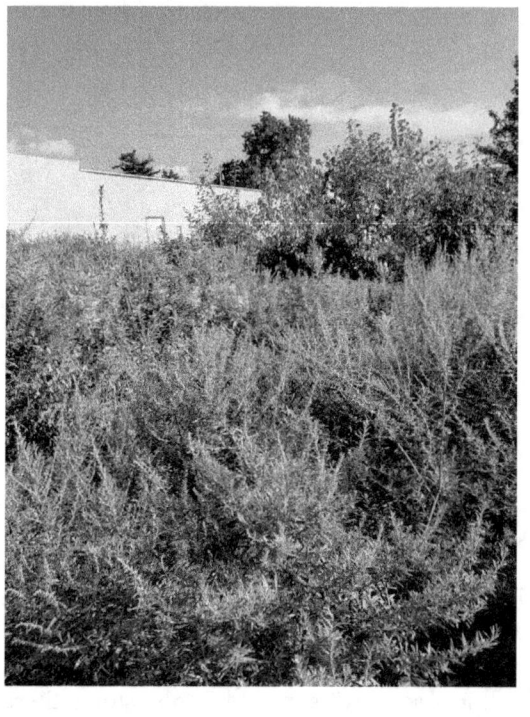

industrial facility that, for almost half a century, churned out comics and other printed products that were distributed nationally and, eventually, worldwide. The complex initially bore the name *Whitman Publishing* on its main sign (after a key subsidiary); by 1949, *Western Printing & Lithographing Company* adorned the building in large, flood-lit letters.[2] The company's name formally changed to *Western Publishing, Inc.*, in 1960, but it rarely used that name until a rebranding initiative in the late 1960s.[3] Throughout this chapter I will refer to the corporation as a whole as the *WPL Company* and to the Poughkeepsie unit as *Western Printing*. Quotations from the WPL Company's internal publication, *The Westerner*, will also frequently use the jaunty nickname *Pokip* when discussing the Poughkeepsie facility.

Founded in 1907 and based in Racine, Wisconsin, the WPL Company played an enormously influential role in twentieth-century mass culture. Comics writer and historian Mark Evanier, who worked for the company as a freelance artist in the 1970s, succinctly summarizes its scale and impact: "However big you thought they were, they were bigger. The sales they racked up in the '50s with the TV tie-ins were astronomical in comparison to the '70s, let alone today. I think they produced a lot of quality comics over the years—and some stinkers, of course—and they employed a lot of people."[4]

As Evanier's comment suggests, exploring the WPL Company's history allows us to think about comics not just as an artistic medium, but also as an economic engine and community connector. Our attention to the company will focus on its sprawling Poughkeepsie branch, Western Printing, between 1934 and 1970—the years in which it created, printed, and distributed millions of comics along with other printed products. We will explore both the products created by Western Printing and the infrastructures that the facility relied upon and supported.[5] Pre-existing buildings, transportation networks, and civic organizations led the WPL Company's management to locate an outpost there. In turn, the plant's products supported the success of animated films, television shows, books, and merchandise in American culture and beyond. Buoyed by its successful alliance with the Walt Disney Company, the WPL Company even served as a primary investor in Disneyland when it was built in the 1950s.

The company's activity in the area supports scholar Paul Lopes's discussion (2009) of an "industrial age" in comics history, a category that overlaps with the Golden, Silver, and Bronze Ages found in many comics chronologies. Encompassing the 1930s through the early 1980s, the industrial age was "an age of a mass market where readers, for a period, seemed to have an insatiable demand for comic books. An assembly-line process was essential to produce product for an ever-expanding market and to generate greater and greater profits" (xiv). Studying Western Printing in Poughkeepsie adds a new dimension to this conversation. Along with impressive technologies and processes, the industrial age reflects the collective contributions of thousands of people who colored, inked, edited, proofread, printed, bound, loaded, shipped, and sold these works. For the people who worked there, the company provided jobs that were steady, demanding, and rewarding. Even area residents who were not employees came into contact with the organization through tours, panel discussions at schools, and annual displays at the annual Dutchess County Fair. Because of its community impact, Western Printing merits an important place in histories of the Hudson River valley as well as in comics history.

A central idea of this chapter is that the interaction worked both ways. The company affected the valley, and the valley's location, culture, and people affected the company. Located on the outskirts of Poughkeepsie and about a half mile east of the Hudson River, the parcel of land that eventually became the Western Printing site had natural features, transportation infrastructure, and community networks that preexisted, and extended beyond, the facility. As we will see in the first two sections of this chapter, the area was a locus of social, creative, and entrepreneurial activities long before Racine-based businessmen laid eyes on it. The ecosystem itself seemed to encourage new ideas.

Exchange, Exclusion, and Transportation

If you want to trace through-lines connecting the valley's present to its past, look no further than the cattail plants that still grow behind the remaining buildings on the Western Printing site (see the plants in the foreground of figure 3.2). As noted in the introduction, the Munsee place

Figure 3.2. Cattail plants behind the former Western Printing site. *Source:* Photo by the author.

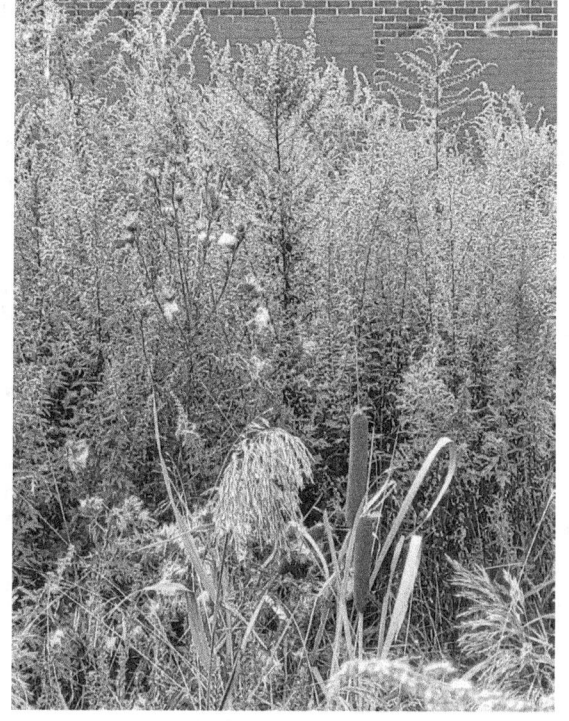

name *Poughkeepsie* denotes "the reed-covered lodge by the spring"—that is, a site defined by water, vegetation, and a human-built structure.[6] The spring offered rest, refreshment, and a hospitable environment for the aquatic plants covering the lodge. The reed in question was likely cattails: Kimmerer notes that they offer "a superb material for shelter in leaves that are long, water repellent, and packed with closed-cell foam for insulation" (228). By covering lodges with this plant, Indigenous people made the most of local materials and technologies.

The fact that *Poughkeepsie* denotes the lodge, the spring, and reeds rather than a single group of people may well reflect the frequent interaction and exchange among different groups of Indigenous people in the area. While Wappinger people to the south were the region's primary inhabitants, evidence indicates that they interacted extensively with Esopus people across the river and Mahican people from points north and west.[7]

Seventeenth-century settlers from Europe transformed this fluid situation into a fixed, exclusionary set of property grants. English officials created Dutchess County in the 1683, and it became a self-governing unit in 1714. The parcel of land that Western Printing would later occupy was granted to Robert Sanders and Meyndert Harmense for farming and milling purposes in 1686.[8] Wappinger leaders such as Nimhammaw responded with strategic concessions, but many Munsee people were forced to move north to the Stockbridge settlement in Massachusetts throughout the eighteenth century, where they met up with Mahicans and other Indigenous people from the region.[9] As detailed in Francis and Alvitre's *Loyalty Betrayed* (chapter 2), after the Revolutionary War, white colonists forced a removal from Stockbridge as well.[10] Members of the settlement moved to Wisconsin, where the seat of the tribal nation now resides. Heather Bruegl (2022), a descendant of Munsee people, notes, "Today, a vibrant community resides in Bowler, Wisconsin, on reservation land secured in 1856. A strong, tribal government leads our community. Our language and culture remain vibrant on this land, where we keep our history alive, too" (114). Recent exhibits in New York, Massachusetts, and Pennsylvania testify to the ongoing survivance of Indigenous creative work and cultural practices in this region.[11]

It is also true that an inexorable process of acquisition and settlement transformed the Hudson River valley in the 1700s. Mile marker 83, placed next to the Albany Post Road in the late eighteenth century and preserved during the administration of President Franklin D. Roosevelt, offers a tangible example of how space was mapped and reconfigured during that period (see figure 3.3).[12] The Western site is just south and east of this spot, on the outskirts of Poughkeepsie.[13] A few decades later, steamboat travel on the Hudson shrank the distance between Dutchess County and the major cities to the north and south: launched in 1807, Robert Fulton's *North River Steam Boat of Clermont* (known today as the *Clermont*) stopped at Poughkeepsie on its travels between New York City and Albany.[14]

By the middle of the nineteenth century, a new network of lines crisscrossed the land. The Hudson River Railroad connected Albany to New York in 1851. In the decades after the Civil War, Cornelius Vanderbilt's

Figure 3.3. Noting Poughkeepsie's distance from New York City, this mile marker sits across Route 9 from the former Western Printing site. *Source:* Photo by the author.

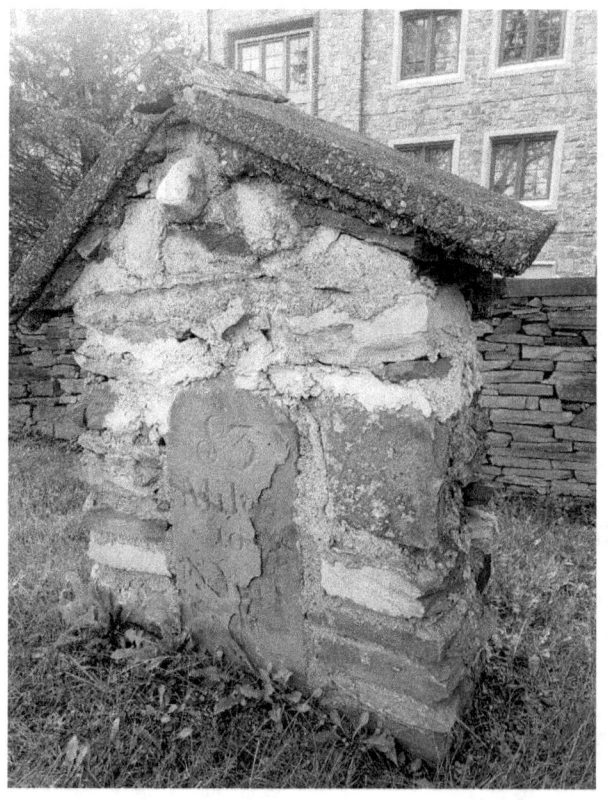

acquisitions and expansions linked the Hudson River valley to destinations across the country and brought waves of Irish, German, and Italian workers to the area.[15] In addition to the north-south lines paralleling the river, the Poughkeepsie and Eastern railroad, which ran to Connecticut, was completed in 1871. While today many of these rail lines now seem like natural features of the landscape, the process of planning and financing them was often unpredictable. A railroad bridge at Poughkeepsie that would connect lines in Pennsylvania, New York, and Connecticut was initially proposed before the Civil War and gained traction as an idea in the 1870s. An 1874 map (see figure 3.4) indicates that the bridge had already been built. This proved overly optimistic, however; because of problems with financing, the bridge was not completed until 1888. Even more significant for our purposes are the converging rail lines visible at the upper left of the map. These depict the "Hospital Branch" spur, a rail line created in

Figure 3.4. The lower left corner of this map optimistically portrays the Poughkeepsie railroad bridge, which would not be completed for another fourteen years. *Source:* Library of Congress, Geography and Map Division. Public domain.

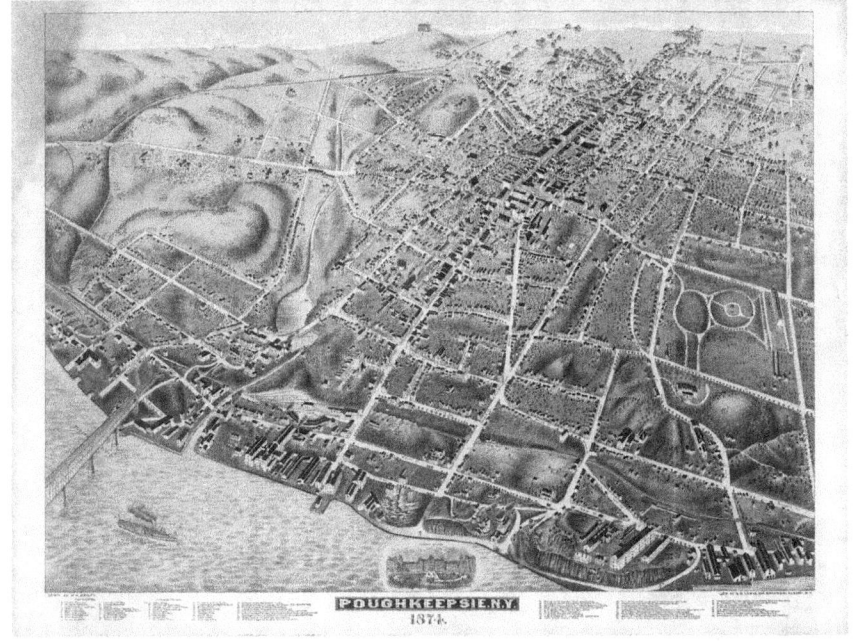

the 1870s to bring coal and other supplies to the Hudson River Hospital, a giant complex designed to house and treat the mentally ill.[16]

The area just to the south of the hospital and crossed by this new railroad spur would become the Western Printing site. It remained a pastoral location—part of an estate owned by Edward Bech—throughout the nineteenth century, even as industry began to dominate the waterfront. Just a small corner of an 1891 map of the region (see figure 3.5) depicts a soap factory, a knitting mill, glass works, a lumberyard, Matthew Vassar's brewery, John Adriance's Buckeye Mower Works, a tannery, and an icehouse. By the turn of the century, however, yet another innovation in transportation would turn this parcel north of the city into a prominent industrial site.

Figure 3.5. The area in the upper right corner, near the converging train tracks, would eventually become the site of the Fiat plant and other businesses, including the Western Printing facility. *Source:* Lionel Pincus and Princess Firyal Map Division, The New York Public Library. The New York Public Library Digital Collections. Public domain.

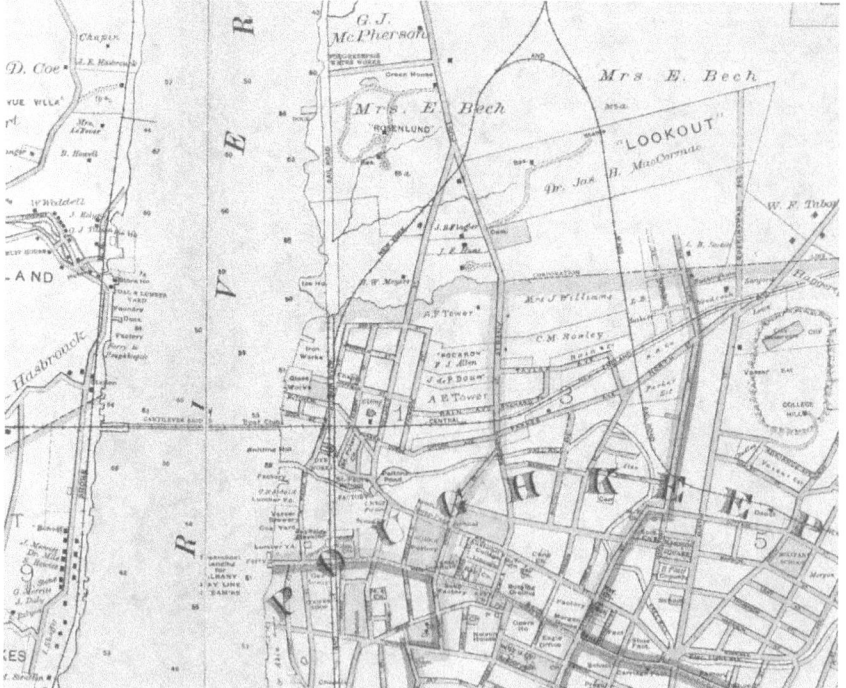

Fast Cars and Big Tents

The Ford Motor Company began mass-producing automobiles in Michigan in 1903.[17] Just six years later, the Italy-based Fiat corporation decided to establish a manufacturing site on the north end of Poughkeepsie.[18] Contemporary reports indicate that Fiat sought to move into the burgeoning American automobile market without having to import all its cars from Europe. The proximity of the site to the Hospital Branch of the railroad was a key factor in the company's decision to build a plant in the area, along with the positive reception that management received from civic leaders.[19]

News organizations celebrated the outcome: a subheadline in the *Poughkeepsie Eagle-News* described the company's impending arrival as a "BIG THING FOR CITY."[20] The facility promised to provide well-paying jobs—"Between 200 and 300 machinists are to be employed at [the] start. All the help will be male and will be well paid"—as well as a bit of glamour: "The great Italian racer, [Felice] Nazzaro, will be located here and will have charge of the try-outs of the cars as fast as they are completed" ("Fiat at Fairview" 5).

Reality turned out to be somewhat less fabulous. There is no evidence Nazzaro came to Poughkeepsie, and he started his own Italy-based automobile company in 1911.[21] Even worse, the community began to perceive test drivers as a hazard. When seven-year-old Harry Weil was "severely bruised" by a car being road tested, the *Poughkeepsie Eagle-News* described residents' frustration: "Many complaints are heard about the reckless driving of the Fiat auto testers on the Hyde Park Road. They send their machines along at great speed and seldom use any warning to rigs and pedestrians" ("Little Boy Hit by Fiat Machine" 5). At first, these drawbacks were counterbalanced by the economic success of the venture: Approximately 350 cars rolled out of the facility in 1912, and by 1913, plans for an addition were in the works.[22] The distinctive design of the expanded two-story structure would remain during later iterations of the facility (see figure 3.6).

The war in Europe brought these promising developments to a halt. Fiat experienced financial difficulties and began to pull back on operations in Poughkeepsie; by August 1918, a classified advertisement in the *Poughkeepsie Eagle-News* offered for sale "new fixture racks from F.I.A.T. dismantling operation" (8). Concerned civic leaders approached the Ford Motor Company, to no avail. The Electric Auto-Lite Corporation took over the space in 1919, but the site was back up for sale by 1921. City

Figure 3.6. The Fiat building in a 1915 postcard. When the Mid-Hudson Plaza was built on the site in 2000, architectural features of one of the buildings evoked those of the Fiat factory. *Source:* James A. Cannavino Library, Archives and Special Collections, Marist University, USA. Used with permission.

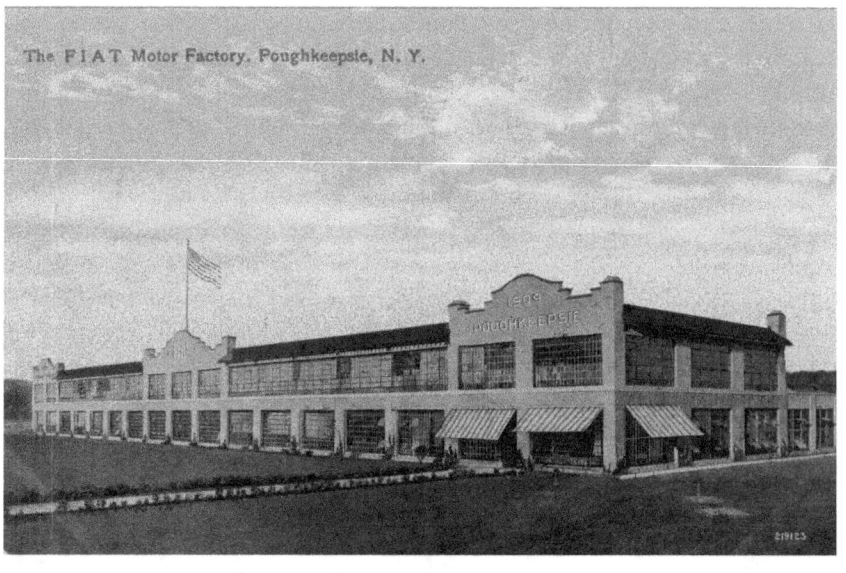

leaders avidly courted new occupants, but without success.[23] A map of Poughkeepsie created in 1931 by Thomas Barrett bleakly labels the site "F.I.A.T. NOW DEFUNCT."

Within three years, the WPL Company would provide the stable, long-term employment to area residents so sought after by local officials. Before that happened, however, the site hosted an additional enterprise whose story prefigures the much longer and more successful tenure of WPL. Let's delve for just a moment, then, into the brief but vivid life of the Jumbo Market.

As early as 1930, the parcel began to be associated with circuses. A front-page story in the July 1930 *Poughkeepsie Eagle-News* noted the possibility that the Ringling Brothers organization could buy the space as a winter residence for the circus, noting, "Ample space is available there for storage of animals and equipment, while the building is also well adapted for training" (1).[24] The presence of an amusement venue, the Woodcliff Pleasure Park, across Route 9 seems to have been a factor in these conversations: The park's owner, Fred H. Ponty, was apparently involved in bringing the site to Ringling's attention. While Ringling never came, the plan may have sparked the imagination of Henry Schaffer, a Schenectady-based immigrant from Poland who gradually built an East Coast network of grocery stores during the middle decades of the twentieth century.[25] In an era when the idea of a "super market" was just gaining currency, Schaffer was a trailblazer.[26]

Signs of a new kind of grocery experience start to appear in February 1934; a newspaper ad from that month solicits tenants for a new market, noting that "preference to local merchants" will be provided. Competitors took note: an April 1934 newspaper ad for the Great Bull Markets proclaims, "We Do Not Favor Misleading Advertising or Circus Bally-ho!"[27] By late spring, the scope of the plan became clear. The "Jumbo Market" would offer a shopping experience that would combine multiple vendors, circus performances, and proximity to Woodcliff Park (see figure 3.7).

Figure 3.7. The Jumbo Market invested the former Fiat site with festive energy. It is unknown whether the large signage pictured in the ad ever actually appeared on the building. *Source:* Public domain.

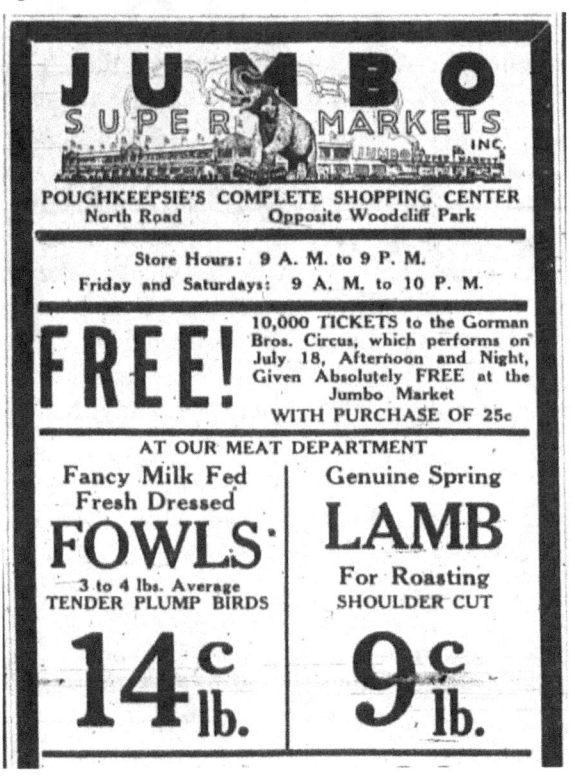

Presumably, the market was designed to attract not just local residents but also visitors to Woodcliff from New York and Albany. Conjuring up both beloved circus elephants and expansive shopping options, Schaffer's idea contains many elements of the shopping malls that would become ubiquitous over four decades later.

It was one circus after another at the Jumbo Market site in the spring and summer of 1934. The Fairview Fire Department sponsored an event there in late April and early May; the Ringling Brothers and Barnum and Bailey presented two shows on June 11; and in mid-July, the World of Mirth circus promised the "World's Fair Here at Your Very Door" and attractions that included a man shot five hundred feet from a cannon. Through it all, more prosaic pleasures were also available at the market, including "Fancy Milk Fed Fresh Dressed Fowls; 14 cents a pound; TENDER PLUMP BIRDS" and other groceries.[28] A *Poughkeepsie Eagle-News* feature article noted that the entire Ringling Brothers entourage traveled to the site by train and were greeted by curious local residents: "The big show attracted large crowds to the Jumbo market grounds last night, and hundreds tramped through mud and puddles to walk close to the tents and wagons, and sense the spell of the huge, dark, potential plant of entertainment."[29] Fulfilling the slightly ominous tone of the article, the market received a blow to its reputation a month later when a doctor heading to the Hudson River Hospital was held up by a possibly intoxicated chauffeur on its grounds.[30]

It is impossible to determine exactly how Poughkeepsie's civic leaders regarded the market, the circuses, or the crowds they drew. What is clear is that they moved heaven and earth to replace the Jumbo Market with the WPL Company. Once the company's management began to express serious interest in the site, the Chamber of Commerce sprang into action, successfully soliciting $5,000 from residents to buy out the remaining months of the market's lease. The Jumbo Market's stock was removed from the facility, and the WPL Company immediately moved in. Chamber of Commerce president Walter W. Kingston was fulsome in his thanks: "I wish at this time to thank all the contributors for their generous support to a fund which was over subscribed and raised in so short a time. This is true evidence of the fact that the manufacturers, merchants, and business men of the city are still willing to back with their money as well as their energy any project which is to be a benefit to this community."[31] Compensation in hand, Schaffer revised his business model and soon established a number of "Empire Markets" throughout Poughkeepsie.

As for the Jumbo Market, it lived on in the reminiscences of people who worked at Western Printing. In a *Westerner* story published in June 1958, Charles Johnson recounts that his first job-related task "was to help clean up the Pokip building which was then called the Jumbo Market, a place where everything from soup to automobiles could be purchased under one roof." Twenty-four years after the fact, his memories of the transition from the Jumbo Market to Western were still vivid: "In helping to get the building ready, Charlie did everything from scraping paint from windows and tearing down old buildings to making new rooms and working with electricians. When he first started, Charlie recalls, part of the market—the meat and grocery departments—was still operating and was fenced off from the rest of the plant. Every time workers had to go through the fenced-in area, a deputy sheriff had to accompany them" (11). Johnson's account suggests that, despite the Chamber of Commerce's efforts, the transition was not entirely without confusion, if not outright tension. Johnson's work cleaning up the market is repeated in an article four years later marking his retirement and in a celebration of the thirty-year anniversary of the Poughkeepsie plant. Noting the building's original construction by Fiat, *The Westerner* recounts that "after another long period of idleness, it became the site of an ill-fated experiment by the Jumbo Markets, etc., which occupied the first floor for a produce market."[32] While refraining from mentioning the circuses, the holdup, and the payout, *The Westerner* implicitly contrasts the market's failure to its own thriving operation.

Nonetheless, some aspects of the WPL Company eventually circled back to the Jumbo Market's heyday. In 1970, *The Westerner* trumpeted the news that the Poughkeepsie facility had produced deluxe souvenir programs for the Ringling Brothers Circus's centennial celebration. Once again, it kept its counsel about the fact that circus performers and elephants had cavorted on that very site in the past.[33] There were deeper forms of continuity between the market and its successor, too. Schaffer's risk taking and creativity were shared by leaders of the WPL Company, even given its conventional corporate infrastructure and culture. Especially during its years of comics production, the spell of commercial entertainment continued to hold sway at the Poughkeepsie site.

An Eastern Plant for Western

The history of unsuccessful ventures at the Western Printing site undoubtedly came as no surprise to the leaders of the WPL Company since its own origin story involved a failing business. The company came into being in 1907 when Edward H. Wadewitz and Roy A. Spencer assumed ownership of a struggling printing operation, the West Side Printing Company, located in Racine, Wisconsin. Originally involving just a few rundown presses in basement rooms, by 1910, the business had above-ground offices, a new lithographic press, and a new name: the Western Printing and Lithographing Company. Six years later, the failure of the Hamming-Whitman Publishing Company in Chicago presented the WPL Company with a key opportunity. Since Whitman owed the company a good deal of money, the latter entity took on Whitman's assets, turned Whitman Publishing into a subsidiary of its own operation, and entered the field of children's and educational publishing. The WPL Company's hybrid identity as a printer and publisher would last until its demise in the early twenty-first century. This decision also set in motion a pattern of growth through acquisition and corporate alliances that would lead to over a half-century of steadily increasing profits. In the 1920s, for example, the WPL Company absorbed two Midwestern engraving businesses. The company's leadership was also willing to take on ever more complex technological challenges: Encouraged by customers to enter the playing card business, the company took on that function in the late 1920s as well.[34]

Continuing to prosper despite the Great Depression, by the early 1930s the WPL Company's leaders began to look toward establishing a company presence close to population centers in the Northeast and publishers in New York City. The factors that led to the selection of Poughkeepsie as the site in 1934 will not be surprising, based on what we have already seen: "The decision at the time was based on rail and water facilities, the distributing possibilities, the availability of such a fine plant and the Chamber of Commerce and the Manufacturers' Association, whose leaders had worked so long and diligently to attract new industry to the community."[35] The company's management team seems to have hit it off immediately with business leaders in Poughkeepsie.

Initially, however, they may have envisioned a relatively limited commitment. In a *Westerner* article about retiring executive Paul Lyle, he recounted that Poughkeepsie was originally "acquired as a shipping facility" and that he only took a job there "three or four months later when it was decided to manufacture there as well."[36] In its own narration of the company's history, *The Westerner* company newsletter remained silent about this original plan. In the event, Western Printing quickly became an indispensable component of the WPL Company's operations. With this facility as with later outposts in Missouri, Maryland, California, and Illinois, the company's leadership consistently highlighted connections between its satellite facilities and its home base in Racine. An illustration from the March 1949 *Westerner* (see figure 3.8) gives Poughkeepsie a prominent place in its visual merging of the company's disparate locations (7).[37]

With its impressive manufacturing capacity and network of transportation connections to New York City and the rest of the East Coast, Poughkeepsie offered the right facility and the right time for the WPL Company. A new corporate partner made the move particularly desirable. At just the same time that the company moved into the Fiat/Jumbo Market site, it embarked on an association with a fledgling entertainment business whose standard bearer was a plucky "five-year-old mouse."[38] This was the Walt Disney Company (WDC), of course, and the WPL Company was a key partner in WDC's emergence as a global provider of child-friendly entertainment. As we will see, comics played an essential role in this process, particularly through the 1950s.

Synergy and Agility in the 1930s, 1940s, and early 1950s

WPL's affiliation with WDC began not with comics but with a closely related product: the Big Little Book, a Whitman Publishing innovation that featured small but satisfyingly chunky volumes with a picture on almost every page.[39] Launched in 1932 with *The Adventures of Dick Tracy*,

Figure 3.8. *The Westerner*, March 1949. *Source:* Courtesy of Wisconsin Historical Society.

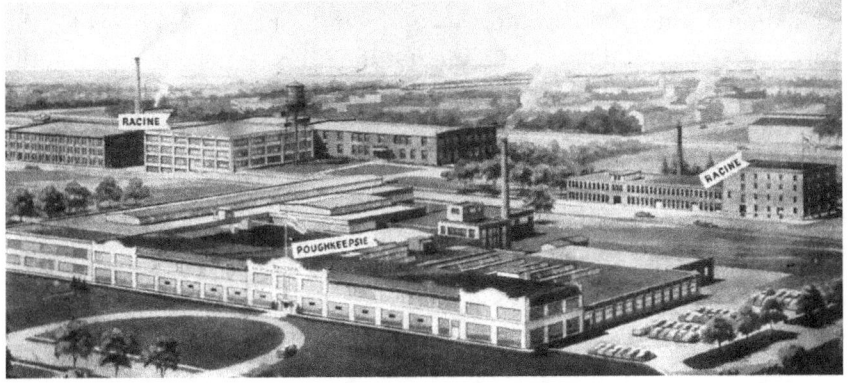

the books quickly gained a devoted following and became a prime venue for publicizing and marketing children's radio shows. They also played a crucial role in the evolution of comics; their lively storytelling and skillful artwork influenced generations of comics creators. Artist George Wilson, who created acclaimed covers for the WPL Company's Gold Key imprint in the 1960s, recalled, "At that time when I was growing up the best [examples of comic illustration] were the Big Little Books and my favorite was Alex Raymond (who did) Flash Gordon."[40] Given Whitman's successful track record with the Dick Tracy book and other volumes, a WDC representative reached out to the WPL Company about the possibility of a Big Little Book for Mickey Mouse. By 1933, this book and a Mickey Mouse coloring book were on the market, and a fifty-year partnership was established. Just four years later, comics produced at Western Printing in Poughkeepsie became an important factor in the two companies' symbiotic relationship.

Beginning in 1937, Western Printing produced the *Mickey Mouse Magazine*, a comics compilation that began in 1933 as small promotional pamphlets. Based on the positive response to that publication, WDC launched *Walt Disney's Comics and Stories* in October 1940 in partnership with Dell Publishing (see figure 3.9). Along with WDC's full-length animated features (starting with *Snow White and the Seven Dwarfs* in 1937), the magazine helped to transform the company into an entertainment empire. By 1942, the WPL Company was printing a million issues a month of *Walt Disney's Comics and Stories* for WDC, primarily out of the Poughkeepsie location. The opening of the company's Beverly Hills office in the early 1940s solidified its connection with WDC's California-based leaders.

Given this situation, it is not surprising that the WPL Company signed on as one of the original investors in Disneyland as plans for the park took shape in the early 1950s. In a 1955 special issue focused on the opening of the park in Anaheim, California, *The Westerner* suggested an ambitious goal for Disneyland: "When completed it will furnish employment to more than 500 people."[41] One of the stores on Main Street, U.S.A. in Disneyland featured the WPL Company's products. It opened on July 17, 1955, as the Book and Candle Shop and in later years (1972–1995) was known as the Storybook Store and as the Story Book Shop.

As the WPL Company's home base, Racine still enjoyed pride of place when it came to WDC-related events such as advance screenings of *Cinderella*, *Sleeping Beauty*, and other animated and live-action films.

Figure 3.9. *Source:* © Disney 1940, October 1940. Used with permission.

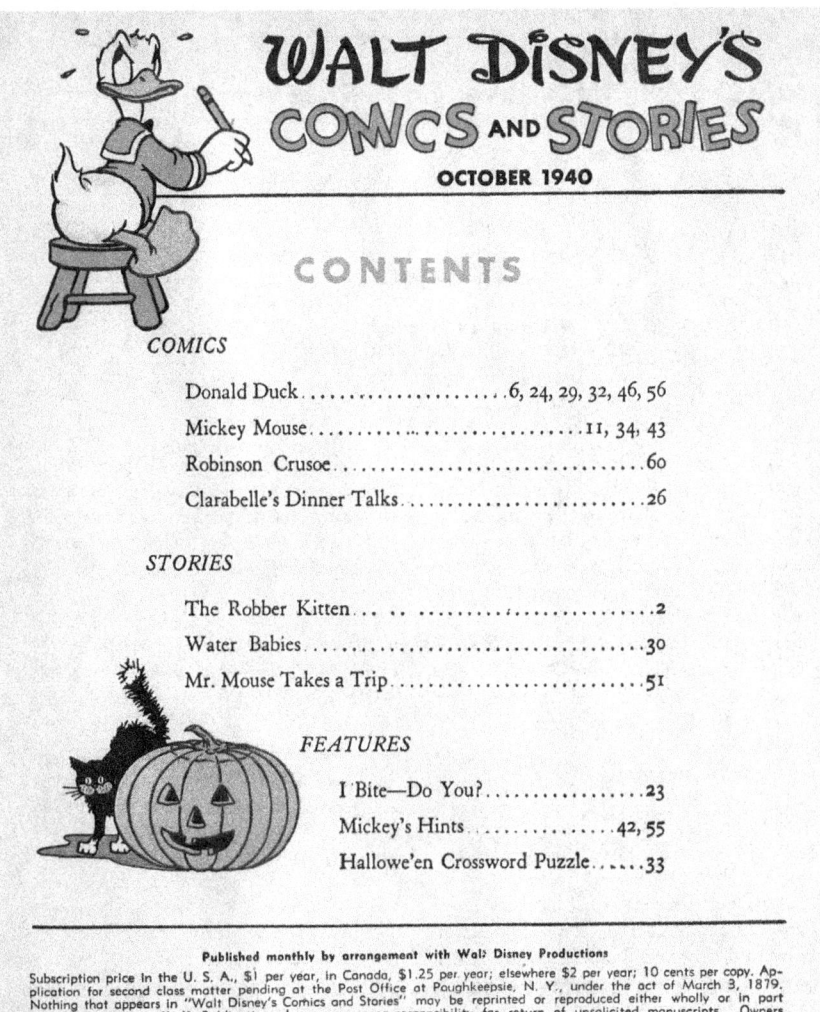

But executives from Poughkeepsie were among the group who traveled to California for the launch of Disneyland in 1955, and several leaders with ties to Poughkeepsie played important roles in advancing WDC-related projects (see figure 3.10).[42] Robert Callender, who worked in Poughkeepsie for seven years starting in 1935, moved to Beverly Hills in 1943 to head

Figure 3.10. *Poughkeepsie New Yorker*, July 1955. Note the final sentence's somewhat tentative description of how Disney characters will appear at the park. *Source:* © *Poughkeepsie Journal*—USA TODAY NETWORK. Used with permission.

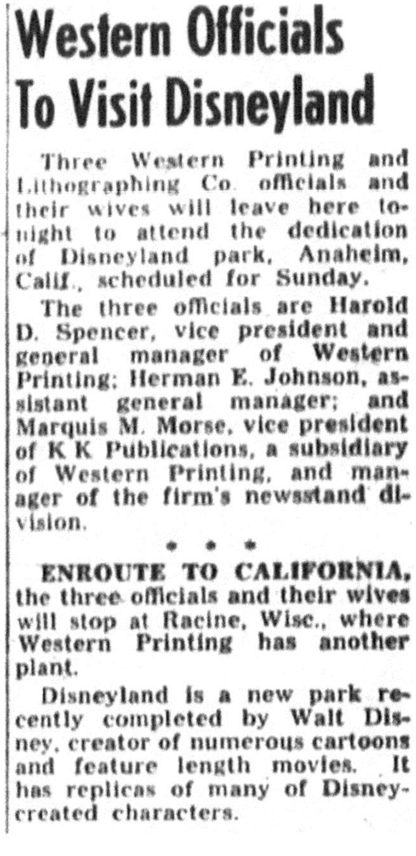

Western Officials To Visit Disneyland

Three Western Printing and Lithographing Co. officials and their wives will leave here tonight to attend the dedication of Disneyland park, Anaheim, Calif., scheduled for Sunday.

The three officials are Harold D. Spencer, vice president and general manager of Western Printing; Herman E. Johnson, assistant general manager; and Marquis M. Morse, vice president of K K Publications, a subsidiary of Western Printing, and manager of the firm's newsstand division.

* * *

ENROUTE TO CALIFORNIA, the three officials and their wives will stop at Racine, Wisc., where Western Printing has another plant.

Disneyland is a new park recently completed by Walt Disney, creator of numerous cartoons and feature length movies. It has replicas of many of Disney-created characters.

operations there. Marquis (Mark) Morse, based in Poughkeepsie, led K.K. Publications, Inc., a unit of Western that focused on comics (including WDC-related ones) for many years.[43]

Many of the WPL Company's interactions with WDC involved another crucial corporate partner: the Dell Publishing Company, a New York–based publisher founded in 1921 by George L. Delacorte Jr. WPL's relationship with Dell eventually became much more convoluted and contentious than its partnership with WDC.[44] Throughout the 1940s and much of the 1950s, however, the synergy among the three companies made them a dominant cultural force. Their achievements in comics emerge vividly in Michael Barrier's *Funnybooks: The Improbable Glories of the Best American Comic Books* (2015), which particularly attends to Carl Barks's brilliant achievements with stories of Donald Duck, Scrooge McDuck, and other characters featured in *Walt Disney's Comics and Stories*.[45] Leonard Marcus's engaging study, *Golden Legacy: The Story of Little Golden Books* (2017), tells how the alliance collaborated on Little Golden Books, which involved many different editorial and printing branches in Poughkeepsie and which remains a forceful presence in publishing today.[46] Another highly successful comics property, *Little Lulu*, did not involve WDC but was produced in tandem by WPL and Dell for almost forty years. Two artists prominently associated with *Little Lulu*, John Stanley and Irving Tripp, lived in the Hudson River valley; we will explore their work experiences later in this chapter.

Western Printing in Poughkeepsie played an essential role in the creation, manufacturing, and distribution of products from the WDC-Dell-WPL alliance.[47] Already impressive in the 1940s, by the 1950s, the numbers were staggering. The 4 billionth Dell comic was printed in 1958, with the majority of these having been printed in Poughkeepsie.[48] Comics from Western Printing made their way to audiences across America and worldwide. The facility's proximity to New York City made it a convenient location for gatherings of representatives from the WPL Company, WDC, and Dell. Particularly throughout the 1950s, *The Westerner* abounds with stories of Hudson River valley golf trips, boating excursions, dinners, and poolside chats among high-level executives from the three companies; as Barrier has written, "The partnership was very sociable as well as very profitable" (334). Legendary Dell vice president Helen Meyer was a regular visitor, as was Delacorte. In recognition of his contributions to the greater Poughkeepsie community, the latter was given an "honorary 14-carat gold citizen's card" at a dinner in 1955.[49] Such events were not only gratifying to the corporate leaders themselves but also proved crucial in the face of increasing scrutiny of comics on the part of psychologists, governmental leaders, and the media.

Navigating Comics Controversies

As has been well documented by comics historians such as David Hajdu in *The Ten-Cent Plague: The Great Comic-Book Scare and How It Changed America* (2009), by the late 1940s, commentators were beginning to cast a cold eye on the graphic depictions of violence, sexuality, and lawlessness present in comics marketed to children. While Fredric Wertham eventually became the standard-bearer for these critics, particularly after the 1954 publication of his work *The Seduction of the Innocent*, others had raised alarms before, and alongside, his critique.[50]

Along with WDC and Dell, the WPL Company navigated this situation with impressive dexterity—and people at Western Printing played a key role in this process from the earliest days of the controversy. After preliminary rules for comics content were proposed by publishers in 1948, Poughkeepsie-based vice president Harold D. Spencer pronounced that the measure was unnecessary for the company to adopt saying, "We have always maintained our comic books on a high standard." His argument drew upon the trustworthiness of the licensed properties held by the WPL Company: "Mr. Spencer said his company held contracts for the Walt Disney, Looney-Tunes, Raggedy Ann, Our Gang, and other movie character books."[51] Two years later, the facility hosted a site visit by members of the comics commission set up in New York following the defeat in the state legislature of a bill designed to regulate comics content. The commission's chairman praised Spencer and other WPL Company leaders as " 'most cooperative' in acquainting commission members with various phases of the comic book business."[52] Industry reassurances rang hollow to Wertham, whose book aimed criticism straight at the "Dell Comics Are Good Comics" slogan: "The whole question of 'good' comics can be summed up in this way: Crime comics are poisonous plants. The 'good' comics are at best weeds" (313). Both Dell and K.K. Publications appear in *Seduction of the Innocent*'s "Bibliographical Note," which listed all the publishers of the comics deplored throughout the book.

Intensifying throughout the first half of the 1950s, the controversy culminated in hearings before Congress in 1954 that led to the formation of the Comics Code Authority, an entity that included DC Comics, Marvel Comics, and Archie Comics among its members. Under pressure from the media, governmental officials, and distributors to adopt the code's list of regulations, publishers began to restrict comics' content. Far from a flash in the pan, the comics controversy of the 1950s had real effects: EC Comics eventually folded altogether, and many talented creators lost their livelihoods.[53]

The WPL Company and Dell steadfastly maintained their opposition to the code. In testimony before New York state and congressional committees, Meyer asserted that the companies refused to participate not because the code was overbearing but because it actually did not go far enough.[54] Similarly, Spencer noted during remarks at a pressmen's union dinner that the company had a "rigid policy of not printing comic books that dealt with crime or violence."[55]

The WPL Company's and Dell's association with WDC (who as a licensor was much less directly involved with comics production) and with other children's content seems to have insulated the companies against the most heated criticism of comics, as shown in figure 3.11. Embracing material with a strong educational component also paid off for the company. When the Thomas Alva Edison Foundation inaugurated national awards for youth reading materials in 1956, winners included a comics version of *Gulliver's Travels* and a science comic named *Beaver Valley*, both produced for Dell. *Walt Disney's Comics and Stories* also received an honorable mention.[56] In addition to printing all three of these products, Poughkeepsie served as a kind of neutral territory for representatives from New York City to discuss the comics controversy with constituencies outside the metropolitan area. In June 1954, for example, Manhattan-based editor Matthew Murphy participated in a Parent-Teachers Association panel discussion at the W. W. Smith School in Poughkeepsie. *The Westerner* noted, "Parents and teachers are interested in comics and their effect on the child and Murphy here has the opportunity to tell about the sources of material and the policies that govern the development of Dell Comics, which are so widely accepted and approved by educators, clergy, and parents."[57] The WPL Company reinforced this message indirectly, too, by sponsoring and bringing editors, writers, and illustrators affiliated with the company to school events, such as a November 1955 "Book Bazaar" at the Violet Avenue School in Hyde Park.[58] Similar events took place in Racine, but Poughkeepsie's proximity to New York City made such meetings easier to coordinate.

Figure 3.11. *The Westerner*, June 1954. *Source:* Courtesy of Wisconsin Historical Society.

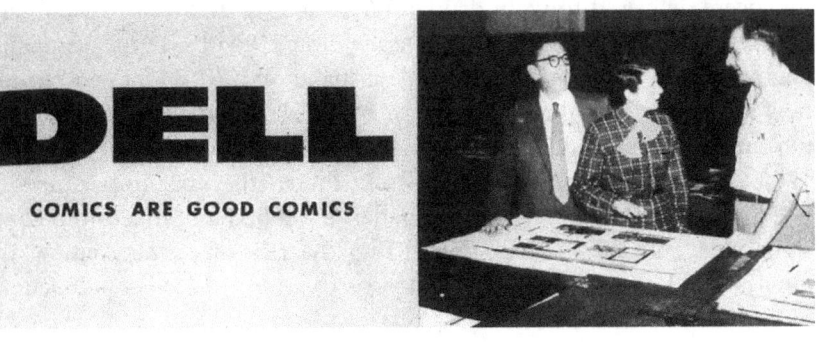

Another layer of protection may have been added by the massive scale and success of the WPL Company's operations. Journalists in Poughkeepsie could not help marveling at the facility's achievements. The 1948 article described above pointed out that the facility printed 18 million comics per month. Similarly, the commission chair referred to the site as "one of the country's finest publishing plants" when he and other members visited in 1950. Comics themselves were controversial. A faith in, and fascination with, cutting-edge technology was not.

Technology in the Community

"Cutting edge" was no mere figure of speech in Poughkeepsie. Five decades after leaving the company for the International Business Machines Corporation (IBM), former employee Barbara McGue (Jones) Carrington spoke enthusiastically about the massive blades that would slice through paper to create comics, paperbacks, and other products. Employment at Western Printing had its challenges, she recounts, including a pension plan that was far inferior to IBM's. But the sight of the "big old knives coming down" was "amazing" (Carrington). A glimpse inside the plant in 1946 provided by journalist Helen Myers gives a similar sense of the plant's dauntingly immense operations: "You see the inner sections of comics magazines, printed in four colors, rolling by the thousand from the giant rotary presses, and sheets that will be cut into the covers, also printed in four colors, coming from the offset presses that are smaller, but still huge pieces of machinery."[59] The WPL Company's push for efficient and precise comics production led to many innovations; for example, Western Printing successfully launched a process by which inks moved directly from trucks rather than having to be stored first in barrels. "Originally comic inks were delivered to us in drums. We ladled the ink into ink fountains on the presses by hand," *The Westerner* noted. By 1951, the company's engineers had collaborated with ink distributor J. M. Huber to create a new system in Poughkeepsie: "Today, Huber delivers our red, yellow, and blue inks from a single multicolor tank truck into our respective 800-, 1200-, and 800-gallon tanks . . . [F]rom there, [the inks are] pumped as need[ed] to our presses where the paper is webbed and inked into comic signatures."[60] In addition to minimizing the risk of contamination, this new method saved the storage space that would otherwise be occupied by hundreds of ink barrels.

According to Jim Robishaw, who worked at Western Printing from 1959 to 1982, the WPL Company frequently launched new technologies in Poughkeepsie, identified problems and best practices, and then introduced them in Racine and other locations (Robishaw). *The Westerner* bears out his claim. When the Miller Printing Machine Company in Germany shipped its new four-color offset press to the WPL Company in 1958, the destination was Poughkeepsie. In later years, the site's proximity to IBM facilitated the early adoption of computerized methods for accounting, mailing, and typesetting.[61] In order to accommodate these acquisitions, the Western Printing facility grew with startling rapidity. Building after building was added to the original Fiat plant, which had had a footprint of about 128,000 square feet. By 1958, it covered approximately 600,000 square feet, or more than ten football fields (see figure 3.12).

Figure 3.12. Aerial view of the Western Printing facility at its most extensive. Company leaders labeled the buildings alphabetically in order of their construction. *Source:* Julianna Gassler. Used with permission.

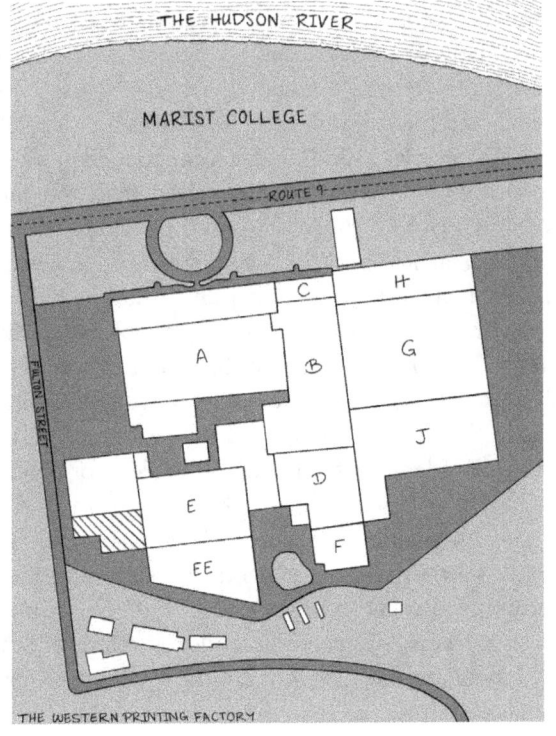

Instead of jealously guarding its technological secrets, Western Printing opened its doors to curious visitors from the region and worldwide. Much as WDC's parks have always foregrounded their own feats of architecture and engineering, so did the Poughkeepsie plant proudly display its sophisticated systems for creating, printing, and shipping printed works. Often working in coordination with the Dutchess County Council on World Affairs, the facility hosted many international visitors. In 1951 and 1952 alone, the plant hosted nine representatives from various countries in South America; Luis Novaro, from Mexico, who published Dell comics in that country; Japanese banker Yoshio Okuno; and George Dhairian, a student from India. There was a startling total of fifteen hundred visitors to Poughkeepsie in 1960, *The Westerner* reported, noting that twenty employees at that site were trained as guides to the facility.[62]

In addition to reaching out to international partners and colleagues, Western Printing cultivated close relationships with the many educational institutions in the area. Vassar College, Bard College, and the State University of New Paltz regularly conducted field trips to the facility. Dutchess County Community College received funding for its library and language laboratory from the company in 1962. Located across North Road from the facility, Marist University developed particularly close ties with Western Printing.[63] Marist allowed the company's leagues to use its softball field, its students served as role players in a 1960 disaster simulation exercise, and in 1961, it too received funding for a language laboratory.[64]

Younger visitors were also welcome. Particularly in the first half of the 1950s, Western Printing made the most of children's enthusiasm for comics. A *Westerner* article in 1952 estimated that between five hundred and six hundred students from kindergarten through twelfth grade visited the Poughkeepsie facility annually as part of school or scouting field trips. "The big attraction, of course, is the fact that 'here is where they make the comic books' . . . to see the four colors, yellow, red, blue, and black combined to produce the finished page is always exciting."[65] One child even requested—and received—a personal tour of the plant for his eighth birthday.

Western Printing's leaders took care to go beyond the confines of their facility, too. As shown in figure 3.13, regular presentations at the Dutchess County Fair in Rhinebeck enticed readers of all ages to look through its tempting display of comics and children's books. In fact, the booth at the fair proved so appealing to children that it became a resource for parents: as the February 1950 *Westerner* recounts, "absent-minded parents who had lost track of their little ones would always return and find them scanning the attractive Western display."[66]

Figure 3.13. *The Westerner*, February 1950. *Source:* Courtesy of Wisconsin Historical Society.

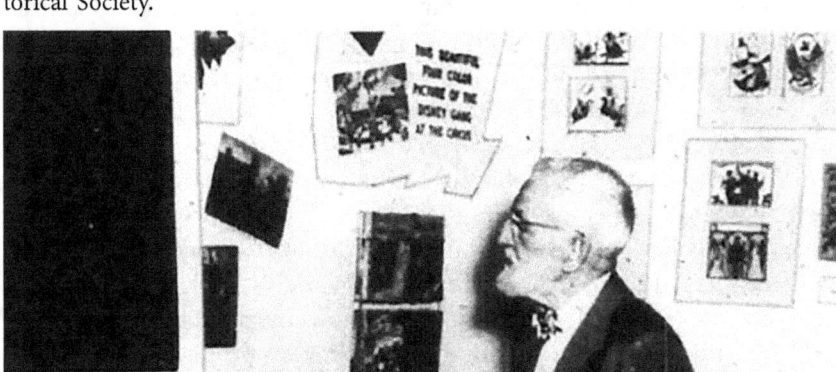

In addition to providing de facto childcare at the fair, Western Printing's employees made substantial and sustained contributions to civic and community life in the Hudson River valley. Executives served on the boards of organizations such as Vassar Brothers Hospital, Dutchess County Community College, and the Catharine Street Community Center. Harold Spencer, brother to the WPL Company's cofounder, Roy Spencer, and a longtime general manager of the plant, was lauded in the *Poughkeepsie Journal* years after his death as "one of the most active and best known civic leaders in the area."[67] Espoused by the WPL Company as a whole, the corporate good citizenship practiced by Spencer and others made them a good fit with the many civic-minded people and organizations in Poughkeepsie and throughout Dutchess County.

Life and Work with the Company

Even as it burnished its external reputation with these activities, Western Printing experienced its share of internal conflicts: A 1954 *Westerner*, for example, noted the resolution of a "prolonged painful work stoppage" in Poughkeepsie.[68] Interviews with former employees indicate that their work was often extremely demanding. When he began work at the print shop, Robishaw recalled, an old-timer took him aside and said, "In this business, you don't sit down." The advice accurately reflected Robishaw's experiences. "It is a challenge to run a press," he recalled, especially one with four colors: "You had to lay stuff out in the proper position. Now you're talking precision." Robishaw also found the culture at times overbearing: when a supervisor said that men working on the floor shouldn't have facial hair, "I started growing a beard that day and kept it for forty-three years." But he also was impressed by the WPL Company's culture of stable, "generational" employment for its workers (Robishaw).

The mid-twentieth-century heyday of comics production at Western Printing presented a mix of positive and negative experiences for artists as well as for those on the production side of the business. The closely related careers of John Stanley (1914–1993) and Irving Tripp (1921–2008) reveal greatly divergent experiences.

Born in Manhattan and a Hudson River valley resident for most of his life, John Stanley is today a revered figure among cartoonists and comics readers (see chapter 5 for a tribute from cartoonist Summer Pierre). One outstanding component of Stanley's body of work is his fourteen-year run with *Little Lulu*, a character created by Marjorie Buell and developed by Stanley with the indispensable contributions of Irving Tripp (as explored below).[69] As the lead writer and drafter of *Lulu*'s stories between 1945 and 1959, Stanley paired narrative adventurousness with a disciplined, decisive artistic style. Whether depicting Lulu, other children in her neighborhood, or newly landed aliens emerging from their spaceship, Stanley makes his characters move and speak in utterly persuasive ways. His achievements are particularly striking given the controversies surrounding comics in the mid-1950s. As arguments swirled around him, Stanley takes Lulu on adventures that are simultaneously familiar, surreal, funny, and surprising (see figure 3.14). The *Lulu* comics amply support a colleague's description of Stanley as "one of the greatest story men I've ever been associated with."[70] It was one of the WPL Company's most successful comics and a true cultural phenomenon in the late 1940s and into the 1950s. There was a Lulu balloon each year in the Thanksgiving Day Parade in New York City, and her face adorned Kleenex boxes, coloring books, and other merchandise.[71]

While Stanley visited Western Printing in Poughkeepsie only rarely, he imbued the strip with locations drawn from life in Peekskill, New

Figure 3.14. "Five Little Babies," story and art by John Stanley and Irving Tripp, with a character created by Marjorie Buell, 1951. *Source:* NBCUniversal. Used with permission.

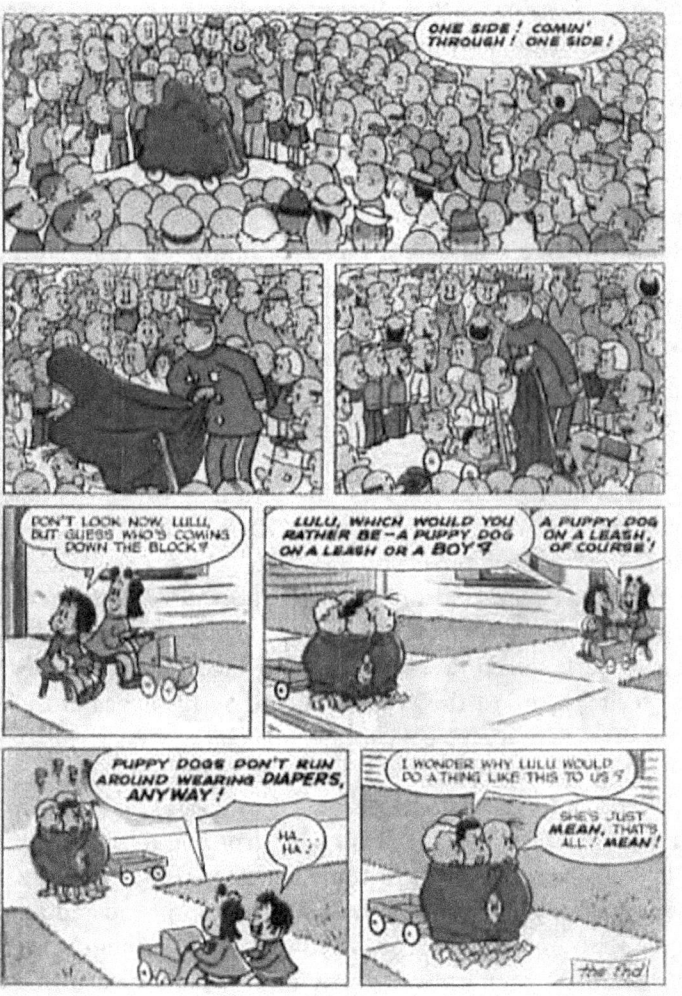

York, the main town center near his Croton-on-Hudson home.[72] Though nominally taking place in the fictional town of Meadowville, Lulu's exploits all reflect real-life locations in the area, as Lulu expert Bradley Tenan has demonstrated. The Sunset Diner in the 1950 story "Great Day," for example, is modeled on Peekskill's Central Diner.[73] Over a half-century later, *Little Lulu* comics are readily accessible thanks to anthologies produced by Another Rainbow in the 1980s and Dark Horse Press in the 2000s. Although he rarely gave interviews, Stanley is the subject of a full-length study, Bill Schelly's *John Stanley: Giving Life to Little Lulu* (2017), as well as thoughtful analyses by Michael Barrier and Frank Young.[74] These sources shed light on Stanley's brilliance and on his struggles with alcoholism and depression.

Working for the WPL Company may not have caused Stanley's health problems, but it definitely left him embittered. Part of the problem may have been Buell's ongoing oversight of *Little Lulu*. Although she licensed the character to the WPL Company and Dell Publishing in the 1940s, she retained a large measure of creative control. As Maggie Thompson explained in a 1985 interview with Buell, "Dell regularly sent a rough draft of each comic to Marge to okay."[75] (This process remained in place until 1972, when Buell finally sold the rights to the WPL Company.)[76] To make matters worse, the WPL Company did not give Stanley a byline in *Little Lulu* comics. He was acknowledged only once, in 1952, as a cover artist.[77] Small wonder, then, that Stanley "maintained a shell of indifference toward the work to which he was devoted for most of his adult life."[78] Stanley stopped working for the WPL Company in 1959 and spent his later years first in New York City, then in a rural area near Cold Spring, another town near the Hudson River. He took a job working as a screen printer for a local manufacturer of precision rulers. Toward the end of his life, he also participated in a few comics-related events, often expressing negative feelings toward the WPL Company in his appearances.[79]

By contrast, Stanley's collaborator on *Lulu*, Irving Tripp, enjoyed a longer-lasting and generally more positive relationship with the company. Tripp was born into a family with deep roots in Poughkeepsie (see the profile of his uncle, Elmer Tripp, in chapter 5). According to his son, Bill, Tripp hoped to study art at the Pratt Institute but took a job at Western Printing immediately after graduating from high school. An undated photograph (figure 3.15) shows him, probably before 1941, grinning broadly in the company of other young artists at the facility. He served in the army as a corporal in the South Pacific during World War II; in 1943, he became engaged to Janet DuBois, who was a Poughkeepsie native herself.[80] Married in 1946, Tripp went back to work at the Comics Department at Western Printing, began to raise a family that eventually included four children, and became an active scout leader and participant in community events.[81]

As detailed in a valuable interview conducted by Bruce Hamilton for a *Little Lulu* anthology published in 1985, Tripp had a varied career

Figure 3.15. *Source:* Reproduced with the kind permission of the Tripp family.

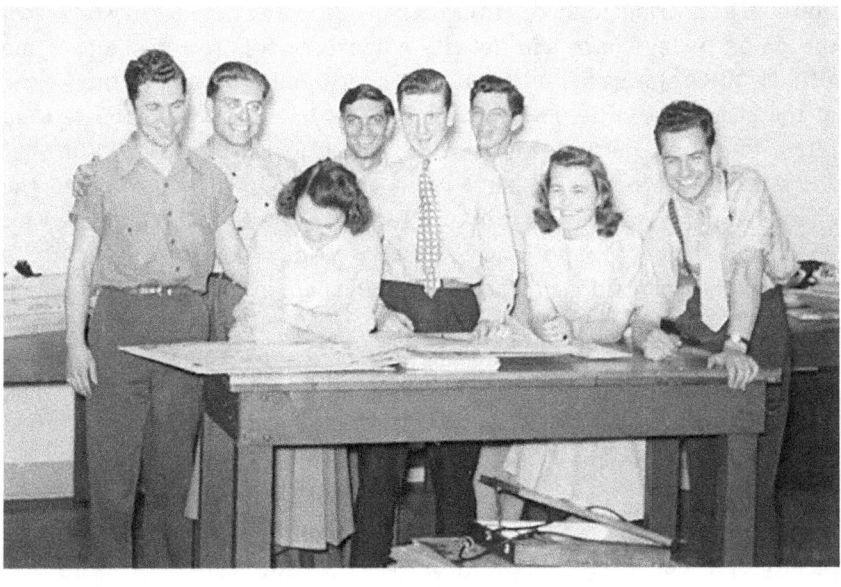

at Western Printing. He produced Disney comics early on, as well as the "snap-action" drawings in Big Little Books: These were small illustrations in the corner of the books that became animated when the pages were flipped.[82] After the war, Tripp and a colleague approached editor Oskar Lebeck about taking on new projects. One of these turned out to be *Little Lulu.*

For over a decade Tripp adapted Stanley's sketches into meticulously rendered drawings, pouring his own attention and emotions into the process. The three collaborators' in-person interactions were minimal. Buell and Stanley met once; Stanley and Tripp met only a handful of times.[83] While Tripp always spoke generously about Stanley's work, the reverse was not always true.[84] Any artist knows the effort needed to bring a draft into actual execution. That difference is where Tripp's achievement resides. His confident line work renders Stanley's drawings with propulsive movement, lively facial expressions, and strikingly skillful crowd scenes, which, as he noted to Hamilton, were time-consuming to produce. Even as he considered himself lucky to work on the comic, the work was very demanding; pressing deadlines and regular weekend work were part of his life as a comics creator at Western Printing.[85]

When Hamilton asked if he got bored drawing for nine to ten hours a day, Tripp replied, "Every day is different because I would feel the mood of the characters myself. When Lulu was happy she gave me a lift. If there was sadness I would feel that too. I would have the feeling of the characters while I was doing the job and this is what made it so interesting . . . I never regretted a day going to work" (13). Asked after his retirement whether Stanley had a feeling of ownership toward the characters, Tripp replied, "I think so. I know, because I feel the same way, you live with them for so long . . . they were my kids."[86]

After Stanley stopped working on *Little Lulu* in 1959, Tripp continued to draw (and often letter and color) the comic for two additional decades. In some ways, Tripp's career recalls that of Fanny Palmer at Currier & Ives. In both cases, talented artists served as a mainstay for a company's production of material that became important parts of American visual culture. But because their works do not reflect the hand-created vision of a single artist, some might overlook their contributions. Nevertheless, Tripp seems to have found satisfaction in his work for Western Printing. The facility even encouraged his work in other artistic media. As with many artists covered in this volume, Tripp's body of work included landscape painting as well as cartooning, as seen in figure 3.16.[87] Along with other Western employees (including those from the WPL Company's Manhattan offices), Tripp regularly participated in the annual art shows held at the plant throughout the 1960s. He was a prize winner at least once, in 1961.[88]

A cartoon Tripp created for his daughter, Linda, during his retirement testifies to his ongoing fondness for the characters he had brought to life for so many years (figure 3.17). Bill Tripp affectionately notes that the photographer looks just like his father, even though Tripp did not choose to depict himself from the loftiest angle.[89] Funny, unpretentious, and skillfully rendered, the cartoon exemplifies Tripp's artistic talent and generosity of spirit.

Tripp was not the only local resident to enjoy a lengthy and satisfying career at Western Printing. Throughout the 1950s, *The Westerner* regularly ran features on Poughkeepsie families who had multiple members working at Western Printing. Its story on the Jones family in 1951 demonstrates that, even during the 1950s, women played an important role in the facility's workforce. In addition to the four Jones brothers, the plant also employed their sister, Josephine Jones, in the Packing and Assembling Department, and two of the brothers' wives, Laura and Edna Jones, in the Comic Finishing Department.[90] Continuing a practice first seen in

Figure 3.16. *Source:* Reproduced with the kind permission of the Tripp family.

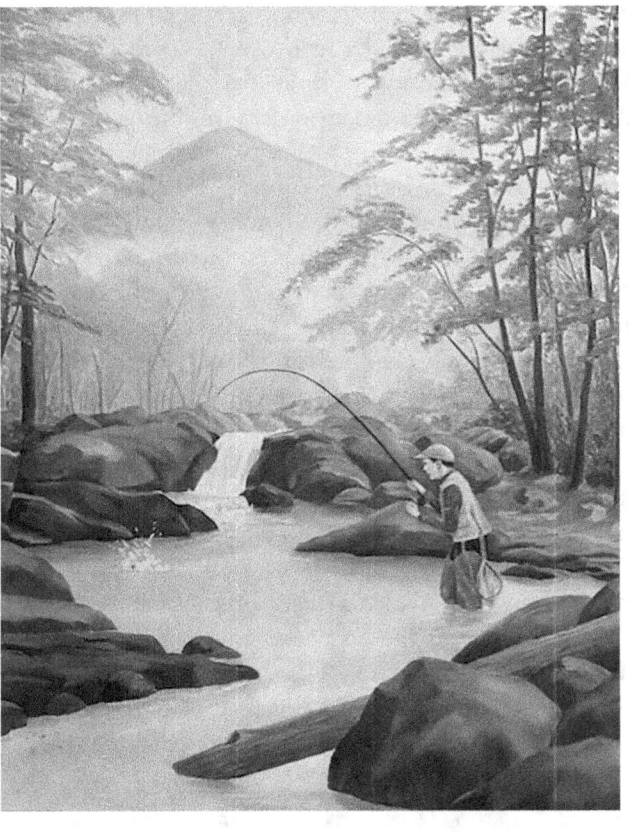

Figure 3.17. *Source:* Reproduced with the kind permission of the Tripp family.

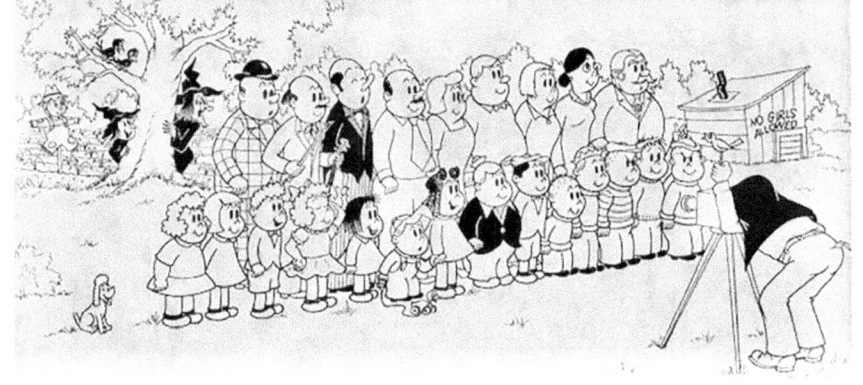

Fanny Palmer's day, comics coloring and masking provided particular opportunities for women; a 1951 photograph of the Photo-Engraving and Masking Department, which helped color *Walt Disney's Comics and Stories*, depicts women hard at work at their desks (figure 3.18).[91] While it was initially unusual for women to achieve journeyman status, Winni Briggs did so as an opaquer in the Litho-Art Department in 1952, and others would follow in the years to come.[92]

Carrington, who worked in the Bindery from 1959 to 1979, offered a mix of reminiscences that echoed those of Robishaw. "I enjoyed working there. I would go back," she asserted, even though annual raises and pension contributions were not as generous as those at her later employer, IBM. Carrington grew to value her interactions with other employees in the Bindery section of the factory, to whom she remains close despite moving to Washington state after her retirement (Carrington). Another employee in the Bindery, Sue Turner, is even more effusive in her discussion of the workforce, which she regards as "one big happy family." Both Turner and Carrington have fond memories of Doris Mack, for example. Often called "Mother Mack" by women in the Bindery who were a bit younger, Mack "was a smart lady" who provided a caring presence at work (Turner). Mack was also a civic leader in the area who later served as a National Park Service guide at Val-kill and who was acquainted with Eleanor Roosevelt.[93] Both Carrington and Turner, who are Black, took part in the sports leagues

Figure 3.18. *The Westerner*, December 1951. *Source:* Courtesy of Wisconsin Historical Society.

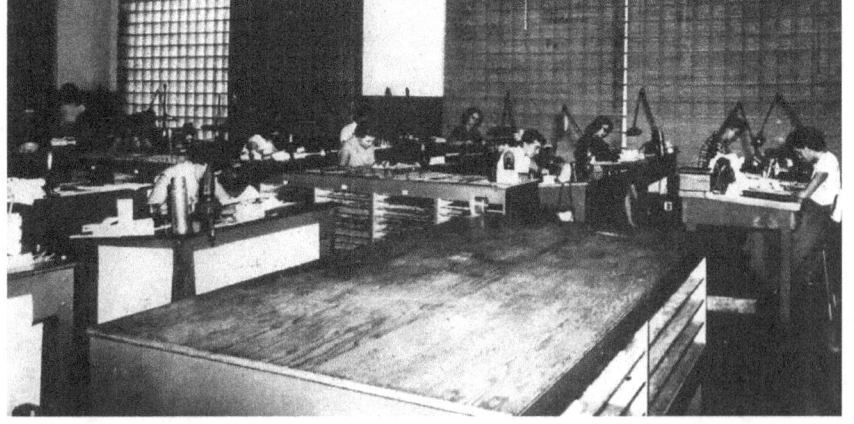

that formed a crucial part of Western Printing's community involvement in the late 1950s and early 1960s. Turner recalled an incident in which the women's basketball team's effort to celebrate their victories with a festive dinner in Poughkeepsie was interrupted by the restaurant's racist owner, who refused to serve her. The team immediately left. The memory of the incident remained vivid to Turner more than fifty years later (Turner).

Other sports teams fielded by Western Printing were integrated as well by the late 1950s. Glenn Henry Johnson, a Black man working in the Shipping and Receiving Department who later became a human resources specialist at IBM, won the Most Valuable Player Award for his division's softball team in 1959 (see figure 3.19).[94] Western Printing sponsored a Little League team with both white and Black players; one of the coaches in the early 1960s was Rupert Tarver, a well-known community activist in Poughkeepsie.[95] But it would take another decade for the pages of *The Westerner* to directly address the civil rights movement or the benefits of a diverse workforce.[96] In its corporate leadership and sales departments, the WPL Company remained relentlessly male and white.

Figure 3.19. *The Westerner*, December 1959. *Source:* Courtesy of Wisconsin Historical Society.

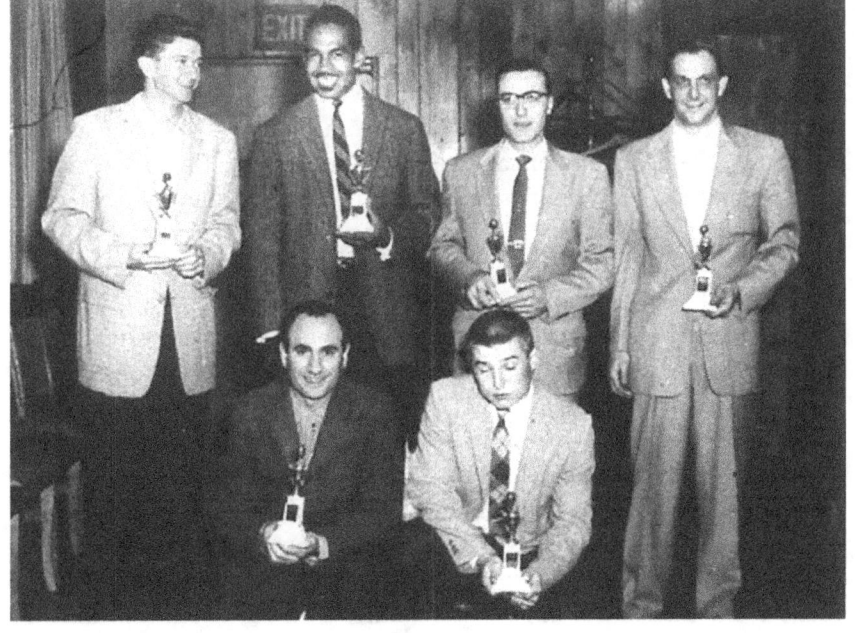

On the other hand, some aspects of the WPL Company's culture contrast strongly, and favorably, with twenty-first-century practices. It acknowledged that employees were not defined exclusively by their productivity metrics. Although employees were expected to maintain a near-superhuman level of consistency and meticulousness, they were also praised for devoting at least part of their time to their hobbies and for expressing themselves creatively in pursuits that had nothing to do with their work output. Hundreds of people attended the art competitions at which Irving Tripp and many others exhibited their work. Pastimes less directly tied to the plant's products were celebrated, too. The "Pix from Pokip" section that appeared in almost every *Westerner* from the mid-1950s through 1964 featured employees who put together gas-powered airplane models, created elaborate robot costumes for their daughter at Halloween, and lived with a menagerie of half a dozen monkeys.[97] Apparently the brainchild of Director of Public Relations and Education John "Jack" Dougherty, these pages feel like a twentieth-century version of a social media account. The February 1954 "Pix" (see figure 3.20) shows Richard Scarry's visit and captures the tempting displays of Western Printing's annual pop-up Christmas store, which was established at the plant in its inaugural holiday season in 1934.

Given these aspects of company culture, it is perhaps unsurprising that the sons and daughters of former Western Printing employees almost unanimously have fond memories of their parents' workplaces. Michael Calenti's father, Achilles "Chilli" Calenti, worked at Western Printing for almost fifty years and could remember a time when "he could count on one hand" the daily tally of cars going by on Route 9. The job supported Michael and his four siblings, all of whom were delighted by a regular perk of their father's work: "He would bring comic books home and it was just a big deal for us. He would bring them home and he would spread them all out, and we would just grab onto them" (Calenti). Carrington recounts that there was usually a pile near one of the main exits, so that employees could pick up some as they headed home (Carrington). Adding to this benefit were annual events such as the summer picnic and the Christmas party, as shown in figure 3.21.

Pamela A. Scarpero recounts another exciting holiday event. Since her father, Harold "Hal" Bittner, helped to lead the Comic Art Department, her family received a Christmas card from WDC one year: "That was a big thing for us" (Scarpero). For her part, Susan Miller valued the chances she had to accompany her father, J. Edward Johnson, into the

Figure 3.20. *The Westerner*, February 1954. *Source:* Courtesy of Wisconsin Historical Society.

PIX FROM POKIP

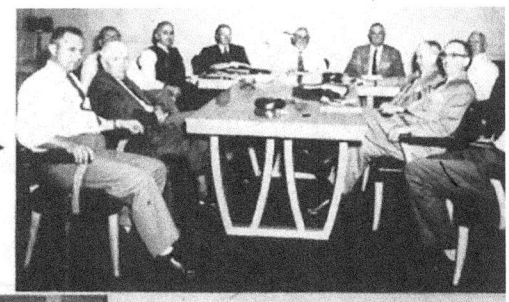

For the first time in its history, the Board of Directors of Western Printing and Lithographing Company held one of its meetings at Poughkeepsie, late in 1953. A full attendance marked the occasion. Seated in the conference room at Pokip, clockwise, from the left, are: Herman E. Johnson, Roy A. Spencer, Jerome C. Wiechers, H. M. Benstead, Emil Stremlau (legal counsel), E. H. Wadewitz, W. R. Wadewitz, H. D. Spencer (background), Elmer G. Voigt, John M. Wolff, Paul Lyle.

Two visiting "firemen" from Racine took time out on a trip to New York to exchange ideas and information with fellow Westerners at Poughkeepsie. Left to right, checking the well-known quality of Pokip reproduction are Elwood Siewert, Foreman of Stereo and Composing Rooms at Pokip; William Reisdorf, Bindery Foreman at Racine; Harold D. Spencer, Vice President in charge of operations at Poughkeepsie; Fred Ragahn, Foreman of Box Department at Racine.

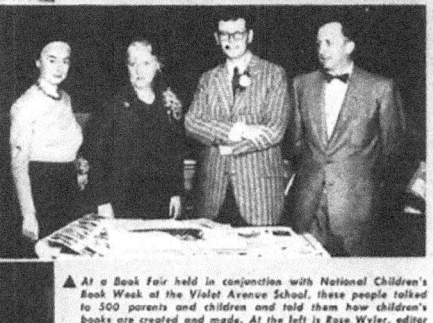

At a Book Fair held in conjunction with National Children's Book Week at the Violet Avenue School, these people talked to 500 parents and children and told them how children's books are created and made. At the left is Rose Wyler, editor of a series of Every Day Science stories, who conducted scientific experiments for the children. Lucille Ogle, Vice President of Artists & Writers Guild, Inc., at New York City spoke about Walt Disney creations and explained how Golden Books are developed. Richard Scarry, author and illustrator, showed the youngsters how illustrations are made. At the right is Edwin A. Juckett, Supervising Principal, Roosevelt High School, Hyde Park, N. Y., who presided at the event.

Friendly competitors often compare notes too, and here are three representatives from Forbes Lithographing Company of Boston, Mass., visiting Western at Poughkeepsie late in 1953, under the expert guidance of Harold D. Spencer, who is coatless. The Forbes men, from left to right, are William Dawe, Superintendent; George Hummer, Quality Control Manager; Arthur R. Hitchings, Chairman of the Board of Directors.

Christmas "shopping" opened with a vengeance in the special Western "store" set up for Westerners at Poughkeepsie. Books, games, greeting cards, gift wrap paper and other items were displayed in profusion and helped to solve some of the gift problems for Western families and friends. Shown in the center is Mary Smith, supervisor in the S & S Shipping Department. Holding the child is Herbert Spaeth, Litho Art Department, an early customer.

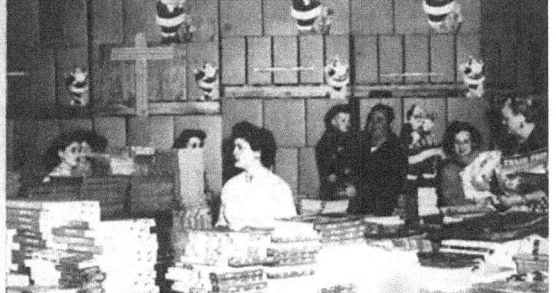

Figure 3.21. *The Westerner*, February 1967. *Source:* Courtesy of Wisconsin Historical Society.

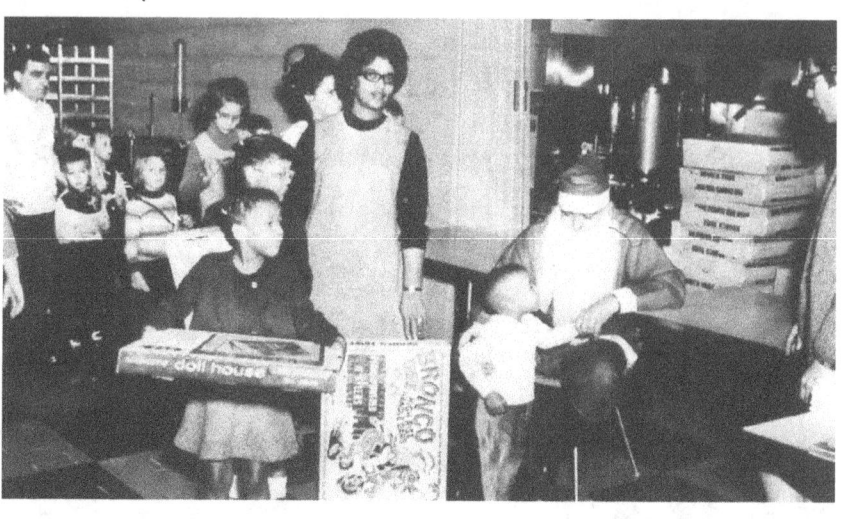

plant when he needed to approve colors coming off the printing press late at night: "Make-ready doesn't happen in the middle of the day," she learned, and she was fascinated to see the plant's operations proceeding throughout the nighttime hours. "As a little girl the whole thing became like a second home to me," she recounted, remembering how plantings of mock-orange shrubs gave off a beautiful scent for everyone who entered or exited the building. Looking back on these experiences as an adult, Miller remains impressed by the "collegiality" and "pride" pervasive throughout Western Printing (Miller).

Through work that was both exhausting and satisfying, workers at Western Printing produced millions of comics in the 1950s, some with a quality still greatly valued today. Slowly, though, the scales tipped away from comics in the WPL Company's cost-benefit analyses. While Western Printing in Poughkeepsie continued to produce comics throughout the 1960s, this product came to occupy a much smaller place in the company's output and corporate narrative.

Comics at the Crossroads

Even before the comics debates of the mid-1950s, the WPL Company at times expressed a conflicted attitude toward the medium that had proven so profitable. While "Dell Comics are good comics" worked well as a slogan, defining the parameters of "good comics" was not always an easy enterprise. An example from *The Westerner*'s own pages illustrates these complexities. The cover of the November 1951 issue (see figure 3.22) features a giant turkey with apparently malevolent plans for the adorable tykes it has entrapped. The cover's humor is a bit edgy compared to the usual subjects found there (flags, beauty queens, bowlers, etc.), and *The Westerner* hedges its bets with an editorial comment within the magazine:

> You will pardon our cover artist, we hope, for going slightly berserk in a topsy-turvy world with his strange interpretation of the Thanksgiving feast. To allay any alarms on the part of the small fry, let us assure them that here in America, at least, it is still our privilege and good fortune to carve the turkey and give thanks for the freedom of learning, worshipping and working in accordance with one's own choice. Let us all keep America a place where we have both the right and the reason to be thankful. (7)

Attempting to counteract the cover's irreverence with a rush of patriotic rhetoric, the commentary epitomizes contradictions within the WPL Company's culture. It often seems unsure how to handle the playful, chaotic elements within its own products.

Perhaps this explains why cartoons appear so rarely in *The Westerner* itself. In 1949, Poughkeepsie-based Harold Bittner created a funny and informative comic about the WPL Company's benefits program, but it turns out to be an exceptional instance in the publication (figure 3.23).

When a repeated cartoon feature does appear in the 1950s, it deploys some of the medium's most harmful tropes: in the mid-1950s, a campaign against employee errors repeatedly uses racist caricatures of Indigenous people to illustrate the workplace sins of inattention, poor communication, and so on.[98] Beyond that, the publication's editors generally refrain from tapping into the communicative power of comics. Indeed, throughout the 1960s *The Westerner* said less and less about comics in its articles. The story the WPL Company wanted to tell about itself became focused on children's literature, educational materials, corporate products, and books produced as rapid responses to major current events, such as the assassination of John F. Kennedy.[99]

A key factor was the souring of the WPL Company's alliance with Dell Comics. Recounting the era in an invaluable special issue of *Comic*

Figure 3.22. *The Westerner*, November 1951. *Source:* Courtesy of Wisconsin Historical Society.

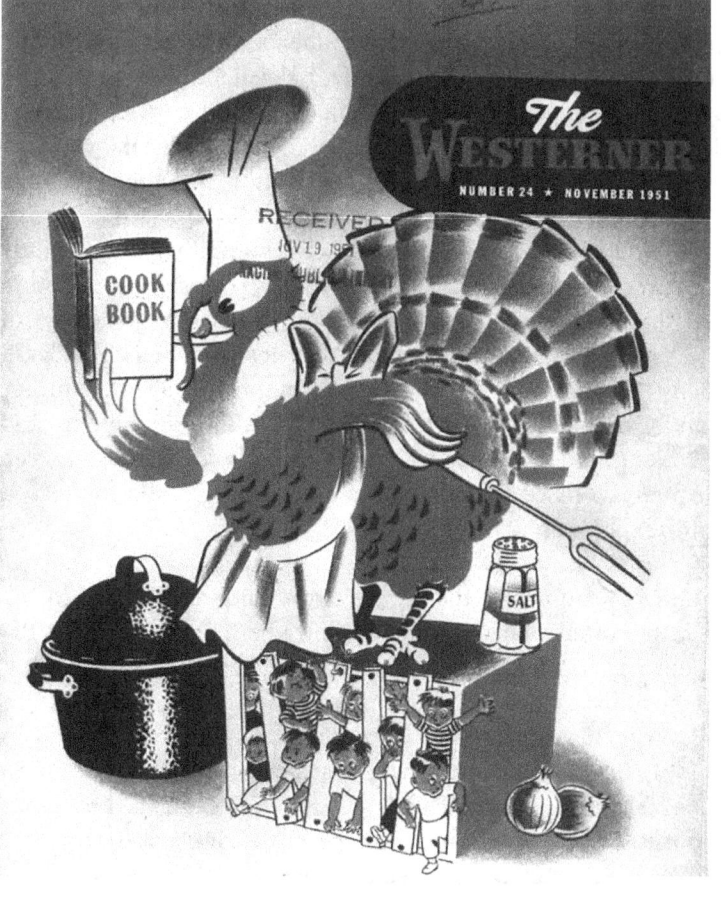

Book Artist focused on the history of Gold Key art and artists, Michelle Miller described the 1962 dissolution of the WPL-Dell alliance as a "divorce" caused by a variety of factors, including increased competition from television aimed at children and the bankruptcy of one of its major distributors.[100] Dell left the comics business for good in 1973; it remained (and remains today) an important player in the book publishing industry, however, and Western Printing continued to produce millions of paperbacks for Dell Books each year.[101] Following the 1962 split, the WPL Company capitalized on its ongoing partnership with WDC and its licensing of *Little Lulu* and *Woody Woodpecker*. Under the auspices of K.K. Publications, the

Figure 3.23. *The Westerner*, December 1949. *Source:* Courtesy of Wisconsin Historical Society and with the kind permission of Pamela A. Scarpero.

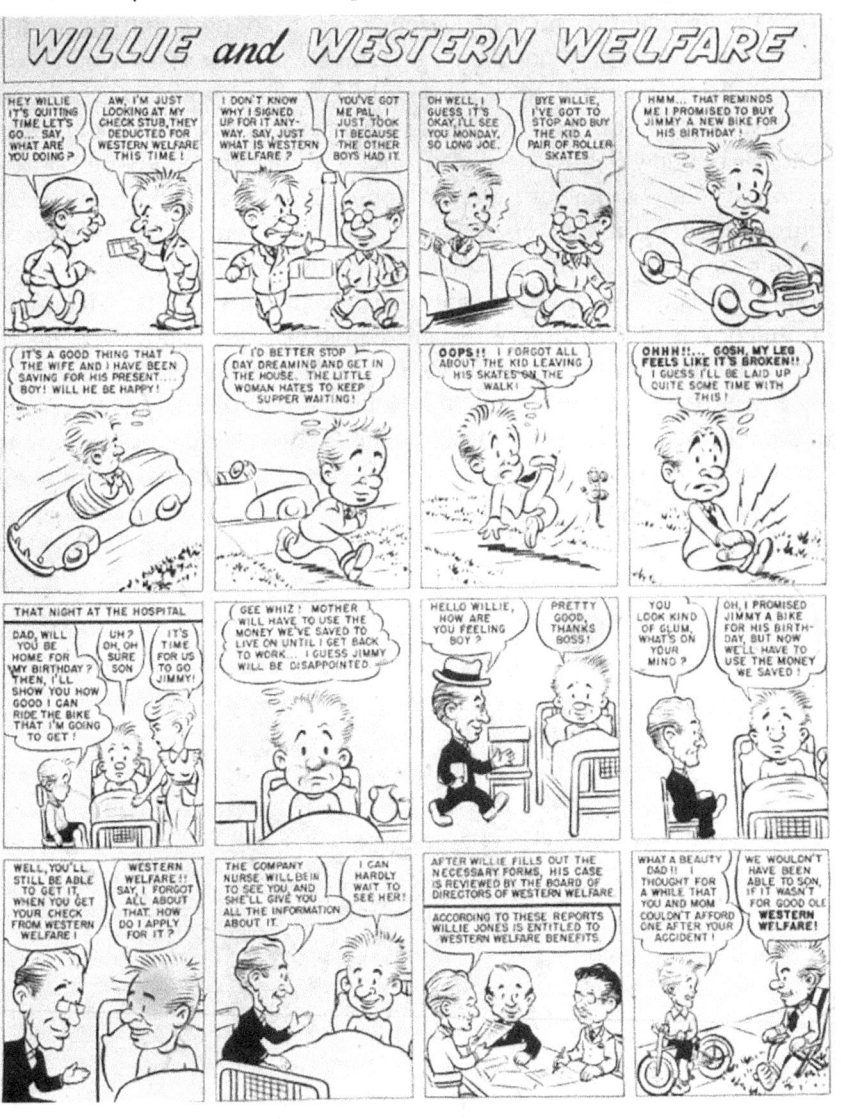

WPL Company began to publish its own line of comics, Gold Key Comics, in 1962, with Western Printing playing a central role in their production.

Some aspects of Gold Key appear unambiguously positive, especially as it was launched. The subsidiary's name gestures toward the commercially successful Little Golden Books while also taking things in an intriguing new direction. There is little straightforward evidence about who deserves credit for the logo, but its design still holds up well today (figure 3.24).

The president of the WPL Company, H. E. Johnson, introduced the venture in favorable, if not glowing, terms in January 1963. Noting "an obvious dip in company sales and profits during the year 1962," Johnson forecasts that "we can also expect our newsstand division to be a growing factor again, now that we have gained recognition, acceptance and distribution for our own line of Gold Key comics and have confidence in their future."[102] Later that year, *The Westerner* describes tours and explanations of "our Gold Key comic operation" for visitors from Mexico and Indonesia—the latter led by newsstand division art director Harold Bittner, creator of the 1948 insurance-benefits comic described above (see figure 3.25). Licensed WDC characters were a crucial part of this division's productions. In 1964, for example, *The Westerner* notes that products related to the new *Mary Poppins* film would include "two special one-shot comic books in two different price classes" produced by "Western's own line of GOLD KEY comics."[103]

At the same time, the line featured content that departed from children's adventure and fantasy. Popular science fiction and speculative fiction

Figure 3.24. Gold Key Comics logo. *Source:* Gold Key Comics. Used with permission.

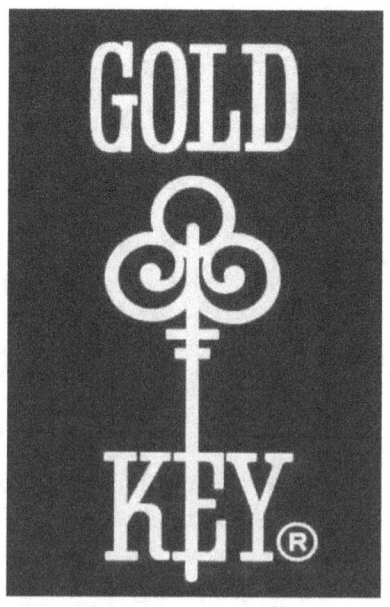

Figure 3.25. *The Westerner*, November 1963. *Source:* Courtesy of Wisconsin Historical Society.

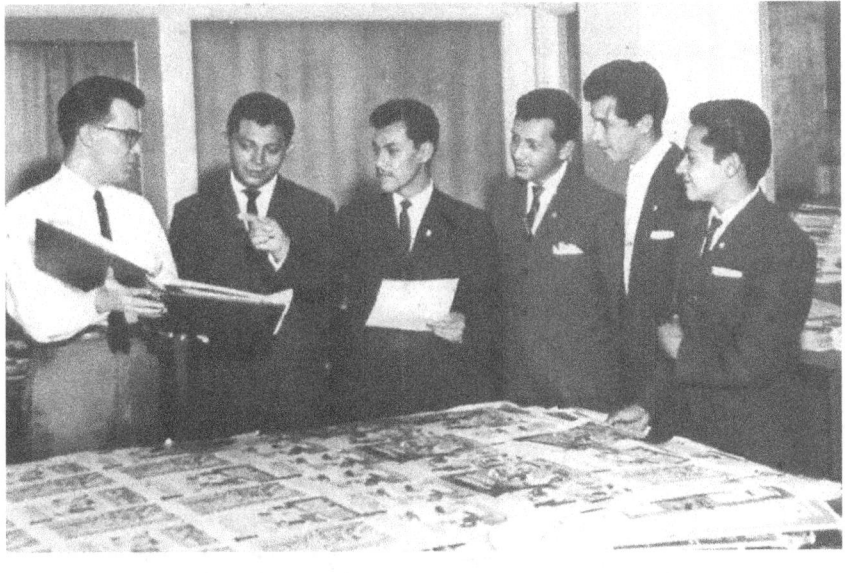

were represented in licensed titles such as *Star Trek, The Twilight Zone,* and *Dark Shadows.* Gold Key artists and writers also generated first-rate original content, such as the prehistoric saga *Turok* and the satisfyingly epic *Magnus, Robot Fighter.* As these pieces were produced, interaction continued between New York–based editors and printers and editors in Poughkeepsie. Freelance artists and writers were located across the country, but some prominent figures were in the area: Yonkers-based George Wilson, for example, gained a devoted following for his painterly covers of *The Phantom, Magnus,* and other titles (see figure 3.26).[104] Noting the high quality of Gold Key products throughout the 1960s, Jon B. Cooke described Gold Key work as "The Place To Be' during his youth": "Maybe Marvel and DC garnered all the glory in that turbulent decade, but some major cool sh*t was coming off the presses in Poughkeepsie, New York!"[105]

But throughout most of the 1960s, the achievements of the writers and artists creating these kinds of comics—particularly the ones not tied to the WDC or aimed at younger readers—go almost completely unremarked in *The Westerner.* Western Printing in Poughkeepsie took a leading role in high-profile projects connected to pressing national events: The quick turnaround and massive distribution of *The Torch Is Passed,* a response

Figure 3.26. George Wilson cover from 1969. *Source:* Gold Key Comics. Used with permission.

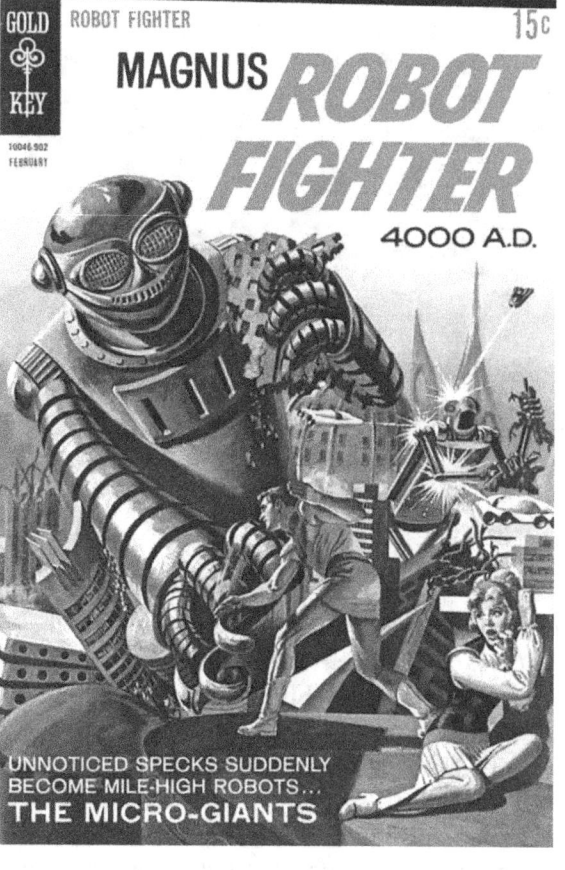

to the life and death of John F. Kennedy, generated a great deal of pride that can still be heard in the memories of employees who played a key role in editing, printing, and shipping it.[106] Educational materials were also touted as a "fast-growing unit"; the WPL Company eagerly signed on to develop and distribute new technologies such as "Projecto-Aid" overhead transparencies.[107] By contrast, the tone of *The Westerner*'s references to comics were tepid at best. Placing K.K. Publications at the end of a long list of other enterprises, the annual report in April 1965 notes that the subsidiary produces "comic magazines to meet high standards that receive the approbation of school and religious circles. Present production approximates 400,000 comics a day. The demand is firm at this level and is carried on at a profit" (6). The report's faint praise aligns with the recollections of Matthew Murphy, a K.K. Publications editor who worked in New York but made frequent forays to Poughkeepsie: "Once I began producing comics at Western, I realized with dismay that management regarded them with disdain. They were considered barely respectable publications for children who had no taste for 'real' books. Yet comics was the locomotive that pulled the newsstand 'train' year after year. Despite the favored position, paperbacks in their best year never brought in as much money as the comics."[108] By 1966, *The Westerner*'s report for 1965 omits comics altogether: "Sales in 1965 increased in important large areas—children's books, children's games, supplemental school-reading books, textbooks, teaching programs, commercial printing and commercial contract printing."[109] Shoppers' move toward supermarkets and away from smaller markets and newsstands posed additional challenges to the distribution and marketing of comics and other printed merchandise—so much so, that in the late 1960s WPL formed an entire department targeting supermarket sales.[110]

But the story of comics at the WPL Company, and at Western Printing in particular, was not quite over yet. After a reorganization in 1968 that gave Murphy a more prominent role—Gold Key became part of a newly formed periodicals division—*The Westerner* begins to mention comics once again, even in connection with slightly edgier material. "Poster comics" containing folded, removable posters were produced as tie-ins not just for the Disney film *Chitty Chitty Bang Bang* comic but also for the film *Yellow Submarine* ("with those ever swingin' and singin' Beatles"), and *Dark Shadows*, "a 'camp' mystery comic thriller which has already had enthusiastic acceptance on ABC-TV."[111] That same year, *The Westerner* quotes Murphy, pointing out "the need for variations in the comic magazine format to present established comic appeals at prices and in sizes that will sell through new outlets and reach wider audiences."[112] In an effort to capitalize on the growing dominance of supermarkets, the WPL Company offered incentives for stores to sell comics in bags of five instead of one at a time.[113] The company also pursued more efficient distribution methods: An article in late 1968 noted that "Comic magazines are being shipped from Poughkeepsie to Australia at less cost and with much less effort these days because of work simplification."[114]

Although these moves improved sales figures, they were not sufficient to save comics production at Western Printing. "Pokip Will Discontinue Comic Book Production," read the page-one headline on *The Westerner*, in an article quoting from a letter distributed to employees by Poughkeepsie plant manager Edward Kaul on May 22, 1969. Noting that "comic manufacturing at Poughkeepsie had been a very marginal operation in terms of profitability and that cost patterns are well above those of Western's competitors," Kaul argued that the change would "best serve the long-range interests of our people and the plant," by involving employees in "other, more profitable kinds of work." After about a year and a half of winding down, "Western will continue to publish its Gold Key comics by having them produced by a supplier," identified later in the article as Illinois-based World Color Press, a printer that "specializes in comics production and is more centrally located nationally."[115] Originally an asset, Western Printing's location in the Northeast had become a liability for comics production and distribution. A year later, as the changes were implemented, WPL Company president W. C. Kidd offered an even harsher assessment: "We have looked at all the activities of our business and decided to trim 'losers' sharply. These actions include . . . the switching of our comic book production from our Poughkeepsie Plant to an outside supplier."[116]

Despite these moves, the WPL Company did not completely extricate itself from the comics industry. Although it had outsourced the printing process, the company continued to publish them until 1984, soon after the Western Printing plant's closure.[117] Well beyond 1970, the publication information of many comics lists North Road in Poughkeepsie as the publisher's address. In 1971, *The Westerner* announced the company's push to license out its own content, such as Wacky Witch, noting that the character was "originally developed for Gold Key comics."[118] Similarly, 1973 saw the company expressing renewed interest in *Little Lulu*, particularly given that she had become a WPL-owned property rather than a licensed one: "Now that we own Little Lulu, our company has big plans for the little girl." A year later, it celebrated a contract with Hallmark to produce *Lulu*-related merchandise and cards.[119] Not one word of these articles mentioned Poughkeepsie-based Irving Tripp, even though by this point he had entered his third decade of working on the cartoon, often taking on the bulk of the work without help from collaborators.

Licensing agreements with WDC kept Gold Key going, too: the WPL Company published *Walt Disney's Comics and Stories* until 1980.[120] But the decision at Poughkeepsie in 1970 was a watershed moment. Noting the centrality of printing to the WPL Company's corporate identity, Evanier argues that once this process was outsourced, "people in the office spoke of that as the beginning of the end for Gold Key Comics."[121]

Western Printing itself remained operational for about fourteen years after the cessation of comics production there. Throughout the 1970s, it was sustained by its production of paperbacks, maps, games, and a best-selling Betty Crocker cookbook with accompanying recipe cards. As late as 1982, it still employed 770 people, as well as high school and college students who took temporary jobs there.[122]

In 1979, however, a painful transition took place. The WPL Company's forty-five-year tenure at the site abruptly concluded when the company was sold to Mattel. When describing the change, both Robishaw and a 1983 *Poughkeepsie Journal* article echoed Evanier's melancholy phrase, "the beginning of the end"—and employees had a strong sense of foreboding at the time (Robishaw).[123] Things limped along for the next few years, resembling the waning years of Fiat's operations on the site. In late 1982, company leaders announced that operations in Poughkeepsie would cease in 1983, a move that devastated employees and others in the community.[124] While a clear rationale for the closure was not forthcoming from the company, employees and local commentators attributed the decision to the economic recession, tensions between management and Poughkeepsie union leadership, and ill will between the Racine and Poughkeepsie sites. "A lot of us could write a book about [the reasons behind the closure], but it doesn't serve any purpose," former Western Printing executive Edgar Zipprich told the *Poughkeepsie Journal* in July 1983.[125] In ensuing years, the WPL Company as a whole changed hands several times before being sold off for parts. Random House bought Golden Books in 2001; that same year, the WPL Company closed its headquarters in Racine.[126]

It wasn't quite the end of artistic activity at the Western Printing site, though. For a few years afterward, Marist University housed its Art Department and several classrooms in the space's front building.[127] Professor Emeritus of Art Richard Lewis recalls the leased section of the factory as a roomy and functional space with beautiful light streaming through the glass blocks that remained in the building (Lewis). Equally memorable, though somewhat less ethereal, was a sign that Lewis retrieved from the building (see figure 3.27). The railroad tracks entering one of the buildings at the back of the site may even have provided a rogue instructor with the opportunity to sneak students into the site for lessons on three-point perspective. Other courses in writing and Chinese history were attended in the space by future comics writer Ron Marz (see chapter 5).

Other artists made use of the site as well. As documented in author John Breiner's fascinating work *Power Kingdom: Graffiti in Poughkeepsie*,

Figure 3.27. Sign salvaged from the former Western Printing facility. *Source:* Richard Lewis. Used with permission.

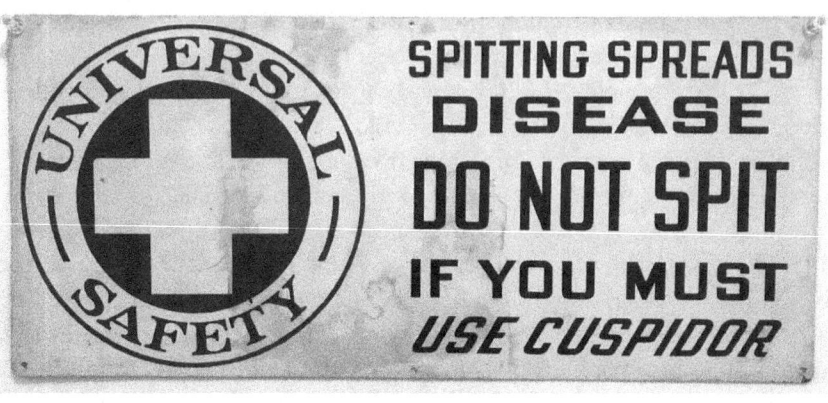

NY (1990s and 2000s) (2022), both the interior and exterior of the buildings served as canvases for ephemeral but sophisticated compositions by graffiti artists from the New York City area and Hudson River valley (see figure 3.28). Breiner recounts that he and other artists developed their "experience and style" through their work on the facility's interior and exterior.[128] Focused on their own art, Breiner did not think much about the site's history during his six or seven visits there. Only once, Breiner said, did an intrusion of light through a hole in the roof give him a feeling of "residual spirit energy" from the people who once worked there (Breiner).

Local authorities probably were no more pleased by the graffiti writers' work than were leaders in 1934 by the doings at the Jumbo Market. All but one of the structures were demolished in the late 1990s to allow for the building of several big-box stores. The remaining building, which still occupies the space today, contained harmful industrial residues that necessitated a 2011 evaluation and cleanup by the Environmental Protection Agency.[129]

But not all the facility's remnants were toxic—far from it. The legacy of Western Printing in Poughkeepsie survives in the rich body of work that was produced there and sent all over the world. Some of these comics have been reissued; others can be found in their original form in secondhand bookstores and in digital retail sites. Other effects are both less visible and more pervasive. Traces of the WPL Company emerge in the ongoing preeminence of WDC as a massive global entertainment

Figure 3.28. Graffiti by the artist MONE created at the Western Printing facility shortly before its demolition. *Source:* John Breiner. Used with permission.

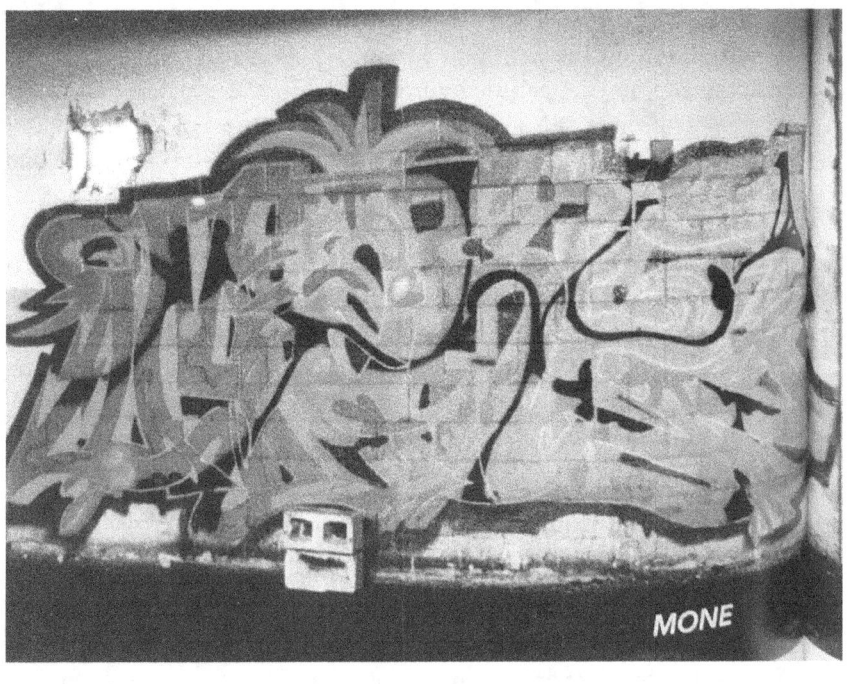

company; in the women cartoonists who chose to call themselves the "Friends of Lulu" when they banded together in 1993; and in the devotion to Gold Key Comics that led four investors to revive the label in 2022.[130] The labor, creativity, and innovation of people in the Hudson River valley played a key role in all of these achievements.

And, as it turns out, it would be inaccurate to say that Western Printing activities have completely ceased in the area. In 1979, the same year that Mattel took over the company, current and former employees in Poughkeepsie banded together to form a new organization, Retirees of Western. Numbering in the hundreds in subsequent decades, the group has hosted dozens of picnics, Hudson River boat cruises, theater outings, and holiday parties.[131] A *Retirees of Western* newsletter has provided lively recaps of these events, indulged in nostalgic recollections, and shared collective sadness over bereavements and other losses, such as the plant's demolition in 1998: "I am still in shock, after all those years, to find that our building has been levelled and is now a huge field of rubble," lamented Retirees of Western president Harold L. Loper in the newsletter later that year.[132] Nevertheless, Loper went on to celebrate the success of the organization and the ability to connect with colleagues near and far by means of the newsletter (see figure 3.29).

Irving Tripp was one such employee. Having moved to Florida after his retirement, he stayed in touch with his connections up north: "I had no idea that you retirees had such a large and wonderful organization," he wrote to the Retirees of Western president in 1999. "I am looking forward to my membership and receiving my newsletter and the directory next year."[133] Barbara Carrington still receives the newsletter in Washington state. Although time has inevitably diminished the number of remaining employees, the July 2023 newsletter, produced by Jim Robishaw using the latest digital software, presents an ongoing schedule of events for the months to come.

All of this suggests that while Western Printing was not a perfect place to work, it did put down genuine roots in its community, leading to connections among employees that persist to this day. It is not just that people in Poughkeepsie helped to create comics. Comics (and the WPL Company's other products) helped to create Poughkeepsie.

And, as it turns out, the region's history as a site of comics innovation was far from over. As the plant's output waned, some former Western Printing employees with decades of experience in printing set up a new company, Fairview Litho, just a few hundred feet from the original facility. They were visited a few times there in the late 1970s by

Figure 3.29. The masthead of a 2023 issue of the *Retirees of Western* newsletter. *Source:* Reproduced with the kind permission of Jim Robishaw.

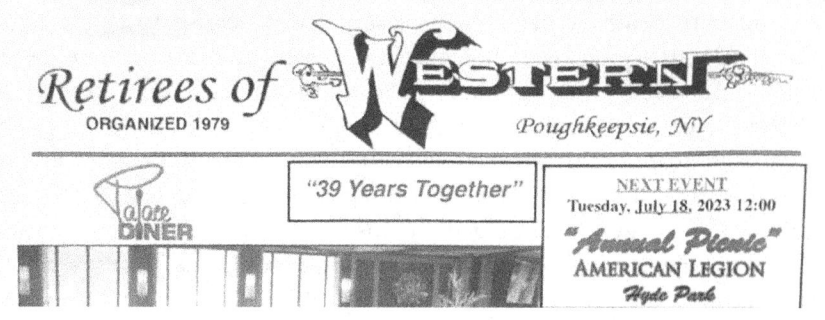

a cerebral young man—a recent transplant to Poughkeepsie—who had many questions about comics printing and publication. Although it might not have seemed like it at the time, that visitor represented one-half of a creative duo who would develop an entirely different model for making and sharing comics with the world.

CHAPTER 4

Thriving Transplants

The Pinis' Epic Adventure

That inquisitive visitor to Fairview Litho, Richard Pini, was engaged in teaching himself the publishing business to advance the fortunes of *Elf-Quest*, the epic fantasy comic he cocreated with Wendy Pini, his partner in art and life. Throughout their work on the series, Wendy has given life to the script and art; Richard has served as editor, publisher, and business manager; and they have shaped *ElfQuest*'s story together. Over the years, they drew upon the contributions of talented collaborators, many located in the Hudson River valley. As with Western Printing, the Pinis' comics creation has been inextricably linked to the region as a natural, artistic, social and commercial ecosystem.

Open an issue of *ElfQuest*, and you will immediately feel removed in many ways from the WPL Company's mainstream, childcentric comics. (Every issue from 1978 to 2013 is, as of this writing, readily accessible in the digital *ElfQuest* Reading Room.)[1] Take up *The Dreamberry Tales*, issue 7 of the Original Quest, published in 1980 (see figure 4.1).

The elves' and trolls' demeanor suggests that the berries in question should be decidedly off limits to kids. In a marked departure from the practices of the WPL Company, who notoriously kept its creators anonymous, this comic prominently features a signature—a woman's name, no less—in the lower left corner. Examine the interior cover, and the elves' large-eyed faces and toned physiques differ from those of protagonists

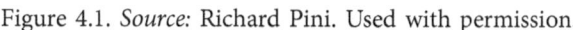

Figure 4.1. *Source:* Richard Pini. Used with permission.

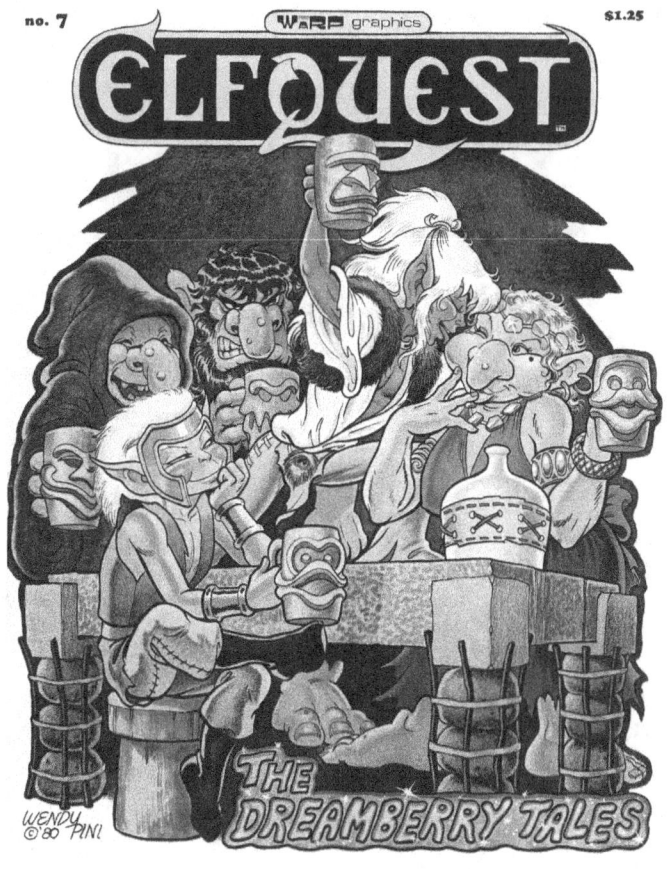

seen in WDC, Dell, or Gold Key offerings. The wolves, too, deserve your attention: Their size relative to the elves and their distinctive and intelligent expressions include them as partners in the action rather than as four-legged sidekicks.

An introductory note speaks directly to readers: "WE'VE ALWAYS TRIED TO BE A LITTLE DIFFERENT WITH OUR BOOK," begins the text, as seen in figure 4.2. Variously identified as "RP" and "Stamplicker," the writer celebrates *ElfQuest*'s success (twenty-five thousand readers and counting, about two years into the comic's run), encourages readers to keep sending letters and candidly discusses the operational challenges

Figure 4.2. *Source:* Richard Pini. Used with permission.

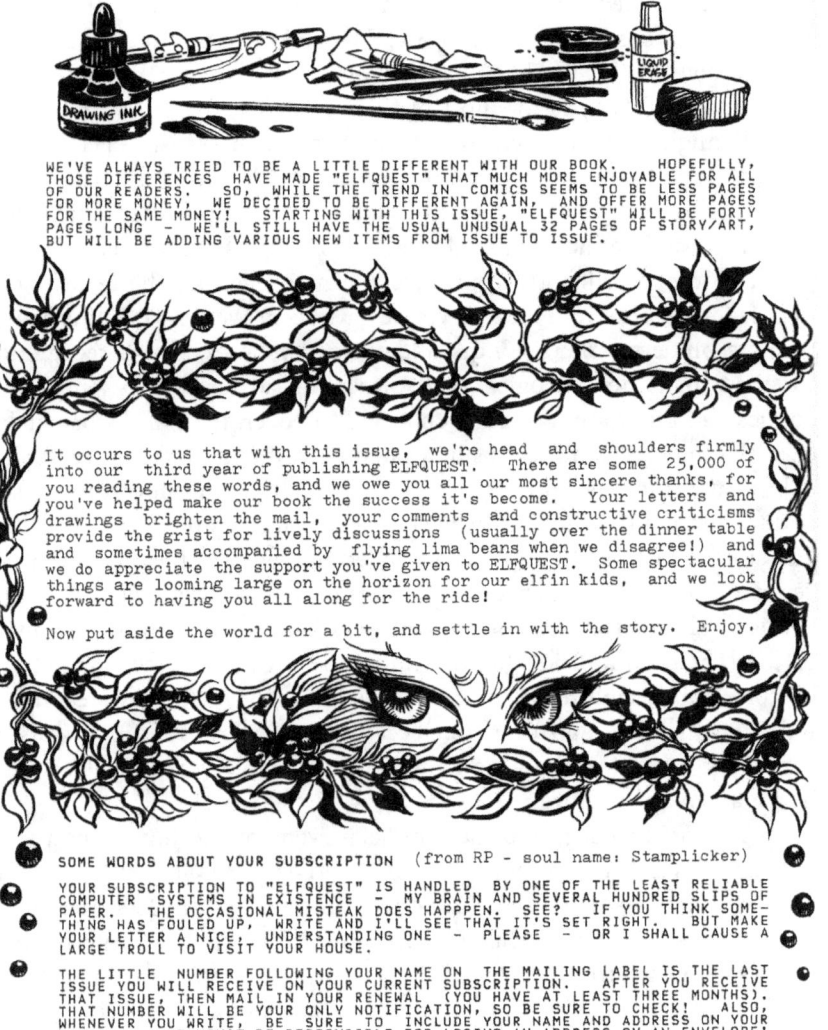

WE'VE ALWAYS TRIED TO BE A LITTLE DIFFERENT WITH OUR BOOK.   HOPEFULLY,
THOSE DIFFERENCES HAVE MADE "ELFQUEST" THAT MUCH MORE ENJOYABLE FOR ALL
OF OUR READERS.   SO,   WHILE THE TREND IN COMICS SEEMS TO BE LESS PAGES
FOR MORE MONEY, WE DECIDED TO BE DIFFERENT AGAIN, AND OFFER MORE PAGES
FOR THE SAME MONEY!   STARTING WITH THIS ISSUE, "ELFQUEST" WILL BE FORTY
PAGES LONG   — WE'LL STILL HAVE THE USUAL UNUSUAL 32 PAGES OF STORY/ART,
BUT WILL BE ADDING VARIOUS NEW ITEMS FROM ISSUE TO ISSUE.

It occurs to us that with this issue, we're head and shoulders firmly
into our third year of publishing ELFQUEST.   There are some 25,000 of
you reading these words, and we owe you all our most sincere thanks, for
you've helped make our book the success it's become.   Your letters and
drawings brighten the mail, your comments and constructive criticisms
provide the grist for lively discussions (usually over the dinner table
and sometimes accompanied by flying lima beans when we disagree!) and
we do appreciate the support you've given to ELFQUEST.   Some spectacular
things are looming large on the horizon for our elfin kids, and we look
forward to having you all along for the ride!

Now put aside the world for a bit, and settle in with the story. Enjoy.

SOME WORDS ABOUT YOUR SUBSCRIPTION   (from RP - soul name: Stamplicker)

YOUR SUBSCRIPTION TO "ELFQUEST" IS HANDLED BY ONE OF THE LEAST RELIABLE
COMPUTER SYSTEMS IN EXISTENCE — MY BRAIN AND SEVERAL HUNDRED SLIPS OF
PAPER.   THE OCCASIONAL MISTEAK DOES HAPPPEN. SEE?   IF YOU THINK SOME-
THING HAS FOULED UP, WRITE AND I'LL SEE THAT IT'S SET RIGHT.   BUT MAKE
YOUR LETTER A NICE, UNDERSTANDING ONE — PLEASE — OR I SHALL CAUSE A
LARGE TROLL TO VISIT YOUR HOUSE.

THE LITTLE NUMBER FOLLOWING YOUR NAME ON THE MAILING LABEL IS THE LAST
ISSUE YOU WILL RECEIVE ON YOUR CURRENT SUBSCRIPTION.   AFTER YOU RECEIVE
THAT ISSUE, THEN MAIL IN YOUR RENEWAL (YOU HAVE AT LEAST THREE MONTHS).
THAT NUMBER WILL BE YOUR ONLY NOTIFICATION, SO BE SURE TO CHECK!   ALSO,
WHENEVER YOU WRITE, BE SURE TO INCLUDE YOUR NAME AND ADDRESS ON YOUR
LETTER — WE WON'T BE RESPONSIBLE FOR LOSING AN ADDRESS ON AN ENVELOPE!

involved in comics publishing. The vagaries of "ONE OF THE LEAST
RELIABLE COMPUTER SYSTEMS IN EXISTENCE," our writer notes,
means that "THE OCCASIONAL MISSTEAK DOES HAPPEN. SEE?"
Playful and idiosyncratic, the front matter of issue 7 makes clear that we
have entered the realm of "indie" comics.

Flip forward to page 33, though, and you'll see from the heading that we've traveled only about five miles south and east of the former Western Printing site on North Road. The elves live on the planet Abode (also known as the World of Two Moons), but their earthly home base has been Poughkeepsie for most of their existence.

It might initially seem that these two Poughkeepsie sagas occupy opposite points on a spectrum: on the one side, the WPL Company's complex global operations, mainstream content, and often-ambivalent attitude toward comics as a medium; on the other, the Pinis' creation and publication of a brilliantly innovative alternative comic. The reality, however, is much more complicated. As we have seen, Western Printing artists, printers, binders, writers, editors, and other employees deserve recognition for the artistic, technological, and marketing advances they brought to comics and other areas of mass culture. Moreover, the Pinis' story makes clear that no creator functions in a vacuum. Although *ElfQuest* represents a departure from the "industrial age" of comics, the Pinis nevertheless have had to respond to pressures in the comics business throughout their long and storied careers. As Lopes has pointed out, even as the later twentieth century saw the emergence of transformative ideas and new voices in comics, "alternative" creators nonetheless "faced the mundane realities of the structural and ideological limits posed by the direct market and by comic book culture" (122). The Pinis have navigated these realities in ways that parallel, and even intersect with, Western Printing's story in surprising ways. Despite geographic shifts over the years, *ElfQuest* is, at heart, a "Pokip" venture.

The *ElfQuest* saga and the Pinis' achievements during the past four-plus decades are epic in scope.[2] Wendy's and Richard's industry accolades include Inkpot Awards from Comic-Con International in 1980, induction into the Eisner Society Hall of Fame in 2019, the 2024 International Adamson Award from the Swedish Academy of Comic Art, and myriad other awards and honors (see figure 4.3). In addition to offering readers masterful art, world-building, and characterization, *ElfQuest* was one of the first comics to engage with the sensibilities and aesthetics of Japanese manga, particularly those of Osamu Tezuka.[3] Describing her sequential animation of a character's thought process, for example, Wendy has said, "I learned it from Tezuka, and I used it . . . [T]he readers seemed to dig it."[4]

They have, indeed: the series has met with impressive commercial success, selling "tens of millions of copies of comics, graphic novels, books, calendars, and other merchandise."[5] More than forty-five years since its

Figure 4.3. *Source:* Richard Pini. Used with permission.

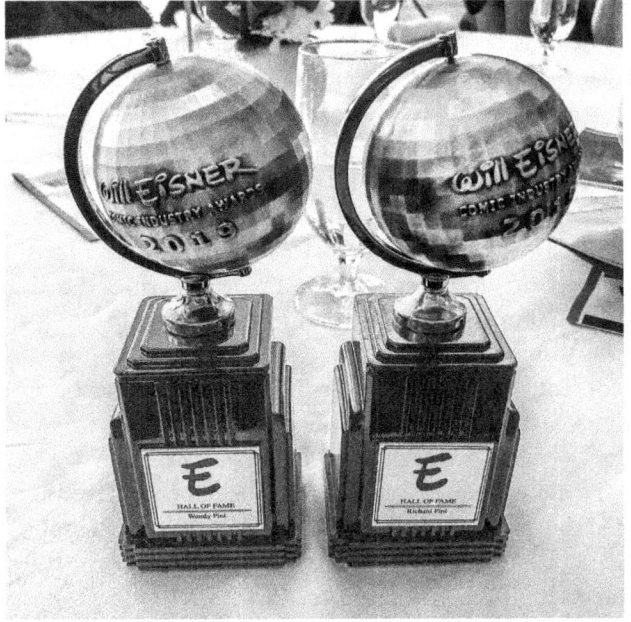

launch, the series continues to attract a joyfully dedicated fandom of readers, gamers, artists, and cosplayers who share their passions online and at conventions; new members can easily join the conversation by exploring the rich trove of freely accessible archival issues, interviews, and other explanatory materials on the *ElfQuest* website. Researchers and others with specialized queries are equally fortunate; instead of selling off their archive, the Pinis donated it to the Columbia University Rare Book and Manuscript Library. Under the superb stewardship of Curator for Comics and Cartoons Karen Green, the Pinis' archive now resides alongside materials from many other comics creators—including their regional neighbor, Irving Tripp.

The Pinis can do exactly what they want with their artistic creations since they own every bit of *ElfQuest* and their other works. Rejected by DC and Marvel when they shopped around *ElfQuest* 1, the Pinis published it with a small company, Independent Publishers Syndicate, in 1978. Unhappy with the quality of the issue, they wrested back control of their content.[6] In a move Richard attributes to the couple's "pure cussedness," they founded their own publishing company, Warp Graphics (originally WaRP to reflect their initials) and never looked back. Today, the company is recognized as one of the first and most successful examples of independent publishing in the comics field. Although they have licensed their work to DC, Marvel, and Dark Horse (their current publisher), they retain copyright over all their properties.[7] This made them an outlier in the late 1970s and a role model for other creators and initiatives in the 1980s.[8]

Complementing Warp Graphics' new publishing paradigms is Wendy's magnificent and inventive art. Although Wendy characterizes herself as "not a fine artist" but as "a cartoonist who carries it to a lavish, sensuous extreme," others beg to differ.[9] Shawn Taylor describes the situation succinctly: "Wendy Pini has one of the most fire pens in the history of the form. That a woman, in the 1970s, was out-penning most (if not all) of her male contemporaries and so many comics fans have no idea who she is, well, that's just criminal."[10] Some readers' inability to appreciate—or even to engage with—Wendy's art because of misogynist assumptions is part of the Pinis' experience.[11] Her achievements have, however, long been lauded by prominent comics organizations and publications, as well as an increasing number of comics-studies scholars and a first-rate documentary film.[12] Positive reinforcement also comes from interactions with fans online and at conventions, as well as in educational settings: The Pinis have heard for themselves the "gasps" from student visitors to the Columbia library when curator Green lifts Wendy's cover art out of its tissue-paper sheathing (see figure 4.4).

Wendy's visual alchemy blends a wide range of elements. A self-taught artist, Wendy recounts, "What I knew of comics was mostly from manga plus I was a Marvel fan. I was a big Jack Kirby fan. So, East and West. *ElfQuest* would give me a chance to combine those styles." Childhood trips to her grandmother's house introduced her to the intricate linework of Gustave Doré and the sweeping strokes of our old friend, Arthur Rackham (see figure 4.5).[13] As an adult, she found kindred spirits in colleagues such as animator Mike Ploog, who created characters for the 1977 film *Wizards*, and artist Sonny Strait, who has served as an important collaborator on *ElfQuest* for the past two decades.[14] Wide eyed and open minded like her alter ego, Cutter, Wendy transforms these influences into a visual style that is all her own. Her lines move across and around the page with an exhilarating, sinuous swagger.

Wendy's art meets its match in *ElfQuest*'s complex characterization. Multifaceted in their personalities, diverse in their appearance, and fluid in their sexuality, the Pinis' protagonists have proved appealing to a broad range of readers. "Queer and/or marginalized readers have recognized

Figure 4.4. As seen in this cover art from *ElfQuest: Siege at Blue Mountain* issue 3 (1986) and in figure 4.5, Wendy Pini's dynamic linework and sweeping ink spots provide an epic feel to the Pinis' stories. *Source:* Richard Pini. Used with permission.

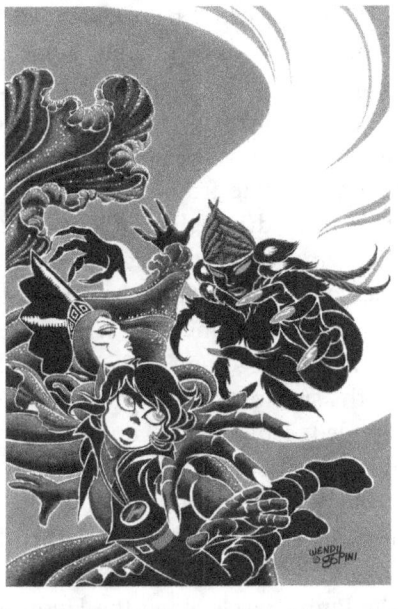

Figure 4.5. Cover art from *ElfQuest: Siege at Blue Mountain* issue 6 (1987). *Source:* Richard Pini.

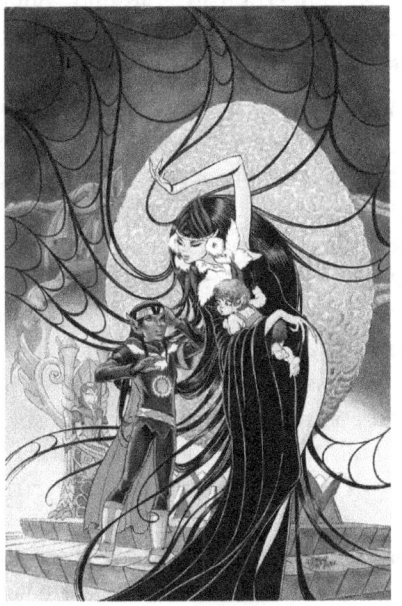

themselves in the Pinis' elves from the beginning," note scholars Madeline Gangnes and Kevin Cooley (2020:172); similarly, Robert Saunders (2019) has described the saga as taking place in "a world defined by multivariate forms of diversity" (4). Four decades before some of the groundbreaking works we have explored, such as the graphic novel *Hollow* and the animated film *Into the Spider-Verse*, *ElfQuest* gave a central place to characters who were female, Black, and brown and depicted individuals struggling to find their home in an often hostile and unfamiliar world. At the same time, the story provides a respite from everyday problems. Abie Ekenezar, who acted the part of Ahdri in the *ElfQuest Audio Movie*, described how her longtime engagement with the saga allowed her to experience "a world that's fantastical, and representative, and beautiful," during difficult circumstances, such as her deployment in Afghanistan while serving in the United States Navy.[15] The ongoing enthusiasm of thousands of readers supports Andrew Smith's succinct 2004 review of DC's *ElfQuest Archives, Volume 1*: "Recommended, especially if you usually hate elves" (F6).

As with the immensely popular comics churned out in the middle of the twentieth century at Western Printing, *ElfQuest* is a globally appealing story produced in the Hudson River valley. If we are truly to understand this saga, we need to trace not just the elves' journeys to Sun Village and Blue Mountain but also the Pinis' travels along the Hudson River, US Route 9, Spackenkill Road, and Violet Avenue. "*ElfQuest* was born in Boston, but it was raised and nurtured in the rural areas around Poughkeepsie, particularly Red Oaks Mill," Wendy explained to *Poughkeepsie Journal* writer Geoffrey Wilson in 2018. "The whole piece would not have been without the inspiration of the scenery and environment of the Hudson Valley."[16] As explored below, the area's people, civic organizations, and businesses also affected the Pinis' work and in turn were influenced by them in serendipitous ways.

Neither Wendy nor Richard was born in the Hudson River valley.[17] Richard grew up near New Haven, Connecticut, and graduated from the Massachusetts Institute of Technology with a degree in astronomy. Wendy grew up on the other side of the continent, on a prune farm in Gilroy, California, about thirty-five miles down the 101 from San Jose. Her interest in drawing manifested itself at an early age, as did her intense interest in other cultures and communities; for example, she often engaged with congregants at a Buddhist temple near her family's property. She was also a keen observer of the natural features of her surroundings. Noting the "knobbly, rough, and twisted" oaks Wendy saw while growing up in Northern California, the Pinis regard them as important influences on her linework: "When you talk about the line of beauty and me, you are not talking about a perfect S-curve, ever. By itself, it's kind of boring."[18] The trees taught her to create "lines that your eye wants very much to be smooth and curving, but which refuse to cooperate."[19]

Herself a youth without much interest in cooperating with others' expectations, Wendy became intrigued by comics and fantasy at an early age: A chance viewing of Tezuka's animated film *Alakazam the Great* in 1961 initiated a lifelong love for manga as an art form.[20] Encountering one another in 1969 through a preinternet social network (i.e., the letters page of Marvel's *Silver Surfer* issue 5), Wendy and Richard realized over time that they were "lifemates," as the elves would have it; they married in 1972 and moved to the Boston area.[21] Richard worked as a high school teacher and director of the school's planetarium, while Wendy pursued opportunities as an illustrator and writer. They soon found a project that tapped into Wendy's talents as a dancer and costume designer, as well as Richard' engineering training: constructing a twenty-pound steel and leather outfit for Wendy to wear as a participant in a Red Sonja look-alike contest held at a small New Jersey comics convention in 1976 (see figure 4.6). Wendy's success led to other appearances, including one on the *Mike Douglas Show* in 1977.[22] Although some have scoffed over the years at this part of the Pinis' experiences, more recent commentators, such those interviewed in Marisa Stotter's 2014 *She Makes Comics* documentary, regard Wendy's performances as Red Sonja as a groundbreaking moment in women's cosplay.[23]

As it happened, Wendy's Red Sonja performances provided her with professional opportunities in the comics ecosystem and satisfying self-expression. Impressed by her understanding of the character, Marvel Comics' editor-in-chief Roy Thomas offered the opportunity to cowrite an actual issue of *Red Sonja*, affording Wendy her first foothold as a comics creator.[24] At about the same time, she decided to share with Richard the extensive outline she had developed for *ElfQuest*. Although she had pondered this world-building effort for years, the recent success of *Star Wars* and the animated film *Wizards* made her feel that there might be a public receptive to the saga. The two decided that comics would be the proper medium for the story. After meeting with rejections from other publishers, as described above, the comic appeared in *Fantasy Quarterly* in February 1978. Although thrilled to see their characters in print, the Pinis were disappointed by the issue's quality and troubled by the unprofessionalism of FQ's publisher, IPS. After a long period of wrangling on their end, and "ghosting" on the publisher's end, Richard traveled to Michigan and retrieved Wendy's artwork for *ElfQuest* issues 1 and 2. Thus began the next phase of their quest: bringing a comic to print as independent creators.

Figure 4.6. *Source:* Richard Pini. Used with permission.

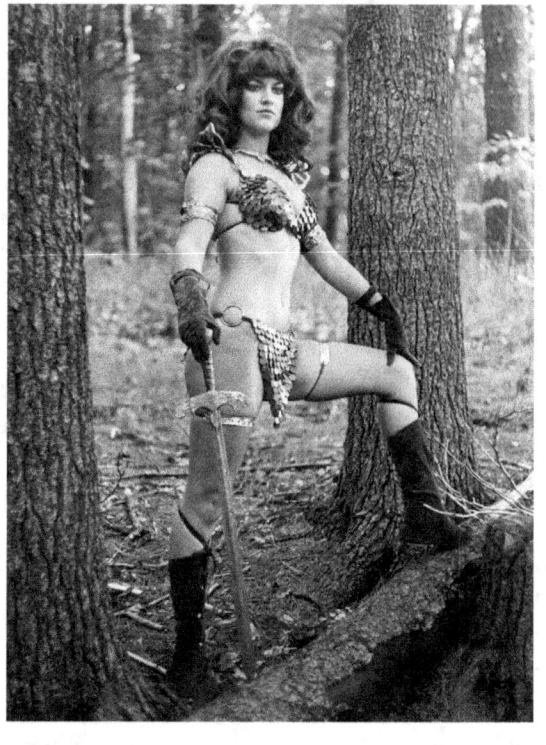

Having identified Massachusetts-area printers for the second issue's inner content and covers—"I opened up the Yellow Pages," Richard recounts—he turned to the question of distribution. Once again, Wendy's Red Sonja performances proved crucial; her work was known by Phil Seuling and Bud Plant, two early leaders in the field of direct-market distribution of comics to specialized stores rather than to grocery stores or newsstands.[25] This new method of distribution was very much in its infancy (at the time, Seuling, like Richard, held a day job as a high school teacher), but the infrastructure was nonetheless emerging. The personal connections among creators in the fledgling independent comics field were just as significant as the rail lines and roads that connected Western Printing in Poughkeepsie with New York City and Racine, Wisconsin. Seuling and Plant bought the entire ten-thousand-copy run of *ElfQuest* issue 2, distributed it through the channels they had created, and sold the whole batch. They took on twenty thousand copies of issue 3, and *they* all sold. The elves had left the holt for good.

By 1979, the Pinis had moved, as well. Although Richard loved teaching and managing the planetarium, red tape at the administrative level impelled him to follow through on a job lead given to him by a friend employed at IBM in Poughkeepsie. Despite the unfamiliar terrain—"Well, I had never touched a computer in my life up to that point," he recalls—Richard took a job as a computer programmer. Both Pinis expressed enthusiasm for the move in the editor's note to *ElfQuest* issue 5: "As of September 1, 1979 we'll be pulling up stakes and moving to a new town, a new job (for me—Richard speaking) and a house (my own studio, hee hee!—Wendy speaking)."[26] It was back to the phone book for Richard, who after a series of unsuccessful attempts found a capable printer in Southern Dutchess News, a Wappingers Falls–based operation whose primary publication was a free regional newsletter with advertisements and coupons. He also contracted with Merchants Press on Violet Avenue in Hyde Park to produce the comic's color covers and acquired a permit from the post office to handle bulk shipping. With that, and their move to a Cape Cod house in the leafy neighborhood of Red Oaks Mill, the Pinis had established a new home base (see figure 4.7).

Figure 4.7. *Source:* Richard Pini. Used with permission.

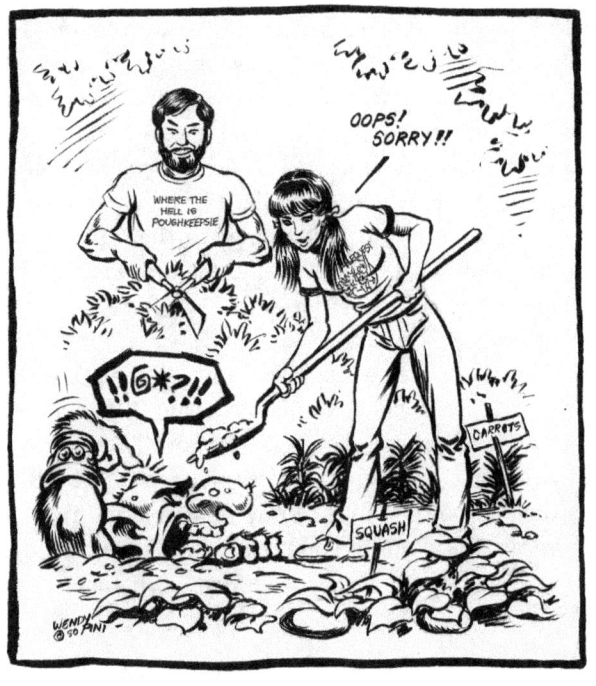

Wendy's relocation to the East Coast had already had a profound effect on her art. She vividly recalls a midsummer evening's stroll during their Massachusetts days. Stepping into a meadow behind their apartment building, the couple found a landscape ablaze with fireflies. "I grew up in California, and we don't have fireflies," Wendy recounts. "It was like seeing God or something, all the stars in the sky falling down and twinkling in this field. And as an artist you want to capture a moment like that. . . . Going to the East Coast gave me a vision for the story." When lifemates Cutter and Leetah reunite in Original Quest issue 10 after a long separation, a landscape sprinkled with fireflies conveys the joyful sensuality of their encounter. It is a lovely scene, though Wendy—who has often expressed a desire to "paint with light" in her art—still expresses frustration that her fireflies did not flash with the same intensity they displayed in real life.

Their move to the Hudson River valley was a significant change for both Pinis, and for *ElfQuest*: Wendy regards it as an integral contributor to "the intense joy that this project has given us." She recalls that when she and Richard needed to talk over developments in the story, "Rather than just sit there in the house, we would take long drives." She was fascinated by the area's vegetation and topography:

> Coming here, to the Hudson Valley, was a complete revelation. The woods—you see, what I knew of the woods was the giant redwoods, and the forest, and it's very beautiful, but it is so different in nature and scale. Giant redwood trees, you don't necessarily think of as places where elves could live. Come here, and you have these thickets and hollows and dells, and my imagination absolutely exploded. From issue 6 on of *Elf-Quest*, you can see the instant change in the artwork, because by issue 6, I was living here. And then you have the fall colors, and you have the seasons—seasons!

These perceptions soon found their way into *ElfQuest*'s landscapes. One demonstration of these changes comes in issue 8, in which Cutter and Skywise enter an intimidating woodland, the Forbidden Grove, after a long sojourn in the desert land of the Sun People (see figure 4.8). "That environment is a distillation of what [Wendy was] soaking in, in the Hudson Valley," Richard asserts. Wendy concurs: "I was not drawing woods like this prior to [to this time]. And [the elves] even talk about it because

Figure 4.8. *Source:* Richard Pini. Used with permission.

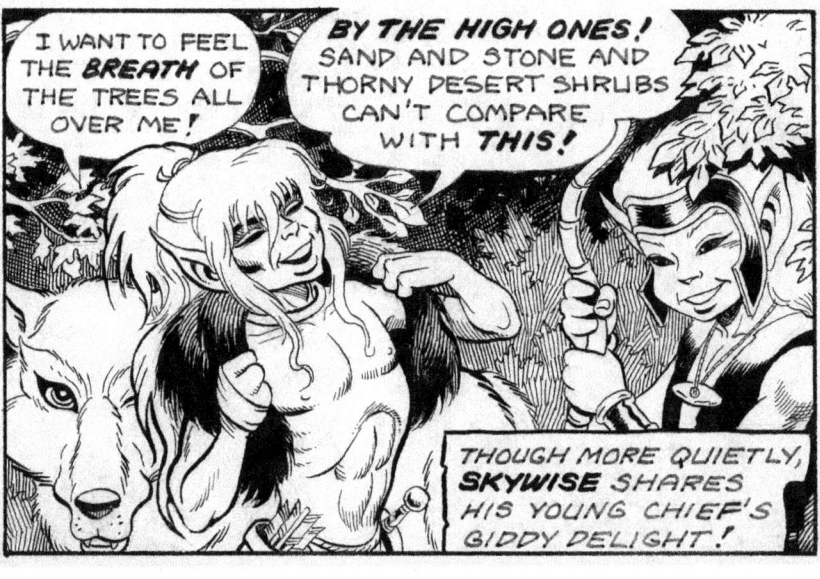

they've been in the desert." Having grown up in a household of cigarette smokers and in a region regularly visited by crop dusters, Wendy enjoyed her new atmosphere of the Hudson River valley in the most literal sense: "The air literally felt different" (see figure 4.9).

While the move was less of a radical surprise to Richard, who in his early years had always enjoyed the beautiful springtime weather of southwest Connecticut, he was struck by the Hudson River valley's functioning as a cultural ecosystem as well as a natural one: "Here you have the forest primeval—what Washington Irving wrote about. [The Hudson River valley and Connecticut] were close but not the same. . . . This is the Hudson Valley of Frederic Church and Rip Van Winkle."

In addition to its literary and artistic significance, the Pinis found themselves attending to the agricultural and industrial history of the area. "When we go on our drives," Richard notes, "one of the things we just love to stumble upon is an old barn that's falling down" and other sites that hark back to older times and people. Urban areas attract them, too: "Poughkeepsie is a little city that is kind of feisty," Wendy asserts.

Figure 4.9. *Source:* Richard Pini. Used with permission.

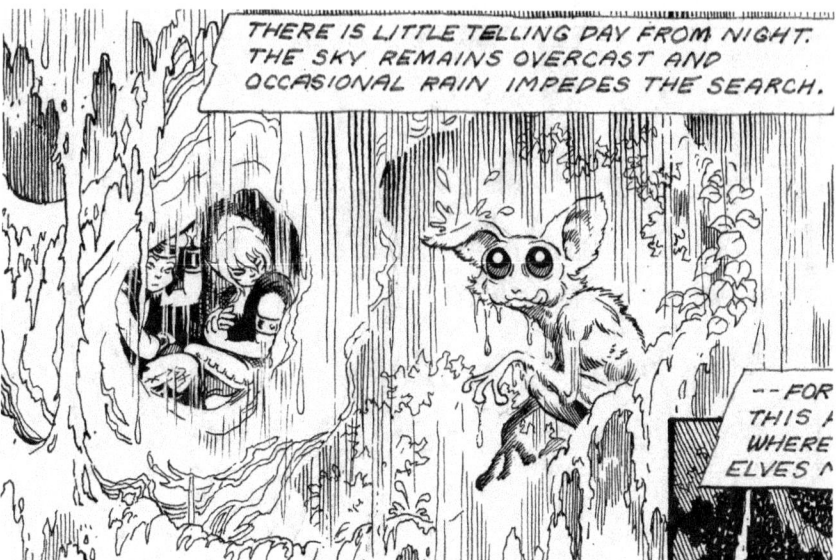

"It has a sense of age about it; it has a sense of history about it; it was once the capital, and therefore there's just this aura of it being connected to everything else in a way." Evoking the same factors that were crucial in the creation of Western Printing's Poughkeepsie plant, the Pinis note that Poughkeepsie is an area "shaped by the water" and the place "where the rail came through. That's where they got the coal from Pennsylvania, and they brought it to New England." The "soothing sound" of the train, audible from their house in Red Oaks Mill, reminded Wendy of the same sounds made by trains passing near her home in Gilroy. While the Metro-North connection to Manhattan proved important to both Pinis, they also cite beloved institutions such as the Bardavon Opera House as evidence that Poughkeepsie is a place "where art matters."

As Wendy made changes to her own art in response to her new context, she received an unexpected boost from a colleague to the north. Having met comics artist Bernie Wrightson at one of his epic Halloween parties, she found herself the recipient of his generosity: "I also had to learn new inking techniques for new effects and new kinds of scenery, and this is where Bernie Wrightson comes in because Bernie out of the blue sent me a box of crowquill nibs. And he said, 'I had all these extras in my studio and I just thought you might like to experiment with them.' I thought it was one of the sweetest things that anyone had ever done for me." The new equipment proved extremely helpful as she added new dimensions to her art in issue 6, the first one created entirely in Pough-keepsie. "So the comic art community really was connected. . . . Almost like he knew. And Bernie was special enough that I wouldn't put it past him. . . . Our fans noticed the difference in my work, I remember."

Such gestures made the Pinis aware of the valley as a social eco-system: they now lived in proximity to fellow comics professionals such as Wrightson, Chris Claremont, and Herb Trimpe (see chapter 5). While they enjoyed interacting with colleagues at conventions and Wrightson's parties, they did not, Wendy recounts, have "all that much chance or time to make friends with, or hang out with, other people in the comics community." Their isolation stemmed both from the sheer workload of drawing and writing the comic and from their position as independent creators: "All those other people were doing something for Marvel or DC. And they had that communal experience to share around a table," whereas they were working in a much smaller operation. When they did have a chance to meet with colleagues, they encountered an admixture of support and "an element of envy." Richard remembers one prominent writer bemoaning exploitative aspects of the industry and then bringing himself up short: "Oh yeah, I forgot, you f**ing *own* your own characters!" Wendy makes clear, however, that independent status did not make the Pinis' experience a simple or easy one. Poignantly, she connects their jour-ney to that of her alter ego, Cutter. Burdened with heavy responsibilities, Cutter "finished what he needed to do," but "he paid a price. Because we paid a price . . . *ElfQuest* happened to us very early on in our relationship. Everything happened extremely fast."

The sheer physical demands of generating a vast quantity of art—and Wendy is an artist who draws with her whole arm—was exacerbated by physical pain from hip dysplasia, a congenital condition.[27] Recalling the rigors of working at Western Printing—"You weren't going to sit down," recalls Jim Robishaw—the Pinis faced grinding and unceasing demands on their time (Robishaw). As sales continued to rise—by the end of the Original Quest in 1984, sales had reached one hundred thousand copies per issue—it became clear to Richard and Wendy that they needed to broaden the scope of their operation. The changes they made in response to this imperative led them to experience the Hudson River valley as an entrepreneurial and commercial ecosystem.

At first, Warp Graphics functioned literally as a cottage industry within their house in Red Oaks Mill. Wendy used a spare bedroom in their new home as a studio, while Richard took over the basement as his base of operations. In 1983, he was joined in an administrative role by Joellyn Auklandus. In 1996, she recalled how she "breathlessly trotted" down the cellar steps of the Pinis' house to see her new desk "opposite the coal bin. Across from the Ping-Pong table" (see figure 4.10).[28]

During this period, the Pinis also brought on other writers and artists to give life to the elves' saga. "There was more work that wanted to be done than I myself could do," Wendy recalled. "We needed to find artists and writers who could come as close to our model as possible." Even as they were key players in the movement toward creator-owned, independent comics, the Pinis recognized the value of collaboration: "We went through a period where we had so much story, and we were working with such

Figure 4.10. Richard Pini's office space in the basement of their Poughkeepsie home. Note the heating unit at right. *Source:* Richard Pini. Used with permission.

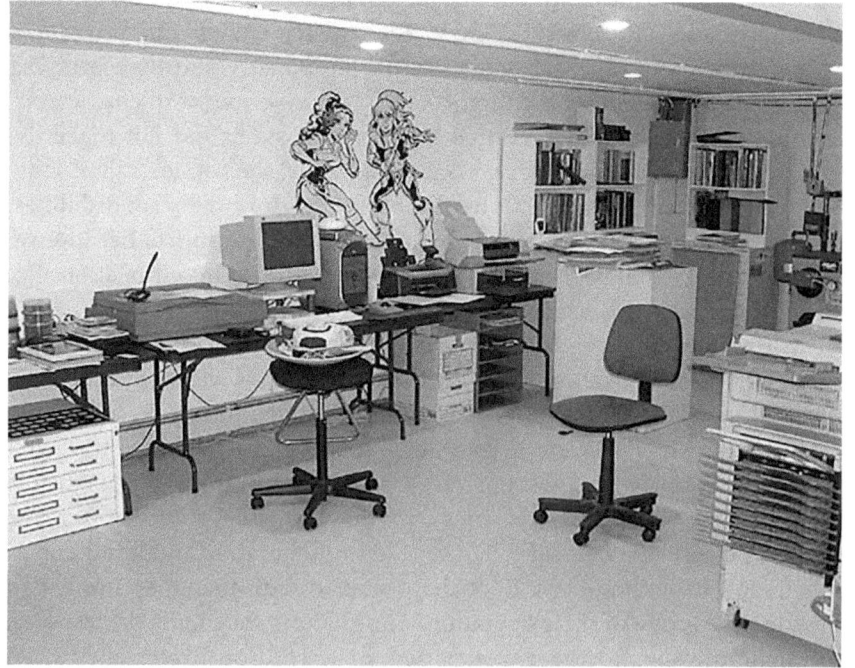

wonderful people, writers and artists, and we wanted their flavoring and spice. . . . We're independent; we're not isolationist," Richard said.

Their move outward provided valuable opportunities to aspiring artists in the area, and several of their collaborators went on to distinguished careers of their own. Joe Barruso, for example, jumped at the chance to help ink and color *ElfQuest* in 1983; he had graduated from John Jay High School in Wappingers Falls in 1981 and learned about the chance to work with the Pinis from a faculty member at the Illustrators' Society in New York. "It was amazing" to watch Wendy work, Barruso recalls, noting that she would typically focus on drawing in the morning, then perform the inking while soap operas played on TV (Barruso). He became an accomplished director credited with episodes of *The Mighty Ducks* and *Where on Earth Is Carmen Sandiego?*, among other works. In fact, a Barruso-directed episode of *Ducks* included the protagonists' encounter with "tip-of-the-hat satires of Cutter and Skywise."[29]

With new assistance came the need for more space. "We had to get the work out of the place where we lived," Wendy recalled. "It was overwhelming." When the house across the street from their own in Poughkeepsie came on the market, they acquired it. The living room became Wendy's new studio; the first-floor rooms were used by artists, writers, and other staff; and the second floor served as a repository for *ElfQuest*'s ever-growing archive. Warp Graphics was expanding in daunting ways as an employer and property manager as well as creators and publishers, but Wendy remembers "a fairly easy transition to a new space," attributing their business's ability to grow to Richard's "ability to learn how to deal with the next step, all the steps one needs to take to go to the next level." For his part, Richard notes that his lifelong interest in solving puzzles made him well suited to address logistical challenges, as did his interest in collaboration: "I love being a facilitator." Recognizing his own need to concentrate, Richard kept his basement studio in the original house, apart from the comings and goings in the new house across the street. He had left IBM in 1981 to focus on Warp Graphics, not without trepidation: "I remember walking out that door without my badge . . . and I went through that door and heard it click shut, and I said to myself, 'I'm not going back in.'"

It was the right decision. By the mid-1980s, Warp Graphics had expanded to the point that another move became necessary. According to Diamond Distributors, in some months during that period, Warp

Graphics was the fourth largest publisher of comics in the United States. "We had eight or ten people employed, and another dozen to fifteen freelancers. We were putting out eight, sometimes nine, titles a month, all *ElfQuest*-related," Richard states. It was about this time that the Pinis' story intersects directly with that of Western Printing. In search of a new provider of color printing, Richard ventured to Fairview Litho, a printing facility near the Walkway Over the Hudson; as mentioned in the previous chapter, the business was staffed by Western Printing employees who had been laid off in the early 1980s. "This was not a small building," Richard recounts. "They had big presses. Six guys with combined four hundred years of experience. And I would sit there and just listen to their stories, and I didn't know half of what they were talking about."[30] Nevertheless, these conversations heightened Richard's sense of the cultural impact of the Hudson River valley: "I knew that Western in Poughkeepsie had done the Dell, the Gold Key, the Disney . . . as a comics fan, as a nascent publisher, as a bibliophile, I realized all this stuff happened three miles from where we lived!"

At one point the, Pinis considered tying their fates even more closely to Western Printing's "gorgeous Art Deco building." Richard recalls, "For a little while, we were thinking about [moving there] because peripheral to printing and comics, *ElfQuest* has almost always been under option for a TV show or movie. And at one point, someone said, 'Why don't you do it?'" The massive space could, the Pinis speculated, lend itself to use as a film and animation studio. "And then we woke up," Richard remembered. "[We were] out of our minds," Wendy concurs, noting that this was one "fantasy" that probably would not have ended well for the couple or their publishing company. A different kind of connection with Western Printing, however, proved both practical and satisfying. Wanting to make their comic distinctive, Richard recalled that "some of the old Dell/Gold Key comics from the 1960s would reprint the front cover art on the back cover, just without any of the type. It was like a pinup you could frame. So we hit upon the idea of Wendy providing a brand-new actual pinup of a major character for each issue." This Western-influenced enterprise was a big success: "Readers went nuts!"[31]

Instead of moving into the massive Western Printing facility, Warp Graphics expanded into office space on Haight Avenue in the Arlington neighborhood of Poughkeepsie, a business district enlivened by students and personnel from nearby Vassar College. The comics professionals who came to use this space included Steve Blevins, Paul Abrams, Barry Blair, and Charles Barnett III. The Pinis made one additional change a year or so later; hearing of an open office on Lagrange Avenue, they rented that out as well. Wendy took over this space as a studio and reveled in the quiet of her first studio detached from Warp Graphics' production and creative staff.

In addition to providing much-needed elbow room for everyone involved in *ElfQuest*, the Arlington spaces provided the Pinis with new opportunities for community and collaboration. As it had when Wendy moved to the East Coast, and when the Pinis as a couple had relocated to Poughkeepsie, this move had an "environmental" impact on their work. Richard points out that when working in a more densely populated and pedestrian-friendly area, "you're going to go to the restaurants, you're going to walk the sidewalks. We would take walks around the Vassar campus, and along Raymond [Avenue], and talk about this scene, or these ideas." Wendy agrees, noting, "Much of *ElfQuest* was created in that area. I worked on two big story arcs: Kings of the Broken Wheel and Hidden Years."[32]

The Pinis' perambulations also led to smaller but undoubtedly satisfying artistic productions. They became sushi devotees and friendly acquaintances of the Nagakawa family, who owned the Tokyo Express restaurant around the block from their offices. Indeed, *ElfQuest*'s characters immediately reminded Henry Nagakawa of the Japanese stories of "Peach Boy," which Wendy had also known and drawn as a girl. Soon, the artists and restaurateurs were collaborating. Drawing upon Richard's emerging expertise in "nascent desktop publishing," Wendy and Richard helped to design new menus for Tokyo Express. Moreover, when the Nagakawas set out to renovate their space, Wendy painted a mural of a samurai, as seen in figure 4.11. Having originally positioned the art in the restaurant's front window, the Nagakawas bowed to town regulations and reinstalled it in the rear wall of the restaurant's seating area. There it remains today, a testament to the careful maintenance of the restaurant's new owners, to the couples' camaraderie, and to the importance of delicious food to everything else in life: "We traded my samurai for sushi. Six hundred dollars' worth," Wendy recounts fondly.

The Pinis forged connections with other entrepreneurs in the area as well. Undaunted by their status as "artistic weirdos" (to cite Richard's self-description), the consortium of small businesses in the Arlington district welcomed the Pinis: "We were the only ones there doing what we were doing, but the fact that this conservative community embraced us, as a thriving business within their community, that was a whole different

Figure 4.11. *Source:* Richard Pini. Used with permission.

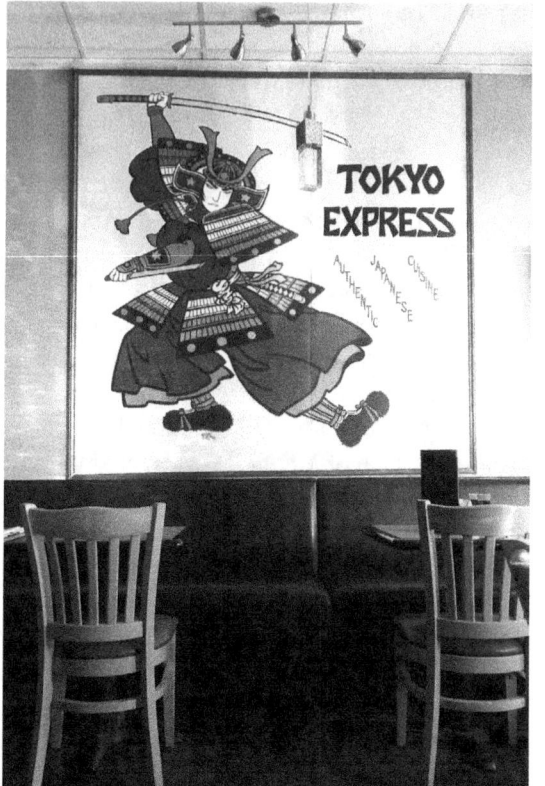

role for us to play in our lives," Wendy recounted. Indeed, it was a commercial property owner's tip that helped the Pinis acquire the Lagrange Avenue studio. They soon became active contributors to the consortium. Richard produced leaflets featuring Wendy's art for the organization, and her art was highlighted in a television advertisement for the group's annual Christmas market. In return, the Pinis gained a new sense of groundedness: "That was the first time that we actually felt like we could make space in our lives to reach out and become part of a community. It was a different role for us to play, a different status, and I think it was an important moment in our life." They also participated in meet-and-greets at retail outlets in the area, such as the local Barnes and Noble, Waldenbooks, and

MediaPlay stores in area malls, and several independent comics shops in the county. A bit further afield, Wendy contributed her work to a mural for the ladies' room of the Museum of Cartoon Art during its residence at Ward's Castle in Westchester County (the museum moved from that location in 1992).[33]

As the 1990s progressed, however, the Pinis experienced changes in the comics industry, just as Western Printing had a few decades before. As Richard had predicted in an early 1990s keynote address to the International Association of Direct Distributors, the field had begun to engage in risky speculation: Distributors and retailers got in the habit of making large, and increasingly unprofitable, gambles on new titles. By the middle of the decade, the Pinis had begun to retrench: "There came a point where I looked up and realized that Warp Graphics was very seriously in debt because I was going ahead and commissioning artists and strips. But the sales figures were going down." Bowing to these new realities, the Pinis let employees go and decided not to renew their leases on the two spaces in Arlington. Over a period of about two years, they paid all their debts to the artists and writers they contracted with, a challenge they are proud to have met.

In tandem with these changes, Wendy's work branched into new areas—most notably, a webcomic and graphic-novel interpretation of Edgar Allan Poe's short story "The Masque of the Red Death," adapting the 1842 story to include a sexually charged love story between male protagonists (see figures 4.12 and 4.13).

The Pinis also decided around this time to engage in earnest with the question of an *ElfQuest* animated film, a prospect that had first attracted interest from Hollywood as far back as 1980. Feeling—as had the managing directors of Western Printing—that such products required for their development a strong on-the ground presence in Los Angeles, the Pinis decided in 1994 to maintain two residences. Wendy spent most of her time in Southern California (including, appropriately, Thousand Oaks); Richard held down the fort in Poughkeepsie; and cross-country flights became a way of life for them. This arrangement held for over two decades. Although an *ElfQuest* film has not yet come to fruition, the Pinis worked with several media organizations to create *ElfQuest: The Audio Movie*, a ten-episode production featuring more than forty voice actors. An American Sign Language version brilliantly interprets the film.[34]

As for so many others, the arrival of Covid in January 2020 necessitated a reevaluation of their work and living arrangements. They had a

Figure 4.12. *Source:* Richard Pini. Used with permission.

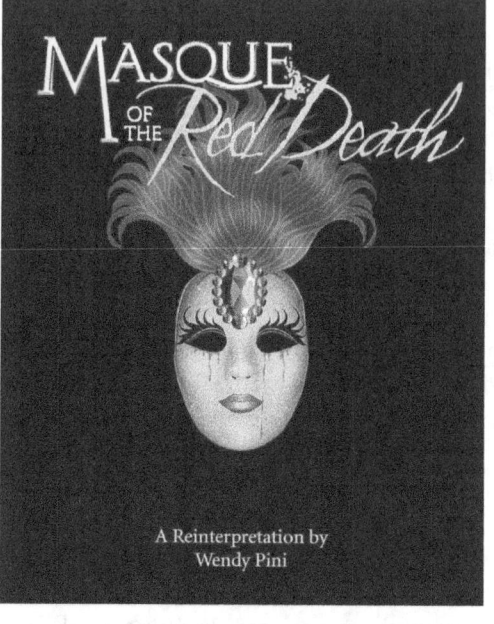

Figure 4.13. *Source:* Richard Pini. Used with permission.

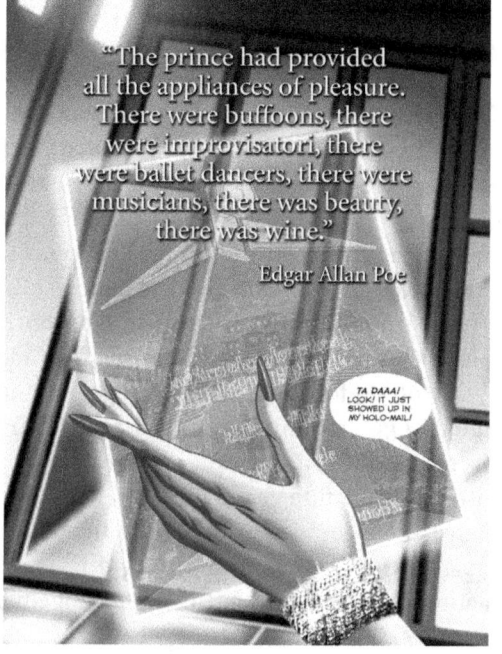

cross-country choice to make, and the winner was the Hudson River valley. Having bought a new house in Dutchess County in 2019 and outfitted it specifically to suit their creative and operational needs, the Pinis made the home their single base of operations in summer 2020 and remain there to this day (see figure 4.14). They still travel to far-flung locations for conventions and talks and complement this work with a lively presence in digital realms. Their enormous online archive continues to draw new readers to the series, and social media allows for enthusiastic commentary.

The Pinis' work includes support of fledgling artists, and they are acutely aware of the ongoing pervasiveness of external and internalized gender bias in the comics industry. In the documentary *She Makes Comics*, Wendy speaks of encounters with women artists who are hesitant about acknowledging their own abilities. Recalling a convention encounter with one young artist who "couldn't accept" praise of her work, Wendy reflects ruefully that "it's scary to know that this discouragement of brilliance—absolute brilliance—still happens."[35]

In encouraging new artists, the Pinis extend to others the same generous support they received from well-established creators during *ElfQuest's* early years. We can see one such moment if we return to *The Dreamberry Tales*, the issue with which we began this chapter. The lower

Figure 4.14. The Pinis' shared office in their current Hudson River valley home. *Source:* Richard Pini. Used with permission.

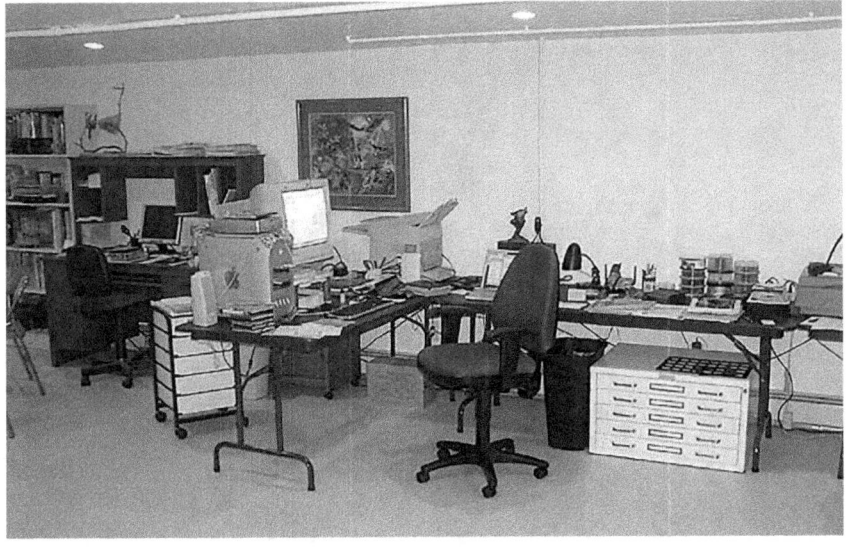

left corner of p. 34 reveals the name *Ursula K. Le Guin*, the celebrated fantasy writer with a Hudson River valley connection of her own. In "From Elfland to Poughkeepsie," a 1972 speech to a gathering of science fiction writers, Le Guin argued that fantasy spaces, or "elflands," needed to serve as distinctive spaces for imaginative activity rather than following the same rules as those found in Poughkeepsie or other everyday locations.[36]

About eight years later, Le Guin reacted with delight to the Pinis' blurring of the boundaries separating the real world from elfin holts. "Thank you for *ElfQuest*," she writes in her 1980 fan letter, published in issue 7. "I am very glad to know this sort of thing goes on in Poughkeepsie!"[37] As their saga moves through its fifth decade (see figure 4.15), the Pinis express similar generosity toward artists just setting out on their own comics quests and remain attached to the place where *ElfQuest* was, in Wendy's words, "grown and sown."

Figure 4.15. *Source:* Richard Pini. Used with permission.

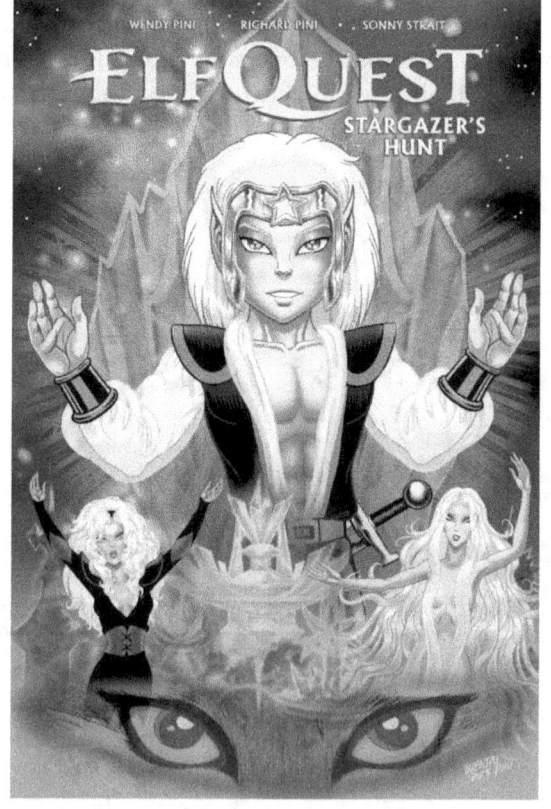

CHAPTER 5

Roots and Networks

Comics Creators throughout the Valley

As we have seen, the comics ecosystem of the Hudson River valley has included both corporate, industrial production (Western Printing) and independent art and entrepreneurship (the Pinis and Warp Graphics). But there are many other local creators and production channels to explore. This chapter will investigate the interplay among individual talent, regional influences, and comics history in the life and work of seventeen practitioners in the field. While a comprehensive encyclopedia of every comics creator in the valley is beyond the scope of our study, my hope is that these stories will whet your appetite for more information about artists in this region or in your own surroundings.

We will proceed in a roughly chronological fashion from past to present. Many of the artists had long careers and overlapped with one another temporally. Launching our journey with the big-picture ideas of Summer Pierre, we will take a trip around the valley that will begin and conclude in Poughkeepsie (*please adopt the voice of a Metro-North train conductor here*), with stops in Elmsford, North Tarrytown, Peekskill, the southern Catskills, Kerhonkson, Newburgh, and New Paltz. We will consider the contributions of an interloper from New Jersey and learn about a riverside region in South Korea with features like those of the Hudson River valley.

Each artist profile will enrich our understanding of the intersecting ecosystems explored throughout this book. We will see evidence of the many different tributaries that have fed into the development of the comics medium: Our featured artists' work engages with everything from vaudeville to newspaper advertisements to webcomics. In terms of the region's cultural and aesthetic history, each story helps us broaden our definition of *Hudson valley artist* beyond the (indisputably beautiful) works of painters such as Church, Durand, and Barstow. Place studies, too, will come to mind: The artists' work cannot be understood without considering the natural and social environments they inhabited. Civic engagement and community support form a vital part of many of the people profiled here. We will also see how bias takes an artistic toll on our culture and on individuals and institutions. This chapter's profiles include people who could have generated more art and improved the valley as a community if they had been better supported and sustained. Woven into all these factors are the individual quirks, priorities, and moments of inspiration that characterize human creativity. Making comics demands both playfulness and tenacity—a combination of traits that is very much apparent in the stories below.

The experiences of cartoonist Summer Pierre will provide us with a useful starting point for our case studies. Her reflections demonstrate the truth of a key idea that Washington Irving expressed over two centuries ago: The Hudson River valley gives both newcomers and longtime residents the chance to "grow imaginative" in unexpected ways.

Summer Pierre: Silence, Space, and Kindred Spirits

Having lived in Northern California, Boston, Vermont, and Brooklyn, Summer Pierre wasn't sure what to think when her husband's job took them to the western shore of the river in the Hudson valley, not far from the US Military Academy at West Point: "This was a foreign space to me," she recalls.[1] As recounted in her Eisner Award–nominated graphic memoir *All the Sad Songs* and her "comic and diary comics" series Paper Pencil Life, Pierre's peripatetic life as a musician and artist continually exposed her to new people, performances, and places. By contrast, her move to the Hudson River valley from Brooklyn in 2012 "converged with a lot of running out of road" in her life. It was initially unsettling for her to think about living in a place that seemed culturally quieter than her surroundings in the city: "You know, New York speaks for itself. In fact, it speaks too loudly. I realized that I was leaning on that. And coming here, there's nothing to lean on. And so, I needed that, because it made me realize, what is it that I'm trying to say? What is it that I actually care about? If I am not looking to other shiny things, how do I shine?" Addressing those internal questions, Pierre states, "was a really important moment" in her evolution as an artist. Before long, too, she found herself asking a new question: "What is it that's here?" As her comic in this volume demonstrates, Pierre answered this question by getting to know the area's artistic history: "That was something sort of amazing to discover: that I had actually landed in the perfect place."

An editor friend living nearby reminded her of John Stanley's ties to the region: "He lived in Cold Spring, which is right across the river from me. He is one of the greatest—not just cartoonists and writers but writers of literature in the midcentury . . . [H]is work inspires me so deeply. You can find Hudson valley stuff all through his work." Although not all of Stanley's experiences in the region were positive ones (as discussed in chapter 3), his legacy provided Pierre with inspiration and a sense of connection to her new home (see figure 5.1).

Pierre's new natural environment changed her perspective as well. She has created brilliant comics about birds, weather, and other natural phenomena in her own cartooning, and she has found another kindred spirit in the writings of the great American naturalist John Burroughs, who grew up in the Catskills and lived alongside the Hudson River in West Park.[2] Burroughs's emphasis on closely observing nature in one's own habitat struck Pierre as particularly relevant during the past few years: "I actually expected him to come back when we were doing the pandemic," she jokes. "Everybody was experiencing the outdoors for the first time. Nobody talked about him but his whole thing was, wildness is in your backyard." During her time in New York City, Pierre loved encountering myriad places associated with artists and writers; now, as a Hudson River valley resident, she values the chance to engage in a close and long-term way with both Stanley and Burroughs's work: "[It] has been so nourishing to work within those bookends. . . . I feel deep company with those two creators."

Pierre has also developed ways to connect with like-minded contemporaries in the area. Approached by the owners of Split Rock Books, an

Figure 5.1. *Source:* Summer Pierre. Used with permission.

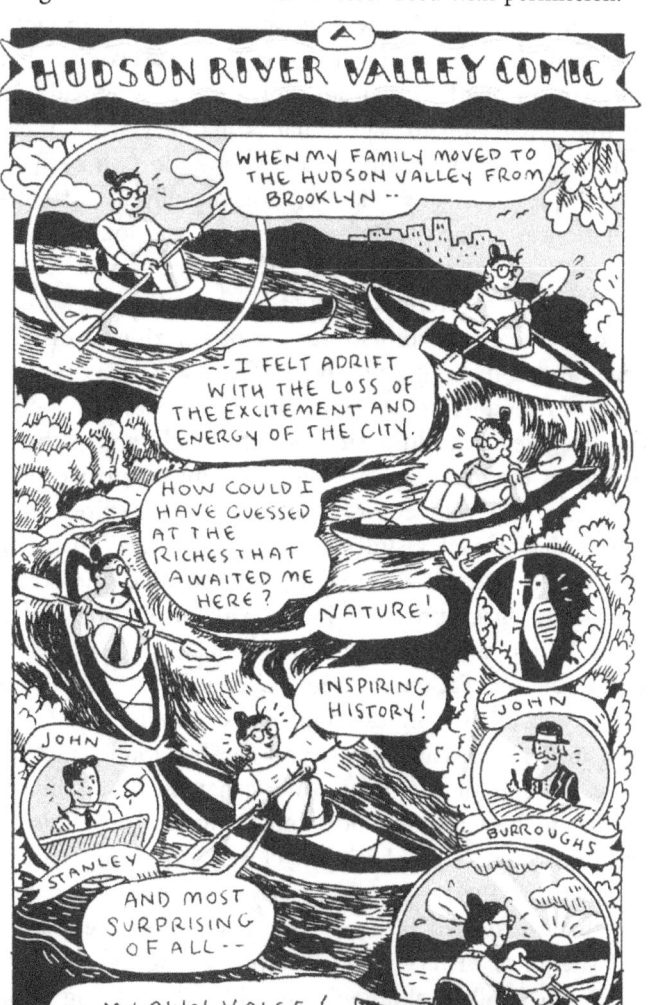

independent bookstore in Cold Spring, with the idea for "drawing nights," Pierre embraced the idea; she has hosted several of these in recent years, aimed at both professionals and amateur artists in the community (including Seth Christian Martel, profiled below). "It's just been great," she asserts. "It's been really nice to see people again. . . . Anybody can stop in." She notes that "comics have invited a lot of people back to drawing." Pierre adheres in her work with students to the teaching philosophy of another kindred spirit, cartoonist Lynda Barry. While it can be intimidating for new or returning artists to expose their ideas "out loud" on paper, Pierre encourages them to tap into their own memories: "The way I've started putting it to people is that you are just meeting an old friend. And the friend has been waiting for you to pick it up."

Encounters with the past are important to Pierre's own work as well: Her current work in progress, *Baby Hold On To Me*, recounts her mother's experiences working as a roadie for the Rolling Stones and other bands. For her part, Pierre feels firmly rooted in the valley after living here for more than a decade: "It is the location of my heart, of my mind, of my life. I think I really needed to come here. What a special place."

Pierre's close engagement with her natural environment and regional history has fed her achievements in creating graphic memoir and biography, comics genres that took off in the early twenty-first century and that continue to have an enormous impact on the publishing industry as a whole. As we begin our travels around different parts of the valley, let's keep in mind Pierre's idea of keeping "deep company" with figures from the present and the past. We'll begin our journey in Poughkeepsie at the very beginning of the twentieth century.

Elmer Tripp: Art, Commerce, and Conviviality

The career of cartoonist, painter, and commercial artist Elmer Tripp (1901–1969) reminds us that the Hudson River valley has long been, and continues to be, characterized not just by beautiful scenery but also by a lively civic and community life. Moreover, with respect to comics history, his work demonstrates that before there were comic cons, there were "chalk talks"—public performances in which cartoonists plied their trade with in-the-minute drawings and witty banter. From the early 1920s all the way to the 1960s, Elmer Tripp made a living in, and injected life into, gatherings in the Poughkeepsie area and beyond.

First things first—no one called him Elmer. Henceforth I will refer to him as *Trippie*, both to reflect how his contemporaries referred to him and to distinguish him from his nephew and fellow cartoonist Irving Tripp, whose career at Western Printing we explored in chapter 3.[3] The Tripp family had a long history in the area. Trippie's grandfather served the Union in Company C of the New York 150th Volunteer Regiment; his father was a longtime railroad worker who "started on the old wooden coaches as a brakeman in 1890" and had seen Presidents Theodore Roosevelt and William Howard Taft on his route; and his aunt Cynthia served as a secretary both to the president of Vassar College and to William W. Smith of the Smith Brothers company.[4]

Trippie wasted no time in making his own contributions to Poughkeepsie's cultural life. A 1967 reminiscence by a local columnist suggests that his first published artwork was shown in *Lone Scout* magazine, a periodical aimed toward boys who lacked a formal scouting organization.[5] Showing an early aptitude for showmanship as well as the visual arts, he composed a poem, drew a picture, and gave a talk on Abraham Lincoln while a student at Poughkeepsie High School (class of 1921).[6] Although he attended the Art Students League in New York City, he did not sever his ties with his hometown. The year 1923 finds him as the team leader at a competition at the Tabernacle Baptist Church geared toward raising money for a new piano. His team won, but there were apparently no hard feelings from his opponent—Phebe Lloyd—and she married him in two years later at a ceremony that included their young niece and nephew: "Little Miss Gertrude Tripp was flower girl and Irving Tripp, ring bearer."[7]

By 1925, an announcement in *The Poughkeepsie Eagle-News* indicated that Trippie had chosen to settle down in his hometown: "Having gained recognition in his chosen work, Mr. Tripp returned to his hometown to place his talents at the disposal of his friends" at his studio, the Art Shop Corner, on Main Street in Poughkeepsie.[8] And did he ever! The Tabernacle Baptist Church provided a hospitable place for his early efforts at entertaining groups with "charcoal sketches": "It was an unusual bit of entertaining that he did, for he would let people in the audience draw lines on the paper and then he would fill them in and make a sketch. He was much applauded."[9]

In adopting this kind of performance, Trippie tapped into a popular form in the early 1920s. In his 1924 work *How to Chalk Talk*, artist Harlan Tarbell defines the practice as a blend of vivid drawings, comedic timing, and skillful storytelling:

> In opening a program it is well to use a novelty picture, one that can be drawn quickly, that carries a laugh, and offers a quick surprise that makes people interested at the very start. There must be something to break the ice, putting the performer and the audience on friendly terms. . . . A short program that is planned for an encore should close with a bang. The

best work possible should be thrown into the closing picture. Make the audience wonder at the skill of the performer or the impressiveness of the subject. (21)

Tarbell's recommendations, along with nationally prominent career of cartoonist and animation pioneer Winsor McCay, remind us that comics history is anchored not just in the two-dimensional world of newspapers but also in the three-dimensional world of theatrical performance.[10]

This format had surprising staying power, even as vaudeville gave way to movie screens. Trippie successfully practiced the chalk talk as a form for more than four decades. Cartooning wasn't just in the funny papers; it was in a wide range of events in and around Poughkeepsie. He delivered "a humorous chalk talk on 'Evolution'" to attendees at the ladies' night dinner for the Dutch Arms Men's Club of the Reformed Church in 1934, provided sketches at a prewedding dinner for Eva Effron at the Vassar Inn in 1936, and entertained seventy-five children at the Poughkeepsie Country Club's Christmas party that same year. He participated in events closer to home, too. A 1927 social article notes that he performed a chalk talk at a surprise birthday party for Phebe Tripp at their home.[11]

Merging his commercial work with cartooning, bank-related events often took Trippie out of town. He designed and entertained at a booth for the Schenectady Savings Bank at the Mohawk Valley Exposition in 1930 and gave an "illustrated talk on thrift" at the Bankers' Club of America that same year. He did similar events closer to home: A 1927 Poughkeepsie Savings Bank ad noted, "As a special attraction," at the Dutchess County fair, "Mr. Elmer Tripp will entertain our visitors twice daily with his clever Chalk Talks and Thrift cartoons." He raised the stakes for eventgoers in 1940 at the Parade of Progress exhibition at the Red Oaks Mill airport hangar: "A sum of $50 will be awarded to any person who can draw a line not more than 2 feet long, which cannot be made into a picture, according to Elmer L. Tripp, sign painter and artist. . . . He will perform nightly at his booth, doing chalk talks and will also make quick portraits." Later, in 1948, he would discuss "the idea of thrift and savings" to middle schoolers in Beacon, in an event sponsored by the Beacon Savings Bank.[12]

Trippie was also an indefatigable supporter of civic institutions in the area. "Elmer Tripp was in charge" of the one hundred plus people attending the Dutchess Scandinavian Society outing at Upton Lake in 1932, and this seems to have been his default mode. By 1937, he was a charter member of the "newly organized Poughkeepsie Business and Professional Men's organization" Even here, he was associated with festivities: He is listed as a member of a committee planning 250th anniversary celebrations for Pough-keepsie, as well as another group drafting a plan to close all area stores for a half-day party at Woodcliff Park. Around the same time, *The Poughkeepsie Eagle-News* reported that "Elmer Tripp, cartoonist, gave a chalk talk on the humorous side of scouting," and this proved an important area for his community work. Throughout the 1940s and 1950s, he lent his talents to scouting events. An article about an awards dinner in Arlington noted that he had been "active in scouting and scoutmaster of Troop 2 for 20 years." Testimony to his years of performing can be seen in the fact that he was a valued host to scouting awards events in the early 1960s.[13]

The YMCA provided another venue for his work. He gave a paint-ing course in 1962 and art lessons to kids for eight successive Saturdays in 1963. He was still offering a "chalk talk" that year at an event for the Arlington Reformed Church. His schedule seemed to have slowed after this, but it is satisfying to see his name listed as a contributor to an art exhibit held at IBM in 1965.[14] As his daughter-in-law, Jane Tripp, recalls, and as this landscape of the Poughkeepsie Railroad Bridge demonstrates (see figure 5.2), Trippie was an accomplished painter as well as a cartoonist.

Figure 5.2. *Source:* Reproduced with the kind permission of Jane Tripp.

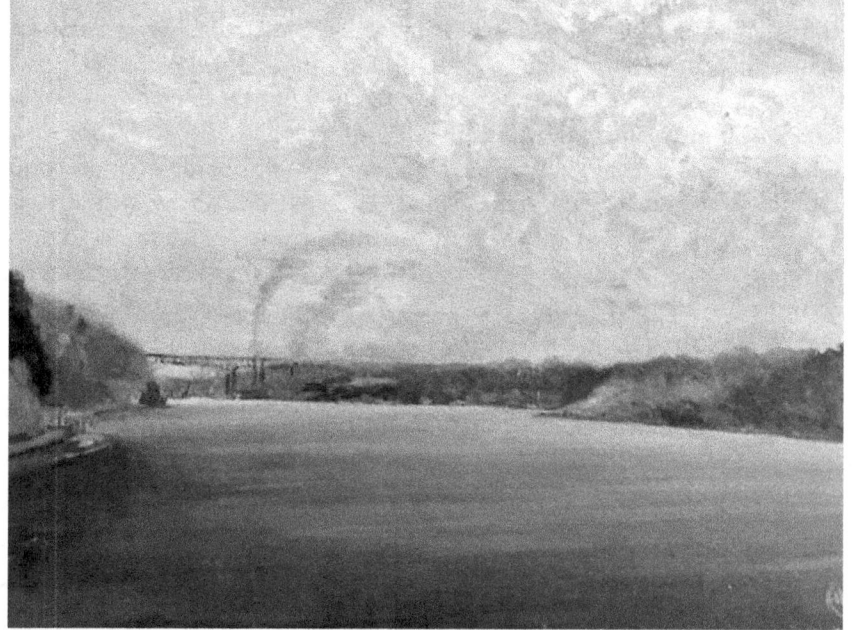

Trippie died in 1969; his wife, Phebe, outlived him by twenty-four years. Several of Trippie's oil paintings, including still lifes and landscapes, occupy honored places in Jane Tripp's home.

None of Trippie's cartooning work seems to have survived, which is a shame. But many good things are ephemeral, when you think about it—laughs at a performance, fun gatherings for children, community picnics. All these things can still work their way into the lifeblood of a place and its people. I have to think part of Trippie still carries on right here in Poughkeepsie.

Amelia "Oppy" Opdyke Jones:
A Poughkeepsie Gig for a Jersey Artist

Before branching out to other areas of the valley, we will consider an intriguing series of comic strips sponsored by a Poughkeepsie-based business and created by an artist who became famous for work she completed in later years. Amelia Opdyke Jones did not reside in the Hudson River valley. She was born in New Brunswick, New Jersey; raised her family in South Orange; and spent her retirement years down the shore. Her most prominent work as a professional cartoonist was featured in the New York City transit system.[15] But, as we shall see, she apparently had a temporary connection to the Hudson River valley as well. Throughout the summer and early fall of 1939, the pages of the *Poughkeepsie Eagle-News* featured a weekly comic strip incorporated into advertisements for the Luckey, Platt, & Co. department store. The ads made space for the strip's title—*Luckey's Lads*—and the name of the creator, Oppy, which was Amelia Opdyke Jones's pseudonym. Exploring these strips not only adds a new layer to our understanding of Oppy's long and renowned career but also shows how a legendary retail establishment in Poughkeepsie tapped into the commercial possibilities of the comic strip as a form.

Born in 1913, Oppy became a published cartoonist while still in her teens. With the help of her mentor, artist and fellow New Jerseyan Fred Cooper, Oppy published her work in *Life* magazine in the early 1930s. By the time of her marriage in 1934 to William Jones, she was creating a single-panel comic, *The Young Idear*, for the United Features Syndicate, though the wedding announcement refers to her as a "Former Local Girl" rather than as a cartoonist.[16] The *Young Idear* did not last long. According to accounts written later in Oppy's career note that she took time off from art when her children, William and Margaretta, were young.[17]

Oppy broke back into public view by 1946, when she began making posters about subway behavior for the New York Transit System. The signs, and the story of the artist who created them, gleaned a good deal of favorable attention in the city: "It was a distinct surprise to this inquiring reporter to discover that 'Oppy' is a woman . . . [I]t is she who decides that a cartoon showing a seat hog with a porcine nose is just the thing to cure said seat hog of his bad manners in overlapping into three seat sections"[18] Some writers still went out of their way to associate Oppy with conventional domestic roles. For example, *The New York Times* describes her as a "New Jersey housewife" even while noting the attention given to her work by hundreds of thousands of commuters.[19]

According to her granddaughter, Elizabeth Opdyke Jones, these attitudes emerged in Oppy's everyday interactions as well: Women in her town would often ask how her "little drawings" were coming along and assumed that her favorite tasks were illustrating cookbooks and fashion advertisements. In reality, Jones recounts, her grandmother was a "maverick" who loved adventurous swims in the ocean, forays to Manhattan, and work related to transportation, science, and technology, such as the Reddy Kilowatt ads she created for electrical utilities (Jones).

In the interim, however, she seems to have created commercial art for Luckey, Platt, a prominent Poughkeepsie retail establishment throughout the late nineteenth and twentieth centuries (see figures 5.3 and 5.4).[20] Published in thirteen successive weeks between May and September 1939, Oppy's linework and style in the strips connect more closely to *The Young Idea* than to her transit work, for which she developed a bolder and cleaner aesthetic. Of course, the details were part of the point for these strips, which were designed to sell boys' clothes alongside promotions for the radios, refrigerators, and furniture also sold at the department store. Clothing advertisements are often a relatively static art, featuring models in poses designed to highlight the clothes rather than the humans wearing them. For her part, Oppy seems to have been working toward two goals: showing boys' outfits in detail and creating comics that would appeal to both children and their parents.

By and large, the strips successfully meet these challenges. The boys boss each other around with slangy irreverence, and their well-tailored outfits do not stop them from blundering into a variety of misadventures. When mayhem breaks out, as in *Chubby Falls for Lady Luck*, Oppy does an impressive job of combining physical action and iconic comics symbols with carefully rendered plaids, prints, and trouser pleats. Her wit

Figure 5.3. Integrated within an advertisement for the Luckey, Platt department store, this comic strip appeared in *The Poughkeepsie Eagle-News* on 16 June 1939. *Source:* Reproduced with the kind permission of Margaretta Friday.

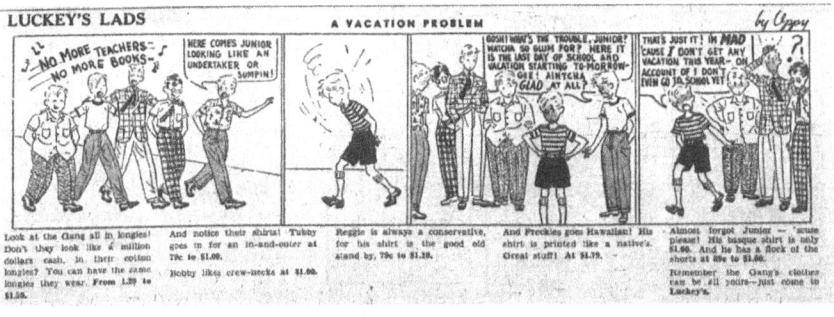

Figure 5.4. *The Poughkeepsie Eagle-News*, June 2, 1939. *Source:* Reproduced with the kind permission of Margaretta Friday.

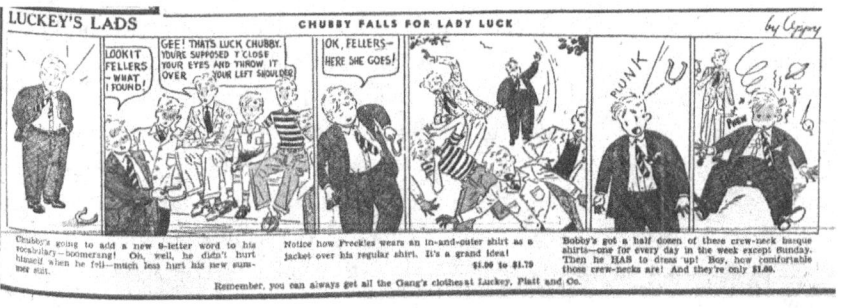

and flair fall short in one strip; when the boys take over the station of a Black shoeshine man, his face, clothes, and speech reflect racist tropes. The strip does not make jokes at the shoeshine man's expense, but his stereotypical appearance resembles the Black workers in Thomas Nast's *Sketches among the Catskill Mountains* (chapter 1).

Perhaps because Oppy herself did not consider *Luckey's Lads* her best work, the strip does not appear in the archive of her work housed at the New York Transit Museum. It would be her later role as "the commuter's cartoonist" that provided her with the opportunity to make a lasting imprint on New York's visual culture.[21] Nevertheless, the marketing savvy of a landmark Poughkeepsie business helped to keep Oppy in the game until she found an ideal match for her talent and determination. Our next profile tells a story that resembles Oppy's in many ways. In the face of daunting obstacles, E. Simms Campbell's versatility brought him success and esteem. Unlike Oppy's story, though, his accomplishments could not be placed into a framework that would be acceptable to American society in the middle decades of the twentieth century.

E. Simms Campbell:
Achievement and Exclusion in the Valley

In an egalitarian world, Elmer Simms Campbell (1906–1971) would be one of the most well-known artists of the Hudson River valley. As a successful Black artist whose work gained global renown, Campbell's achievements constitute a step forward from, and a rebuke to, the caricature in Oppy's strip and the aggressive racism found in "The Legend of Sleepy Hollow," Darktown Comics, and other works we have discussed. But his story also shows that old attitudes die hard and that a feeling of ownership and home in the valley has not been equally extended to all its artists.

In 1953, artist Thaddeus "Teddy" Shearer published an article in *The New York Age Defender* that celebrated the increasing prominence of Black artists in the fields of commercial art and cartooning.[22] Shearer lists Campbell as one of the figures who "helped to break hard ground on a path that many of us were to follow eagerly." Born in St. Louis, Missouri, in 1906, Campbell trained at several institutions in Chicago, moved to New York in 1929, and quickly became a fixture in the city's culture; he collaborated with Langston Hughes and Arna Bontemps and made friends with Cab Calloway.[23] His *Night-Club Map of Harlem*, created in 1932, offers a lively look at the area's rich musical and social environment.[24]

Campbell also met with immediate success as a cartoonist and illustrator. With boosts from white cartoonists Ed Graham and Russell Patterson, Campbell "made the leap into White media," as Ken Quattro has written.[25] For more than two decades (1933–1958), Campbell's cartoons were a mainstay on the pages of *Esquire* magazine; these offered sardonic glimpses of the social and sexual mores of the city, almost invariably depicting white characters or "Harem Girls."[26] He published in other prominent magazines, including *Life*, *The New Yorker*, *The Saturday Evening Post*, and others; moreover, his syndicated comic strip, *Cuties*, appeared in 145 newspapers and was published in three anthologies. An archive of his photographs and letters resides at the Billy Ireland Cartoon Library and Museum at The Ohio State University.[27]

As indicated in his obituary in *The Crusader*, a newspaper in Illinois geared toward Black readers, Campbell had a longstanding but somewhat distanced relationship to Black advocacy movements: "Although not a civil rights activist, Mr. Campbell did support the civil rights movement through his art."[28] When the NAACP and College Art Association collaborated on "An Art Commentary on Lynching" in 1935, Campbell contributed a haunting charcoal illustration, *I Passed along This Way*, that implicitly connected lynching with Christ's crucifixion.[29] He wrote and illustrated a thoughtful reflection on the blues in *Esquire* in 1939 and participated in benefits such as the October 1949 event in support of the Harlem Hospital Library Fund.[30] His woodblock-style illustrations to Sterling A. Brown's anthology *Southern Road: Poems* (1932) offer gorgeously rendered visual narratives of Black history. And, as Shearer's article makes clear, he served as a leading light and a practical mentor for other Black artists entering the field.

Amid these activities, Campbell encountered racist hostility in the Hudson River valley that eventually led him to leave the area, and the United States, altogether. When he sought to buy what *The Daily News* (Tarrytown) called "a swanky country estate" in Pleasantville in 1938, including twelve acres of land and a ten-room house, he was thwarted by a series of strategic counteroffers.[31] Although the estate was in foreclosure, the white former owner of the property somehow managed to find the funds to offer higher bids than Campbell. Neighbors in the area included Arthur Choate and John D. Rockefeller Jr.[32] Claiming racial animus, Campbell brought the matter to court and lost his case in 1938. References to Campbell in *The Daily News'* headlines (e.g., "Negro Can't Buy Property") indicates the lens through which whites saw Black artists, even those known for "svelte drawings of women" in "nationally circulated magazines."[33] *The Daily News* did not lend support to Campbell's case in any way. Editorials in the ensuing week focused instead on plans to resurface Main Street and to prepare for the annual Soap Box Derby.[34] Ten days later, the newspaper's glowing description of commercial artist Gustave Pernod's creation of a modernist, cinderblock house in Mamaroneck starkly shows the contrast between the leeway for a successful white artist and that afforded to Campbell.[35]

Campbell remained in the area for almost two more decades; the 1940 and 1950 censuses find him living in Elmsford, New York. In 1956, however, he moved to Switzerland and lived there until returning to the area in 1970; he died in 1971. The fact that he was not inducted into the Will Eisner Hall of Fame until 2020 demonstrates the slow pace of racial reckoning in comics as a field and in the United States in general.[36] The story of a near-contemporary of Campbell's provides an even more striking reminder of the challenges facing Black artists in the early and middle decades of the twentieth century.

An Incomplete Story: John F. Parker

A poignant sense of missed opportunity emerges in the intriguing but incomplete history of John F. Parker (1910–?), a Tarrytown-born cartoonist who met with early success before disappearing from comics history. Census records indicate that he was born in 1910 to George and Mary Parker. The 1920 census lists John along with four siblings, noting that George was employed as a porter for the railroad out of Grand Central and that Mary, who worked as a laundress, was born in Bermuda.[37] By 1930, Mary is listed as widowed, and John is working as a chauffeur and delivery man.[38] Parker first surfaces in an artistic context as the author of *Goodhair*, a comic strip syndicated by Stanton Features in 1933 and described by *Pioneering Cartoonists of Color* author Tim Jackson (2016) as "an inexplicable throwback to the blackface minstrel image" (39–40). The next piece of evidence suggests a career breakthrough for Parker. He has been hired as a cartoonist by *The Daily News* in Tarrytown, just two months after Campbell was denied the opportunity to buy the estate in Pleasantville (see figure 5.5).[39]

The laudatory piece mentions his parents and his father's death, as well as his talents as a baseball player and caricaturist of the teachers during his time at Tarrytown High School. Unlike the headlines or text of the paper's articles about the E. Simms Campbell suit, the article identifies Parker as a "youthful artist" without reference to his race; only the accompanying photo indicates that he is Black. Confirming Parker's connection to *Goodhair*, the article mentions that he "had done comic strip work for the Stanton Feature Service"; it also notes that he had been mentored by *Reg'lar Fellows* cartoonist Gene Byrnes after Parker showed him his work in 1931.

"The Daily News is enthusiastic about the local cartoonist and plans to make his drawings a regular feature," announces the July 15, 1938, article. Sure enough, Parker's cartoon appears in that same issue. Fulfilling the article's characterization of his work as aimed at those "who love the red-blooded American 'kid,'" the cartoon shows two young white boys

Figure 5.5. *Source:* © Tarrytown *Daily News*—USA TODAY NETWORK. Used with permission.

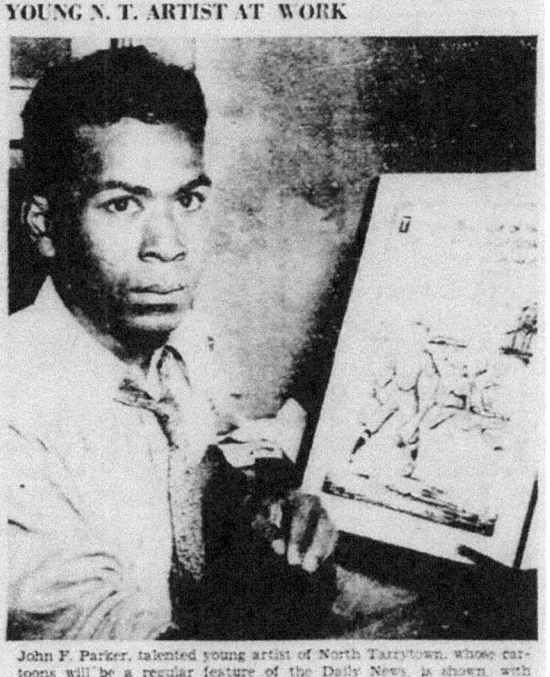

John F. Parker Draws for Daily News; Gene Byrnes Aided Talented N. T. Youth

First Cartoon by Local Man Is Published Today

Making his debut today as a cartoonist for The Daily News is John F. Parker, a solemn-faced fellow who sees the humor in things and has the ability to put his impressions on paper.

One cartoon by Parker is printed in today's issue of this publication. This cartoon has a special appeal to those who love the red-blooded American "kid." Two young fellows, in the shadow of a "No Fishing or Swimming Allowed" sign, are at odds because one wants to plunge into the lake and the other is set for a bit of angling.

A Native of N. T.

Parker is no stranger in North Tarrytown. The son of Mrs. George Parker, of Depeyster Street, he has spent most of his life here. He went to the North Tarrytown schools but was unable to complete his high school course because of the death of his father. Parker left school after finishing his sophomore year and went to work.

Unsmiling, like Buster Keaton, Parker has the ability to make others laugh. As a high school student more than 10 years ago, he used to make his class mates chuckle at his drawings. Especially favored by his school mates were his caricatures of members of the faculty. When several of the sketches were printed in the school annual, some of the officials raised mild objections but it was all good clean fun and

YOUNG N. T. ARTIST AT WORK

John F. Parker, talented young artist of North Tarrytown, whose cartoons will be a regular feature of the Daily News, is shown with pencil in hand, at his drawing board. This newspaper publishes the first of his cartoons today.

Staff Photo

sparring over fishing privileges in a location with a large sign that warns against trespassing. The focus on summer pastimes continues in Parker's cartoon published about a week later, which celebrates the baseball triumphs of the "First Half Champs" of the Twilight League. In a third cartoon published on July 25 (see figure 5.6), Parker moves to four panels to show boys "sifting dump piles, invading attics, and raiding cellars" to build their soap-box-derby cars. This cartoon is especially successful. In one panel, a silhouetted boy braves a darkened cellar to find a useful baby carriage; in another, a bystander comments to his pal that the car looks "like a dead catfish on wheels."

Figure 5.6. *Source:* © Tarrytown *Daily News*—USA TODAY NETWORK. Used with permission.

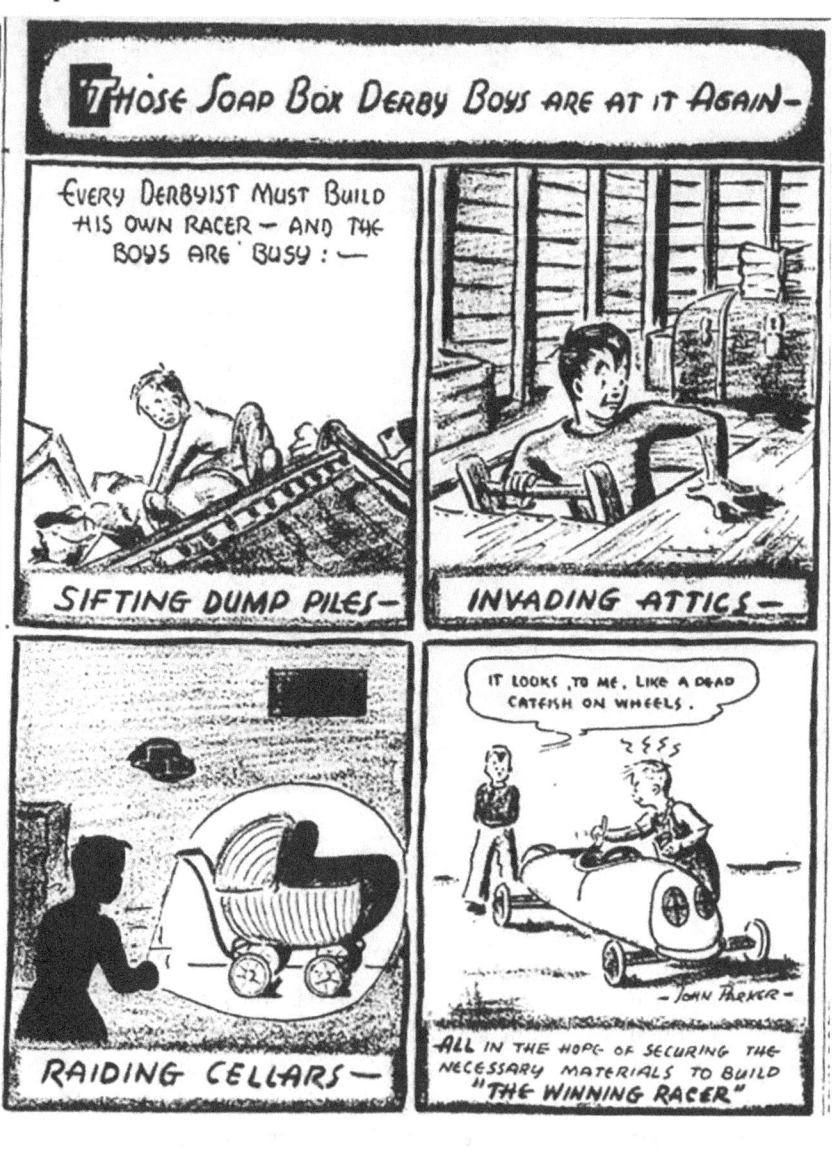

Strangely, however, these three cartoons seem to be all Parker published in the newspaper; nothing appears after July 25 for the whole remainder of 1938. The original article about Parker came up again in August 1938, in a more tense and tragic context. Following the death by drowning of Columbia University graduate and aspiring doctor Zebdee

V. Jones, *Daily News* reader Marguerite Nixon wrote a letter to the editor criticizing the paper for not identifying him as a "Negro": "Some people may think that it was a great thing for an article to appear in the paper which concerned a colored person and not refer to his race, but I can see through the act." To Nixon, the omission reflected the paper's desire to "keep the colored race down and to keep the majority of people from learning of its progress." *The News* responded in an editor's note calling the omission an "oversight," pointing out that the article had mentioned Jones's studies at Howard University, "which is widely known as a Negro institution," and using Parker's employment to support its argument: "The charge, by implication, that the Daily News is prejudiced against the colored race is so ridiculous that it seems hardly necessary to mention that several weeks ago we hired John F. Parker, a talented young Negro artist of North Tarrytown, as a cartoonist," citing the article and the photo.[40] By this point, though, it had been almost a month since any of Parker's cartoons had appeared in the paper. Notably, the newspaper did not say anything about Parker's ongoing work or the number of cartoons that had appeared.

The headline affixed to Nixon's letter by the newspaper—"A Ridiculous Charge"—reveals that *The News*' leadership reacted angrily to her criticism. Could a similar conflict have led to Parker's dismissal? It is impossible to determine exactly what happened. He appears in the 1940 census living on Depeyster Street in Tarrytown with his mother and brother, with his occupation as a self-employed "sign painter." He is not listed in the 1950 census, though his siblings still are. Many questions remain unanswered: Did Parker move somewhere else and continue to work as an artist? Did he ever cross paths with Campbell, who lived only about three miles away in Elmsford? Did he try to get a job at Western Printing, which was just starting up its massive production in Poughkeepsie in the late 1930s? In any case, Parker's talents were unmistakable. Perhaps other evidence will surface in local records to explain what happened to this Hudson River valley artist. We will turn now to a cartoonist on the opposite side of the spectrum. A rich record remains of Melvin Tapley's lengthy career as a cartoonist, editor, and community leader.

Melvin Tapley's Art and Activism

Born only eight years after Parker and residing fewer than twenty miles north of him, Melvin Tapley (1918–2005) spent his long life addressing the factors that may have derailed Parker's career and that certainly led Campbell to leave the country. When someone finally writes a full-length biography of Tapley, it will be fascinating.[41] He combined a prolific career as a cartoonist with full-time work as an editor and with numerous commitments to Black causes and other aspects of community life in the Hudson River valley. His career was anchored in Peekskill, where his family had already lived for generations before his birth, and he became a mainstay of civic life in the city while, at the same time, editing the Manhattan-based *Amsterdam News* and creating comic strips that were published in Black newspapers all over the country. Lauded with an NAACP Lifetime Recognition Award in 1996 and commemorated posthumously by Peekskill's NAACP chapter, city leaders, and the Field Library with a "Mel Tapley Day" celebration and exhibit, Tapley was remembered by a longtime colleague as "the kindest, gentlest, most easygoing person I've ever met."[42] His granddaughter, Imani Montgomery, offers an even more heartfelt tribute: "He was just my favorite person."

Tapley's skills in advocacy and communication earned recognition early in his life: in 1936, he won second prize in a local oratorical contest with his speech "Booker T. Washington and the Constitution."[43] His talents as an artist and writer secured him early professional success, too: having graduated from New York University, he began over a half-century at work as both an editor and staff cartoonist at the *Amsterdam News* in 1941. In that role, Tapley produced a stunningly wide range of work: editorial cartoons, an adventure series called *Jim Steele*, the single-panel cartoons *Spoffin* and *Dos and Don'ts*, *The Brown Family* comic strip, and *Breezy*. Tapley published these comics using a variety of names, including *Tap Melvin* and *Stann Pat*, to efface the fact that one person was creating so many seemingly disparate works.[44]

An anthology of Tapley's work across these comics genres is sorely needed. As a recent collection produced by About Comics demonstrates, *Breezy* is a great comic strip.[45] About a decade before Charlie Brown donned his zigzag-printed shirt, teenaged protagonist Breezy Biggins sports a distinctive sweater with stripes on the midriff and sleeves. Although he wears glasses, he is by no means a nerd; he navigates girls, friends, schoolteachers, and his parents with a sanguine and irreverent outlook. At times, Tapley incorporates Black history directly into the series: One strip (see figure 5.7) finds Breezy becoming so "swell-headed" from reading about Black achievements in *The Negro Is a Man* that his hat no longer fits. Other strips contain even more pointed social messages: One strip

Figure 5.7. *Source:* Reproduced with the kind permission of Imani Montgomery and About Comics.

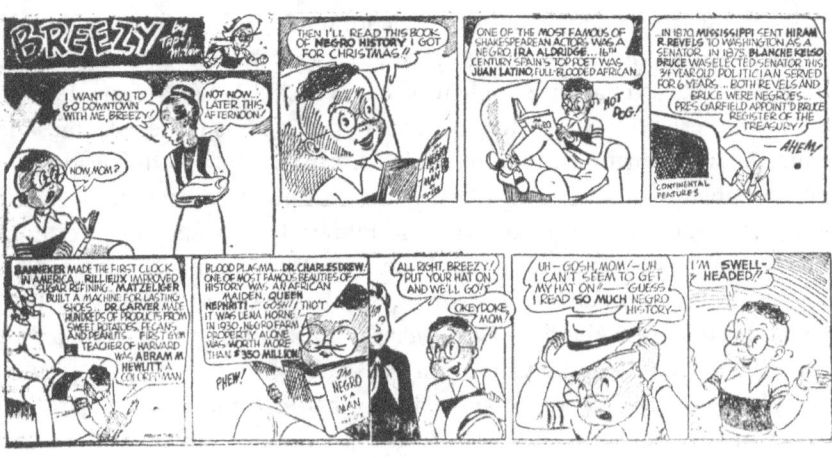

depicts a white woman threatening to call the police on Breezy when he helpfully picks up a toy gun dropped by the woman's son. Still others allow Tapley to move from social realities into Herriman-like surrealism: After overeating at Easter, Breezy is pursued in his dreams by malevolent bunnies and humanoid hard-boiled eggs.

Even as *Breezy*'s reach widened—the strip appeared in Black newspapers nationwide such as *The Chicago Bee*, *The State Press* in Arkansas, the *Jackson Advocate* in Mississippi, and *The Ohio State News*—Tapley generously acknowledged his neighbors in the valley. A note in the fourth panel of a 1944 strip renders "thanx to Navy draftee, Len Carrington, Peekskill, NY," suggesting that Carrington gave him the idea for the gag (see figure 5.8).[46] Tapley collaborated on a work of local history, too: He

Figure 5.8. *Source:* Reproduced with the kind permission of Imani Montgomery and About Comics.

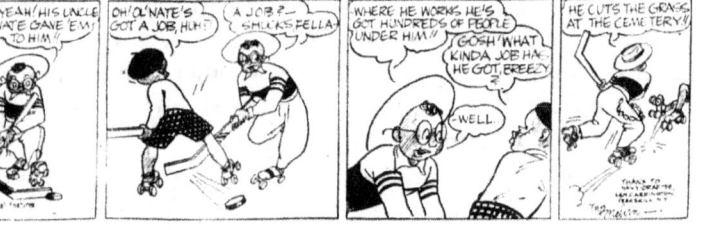

served as an uncredited illustrator in Joseph M. Fox's *The History of Early Peekskill, 1609–1876* (1947).[47]

These artistic connections to the community complemented Tapley's editorial work and his dizzying array of civic activities. The biggest role he played was as chapter president of the Peekskill NAACP from 1952 to 1968, where he advocated for job creation, fair housing legislation, and educational opportunities for all students.[48] In addition to this leadership position, he took on a variety of other commitments and activities—some long term, such as his service as a Field Library trustee and Board of Education member, and others as standalone events.[49] At times, he merged his interest in arts with civic engagement, as when he participated in a 1986 panel discussion of the film *The Color Purple* at an event coordinated by the Mount Olivet Baptist Church in Peekskill.[50]

Tapley earned many honors during his lifetime. He was named a fellow of Columbia University's Intergroup Relations Project in 1966 and was an award winner at the Peekskill NAACP's annual dinner in 1996.[51] Amid all these activities, he never seemed worn down by his obligations. He always had time to draw, finger paint, or have tea parties with his granddaughter (Montgomery).

How was Tapley able to coordinate his work as a family man, cartoonist, editor, and community leader with such verve and grace? Perhaps these roles were mutually reinforcing. The accomplishments of his wife, Arline J. Tapley (1932–1990), suggest that civic engagement was a key part of his family's ethos and his personal convictions, an idea backed up by Montgomery: "He wanted to share the news and fight against injustice where he thought it would matter."[52] Whereas Stanford W. Carpenter has noted the painful contradictions experienced by many Black comic creators—"leading double lives, living on both sides of the color line, shifting between living in Black communities and working as cogs in a very White machine tasked with crafting fantastical stories"[53]—Tapley was firmly grounded in his community. He seems to have known exactly who he was and what he stood for: "He was very big on our knowing our own history," Montgomery recalls. Through his community leadership, his journalistic work, and his comic art, he channeled his own talents into sustaining and motivating others. His example could guide twenty-first-century efforts to make the Hudson River valley a healthier social, economic, and cultural ecosystem.

As much as communication in the digital realm can facilitate this work, there is probably no substitute for in-person gatherings for people to support and sustain each other's efforts. In terms of artistic achievement, we can see ample evidence for this in the stories of three comics creators who interacted as neighbors and comics colleagues in the later decades of the twentieth century.

The Catskills Crowd: Linda Fite, Ron Marz, and Herb Trimpe

To consider these next three individuals, we need to cross the Hudson River, travel north on the New York State Thruway, and head west into Ulster County. Bounded by the river on the east and the Catskills to the north, the region we might call "the greater Woodstock area" has served, and continues to serve, as a home base for many writers, artists, editors, letterers, and colorists in the industry.[54] The experiences of Linda Fite, Ron Marz, and Herb Trimpe will serve as our inroad into this creative ecosystem.

"Like metal filings and a magnet, they kept coming up," recalls Fite, referring to comics creators' moving into the area and displaying her talent for the apt turn of phrase. Her verbal skills earned her a job as Stan Lee's assistant at Marvel in the 1970s; eventually, she wrote the entire four-issue run of *The Cat*.[55] In addition to the benefits of living near industry colleagues, the relative affordability of Ulster and Greene Counties was also a key factor. "A whole raft of people, both comics as well as illustrators, ended up in the Hudson valley because it was still a close enough drive, or train ride, that you could go to the city to conduct your business and turn in your pages, but you didn't have to be in Manhattan or Brooklyn or Queens," recounts Ron Marz, whose career as a comics writer includes long runs of *Green Lantern* and *Silver Surfer*, among many other titles. Even in the pre-internet era of the 1970s and 1980s, Marz adds, "remote" work was possible: "As long as you could be reached by FedEx, you could work in comics."

Individual preference and happenstance had their role to play, as well. For Marz, opportunity came knocking when, as an undergraduate at Marist University, he conducted an interview with Bernie Wrightson for the campus newspaper.[56] When Wrightson kindly invited him to his annual Halloween party, Marz was both thrilled and overwhelmed: "I waffled right up to almost the last minute, but I finally pushed myself into going. I had no way of knowing it at the time, but it was a decision that changed my life. . . . I'd likely never have met Jim Starlin [see figure 5.9],

Figure 5.9. Marz with his good friend and fellow Hudson River valley comics creator Jim Starlin. *Source:* Courtesy of Ron Marz.

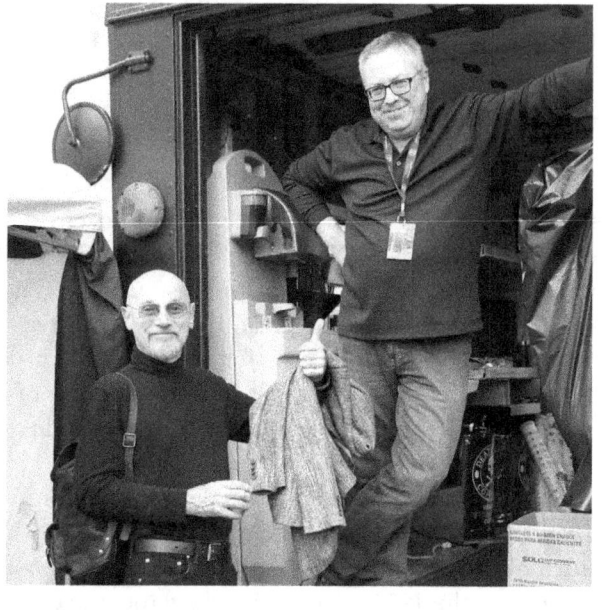

meaning Jim never would've suggested that I write comics, or showed me the ropes of writing comics, or led me by the figurative hand into Marvel Comics."[57] In addition to setting his career in motion, the interview and party introduced Marz to an area that he would call home: He lived for years at the base of Overlook Mountain, near Woodstock.

Herb Trimpe's story also connects both to multiple parts of the Hudson River valley. Renowned for his artwork on *The Incredible Hulk* and for his creation of the first published Wolverine art, Trimpe grew up in Peekskill, a city his family had lived in for generations. (I have found no evidence of interaction between the Trimpe family and the Tapleys or with John Stanley during his time in the town, but it is intriguing to think about.) In Jon Michael Riley's documentary *Herb Trimpe, We Love You!* Trimpe is seen at home in Peekskill and hiking next to the river (see figure 5.10).

During Trimpe's marriage to Linda Fite, the two lived briefly in England before deciding to move back to the United States. Their daughter, Amelia Trimpe, described how comics were not her father's top priority

Figure 5.10. Herb Trimpe (right) and Linda Fite (second from right) enjoying the Hudson River valley with friends Jon Michael Riley, Catherine Riley, Kay Barthelmes, and Bob Barthelmes. *Source:* Courtesy of Jon Michael Riley.

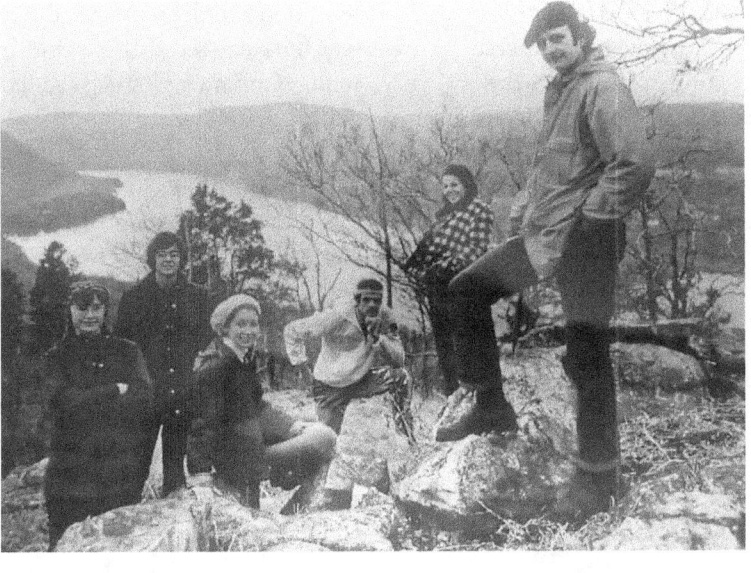

when deciding upon a new home: "He had a very particular process" for making the decision, she recalls. A certified pilot and owner of a biplane, "He marked all the small airports in the New York City area, then took out a compass and measured everything within a thirty-mile radius. Kerhonkson, New York, ended up being the place with access to the most small airports." The area appealed to Fite, as well; a committed Anglophile, she found Ulster County scenery like the English countryside.

Fite also lured British artists to the region. While opening Stan Lee's mail during her time working for him in Manhattan, Fite noticed a letter from Steve Parkhouse and Barry Windsor-Smith. Although there were no positions open for them, Fite encouraged the two to come to the United States and "give it a go." It took a while for the guests to find their way—"They slept in our living room . . . [T]hey would be sitting there glumly strumming the guitar," Fite recalls—but both became prominent artists in the field. While Parkhouse eventually returned to the United Kingdom, Windsor-Smith settled in the area, was godfather to one of Fite and Trimpe's daughters, and remains one of Fite's close friends.

There were ample opportunities for comics writers and artists in the area to talk shop with one another. Wrightson continued to throw his Halloween parties for many years. Wendy and Richard Pini occasionally traveled up from Poughkeepsie for them, and children attended as well: Amelia Trimpe remembers marveling as a ten-year-old at the "mind-blowingly good costumes" worn by everyone in attendance.[58] Other events took place on a regular basis, as Marz recounts:

> For a number of years, we had what were called First Friday parties. That was a tradition that was a holdover from the seventies and eighties in the city, where all of the comics people would get together on the first Friday of the month [and share] what they were working on and have sort of a potluck dinner and hang out and see what each other were working on. That sort of got revived up here, a lot of times at Bernie's place, because he had the big studio in the back, but at any number of places . . . [in addition to comics writers and illustrators] it was also artists, writers, some musicians, some photographers, everybody who did something creative was welcome.

Fite also has fond memories of these gatherings, which usually involved spouses and children. She notes that there were other get-togethers specifically for artists and writers and that this group sometimes included celebrated comics artist Ramona Fradon.[59]

Many members of this crowd also convened for athletic events. Both Fite and Marz recall racquetball games with Jim Starlin and others, and Marz's experience included team sports: "We had a volleyball game that ran for years that all of us participated in at the Woodstock Elementary School." Marz also counted Herb Trimpe as a teammate: "I played on the same softball team with Herb for a number of years. We were the two comics guys on the team. . . . The second baseman wrote comics, and the right fielder drew them." Marz's on-field bonding with Trimpe did not, however, extend to another of Trimpe's avocations:

> We were at a party at Herb's house . . . [W]e're sitting around eating and drinking and Herb's taking people up for biplane rides, and I'm thinking, "Shit, that's cool; I should do that," and so I start to head over to the hangar. . . . And [Jim] Starlin grabbed me by the arm and said, "Don't do that. . . . Yeah,

that thing's going to fall apart in the air at some point, and you don't want to be on it when it does." So I said, "OK, fair enough." . . . I went back and had another beer.

Despite Starlin's warnings about the plane, Trimpe undoubtedly knew what he was doing as a pilot: His four years of service in the Air Force included a year-long stint in South Vietnam.[60]

Amelia Trimpe remembers her father as someone with a strikingly broad range of interests and talents: "He was into stuff," including creating whole battalions of Civil War model soldiers and serving as a deacon in a local Episcopal church and, eventually, as a chaplain at Ground Zero after the 9/11 attacks. When Marvel fired him in 1996, Trimpe reinvented himself as an art teacher, eventually teaching seventh-grade art at the Eldred Middle School in Sullivan County as well as leading sessions at the Poughkeepsie Day School in collaboration with his third wife, Patricia.[61] The transition away from comics to a career in education was not an easy one, as Trimpe recalls in a candid essay in *The New York Times* education section in 2000. But he gained insights that merged his on-the-ground work in the valley with his airborne adventures: "Teaching is like flying a plane. You leave school one day feeling like you're spiraling down toward the trees, expecting that the next day the crash will come. You brace yourself for the impact, only to find out that things have leveled out at treetop height, and you climb and enjoy the remainder of the flight."[62] Trimpe's flights above the Hudson River valley landscape helped him come to terms with his rupture from comics and movement toward a new career. For her part, Fite had moved away from the industry after she became alienated from it: "I always thought of comics as fun. Then when you had a new wave of serious writer types, I didn't want to do that." She continued her involvement in the publishing industry, though, by serving as the managing editor of the community newspaper *BlueStone Press* for many years. Recently retired, she has overwhelmingly positive memories of her connections to the comics community: "It was a delight back then; it really was."

Ron Marz remains a busy comics writer, although he notes that comics have become less local than they were in previous decades: "I work with artists who live in Albany, and I work with artists who live in India." Conferences still give creators a chance to get together, though, and the Hudson River valley still has a powerful sway over him: "You take a notebook; you take a laptop; you go somewhere that it's quiet. I've done that on both sides of the river, in the mountains, in the hills overlooking the river. There's a peace and a tranquility to that and frankly, if you are disciplined, and you can leave your phone in the car, there's no internet, none of that stuff infringes upon the fantasy world that you're creating." Echoing Pierre's ideas, Marz notes that solitude, as well as community life, can be a gift. A little quiet, a little space—we shouldn't overlook these as factors, even when trying to tell a story located in a far-off place or alternate universe.

While Ulster County has, as we have seen, hosted many creators involved in the production of superhero narratives, the region also is called home by writers and artists working to develop another dimension of the medium: the expanding market for graphic novels designed for children, young teenagers, and young adults. To learn more about these creators, we will travel to New Paltz, a town in southern Ulster County that sits alongside the Wallkill River.

Kayla Miller and Jeffrey Canino: Finding a Neighborhood That "Clicks"

For Kayla Miller and Jeffrey Canino, a sense of creative community begins at home. Miller is the author and illustrator of the middle-grade Click series of graphic novels, while Canino has written several forthcoming graphic novels for young readers. Partners in work as well as in life, Miller and Canino cowrite Besties, a series for the tween crowd about adolescent friendship (comprising three volumes so far) with illustrations by Vancouver-based artist Kristina Luu.

Even a successful partnership, however, occasionally necessitates someone's "taking a hike," and that is what Miller and Canino do: "Every time I need to clear my head is I end up going for a walk or a run on the rail trail," Miller asserts. Canino agrees: "We've actually broken down a lot of the books in the planning stages while going on walks on the rail trail." In keeping with these experiences, Miller's contribution to this volume (see figure 5.11), which they produced for a children's literacy campaign, depicts the joy of reading, performing, and playing in outdoor spaces.

The couple's chosen hometown of New Paltz provides a similar blend of stimulation and support. A native of bucolic Vernon, New Jersey, Miller earned their degree in illustration from the University of the Arts in Philadelphia and loved the vibrant "alt-comics" community there. When

Figure 5.11. *Read beyond the Beaten Path. Source:* Kayla Miller. Used with permission.

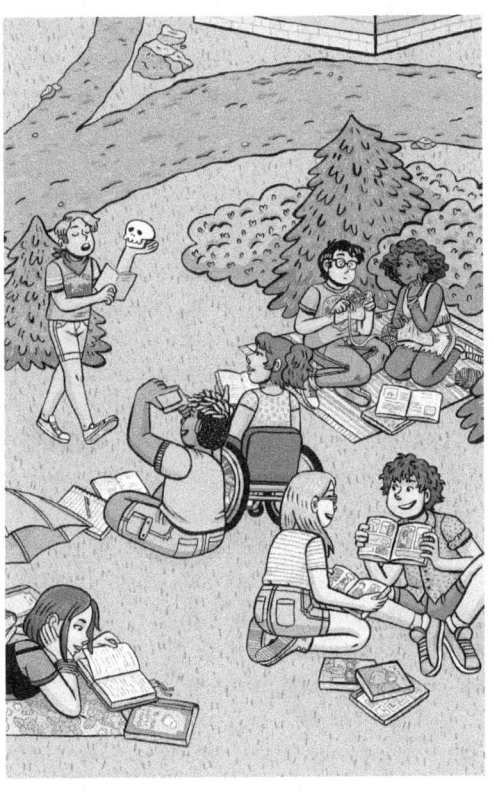

it came time to settle down, Miller was eager to live in a place with a " 'sit down and write here' atmosphere. When we were looking for places, I wanted to live in a town. . . . People at the library are super-friendly, and having two bookstores in town is great." They note that area cafes such as the Gunks Gaming Guild are "welcoming places" that host writing groups and gatherings for artists, filmmakers, and writers. These benefits of the area were well known to Canino since he earned both his undergraduate and graduate degrees at SUNY New Paltz. He notes that their house, near Huguenot Street, offers a rich array of historical associations as well as social connections. The neighborhood has been designated a National Historic Landmark District and holds many community events centered around the histories of the Indigenous, French, Dutch, and enslaved Black people who have lived in the area.[63]

Canino says that one of his recent graphic novels directly invokes the Hudson River valley: "It's set in the fall, it's right around Halloween, [and] most of the action is set at a farm stand, much like the farm stands here, . . . I think this is something that Kayla feels too, that this is a perfect atmosphere for mystery." Harking back to Irving's descriptions of the area, Canino invokes the valley's combination of spookiness and domestic delights: "[There is a] cozy vibe, too, which I think helps with these softer mysteries." Similarly, Miller envisions "intentionally basing" a future comic on life in New Paltz: "I want to have an old cemetery, all the shops in town, [and a plot] centered around an antique store."

Despite the couple's shared appreciation of the area's natural beauty, Miller notes that representing the outdoors is not their primary preoccupation as an artist: "I like drawing backgrounds but . . . I like civilization. I like interiors and architecture; I do draw nature, but usually it's trees and not specific landscapes." Their primary inspiration comes from the people they encounter. "Sometimes people ask me, 'Why do you draw so many characters in your book or different types of people who are dressed different ways?' Because that's what I see in the world, and I want to reflect that. I'm glad we live in a place like that." Canino concurs: "We're in town," he says. "That matters a lot."

While Canino and Miller draw upon New Paltz for mass-market books created for young readers, the town's thriving artistic community has played a role in developing new forms of independent creation and publishing as well. Knowledge and inspiration from New Paltz, among other Hudson River valley locations, also influenced comics artist and writer Harry Sheridan, the writer and artist of the Tricky Style series and the founder of Amekomi Comics.

Harry Sheridan: Local and Global Influences

Encouragement from teachers played a key role in Sheridan's development as a comics creator. "I had a lot of really good influences in the area," he recounts, noting that art teacher Rocco Manno at Warwick Valley High School served as a particularly valuable mentor:

It wasn't just doing still lifes and stuff (which we also obviously did). [Manno] really encouraged doing the comics work. He had friends who did comics, and he would introduce me to them; they would give me their work and give me signed copies of their work. . . . I feel like you don't get that everywhere in a lot of schools where I feel like, if [a student] were pursuing art, they would actively discourage doing comics and more encourage traditional painting and whatnot.

Some of the characters, ideas, and drawings from that period continue to find their way into his comics.

Sheridan strengthened his skills as a storyteller and artist by earning degrees in English and visual arts (with a concentration in illustration) from SUNY Fredonia and in video production and communication from SUNY New Paltz. As with Miller and Canino, Sheridan enjoyed the sense of creative community offered by New Paltz: "It was a great school—I loved it there. I loved the area, too, the town: I lived right across the street from the campus. . . . It's a very artsy town. They do a lot of music events and stuff. I have friends who would do improv events and stuff. It's a great environment."

Back home in Warwick during the Covid lockdown in 2020, he realized that the pandemic's circumstances, however difficult, also provided him with an opportunity: "I was like, 'OK, I have all this free time now, I have all these ideas, let's get them on paper. Let's start actually doing something.'" The "something" that Sheridan started was the Tricky Style series, an action-adventure comic featuring the exploits of youthful vampire Ammi Punkin and her comrade the Wily Wolf-Man (see Figure 5.12).

Irreverent and vividly drawn, the comic now has seven issues; once Sheridan has published ten, he hopes to assemble them into an omnibus volume. Working with a California-based printer, Sheridan has self-published all his comics under the auspices of his imprint, Amekomi Comics. He also works remotely at his day job as a communications manager for a school district on Long Island.

Although the Tricky Style series is produced as a conventional comic with a glossy cover and professional binding, Sheridan also finds kindred spirits at zine fests. These gatherings feature independently produced, often idiosyncratic comics and written texts. "It's fun because I'll go to zine fests, and my work will look kind of out of place. But it's cool: that's a space I would like to be a part of," he says, noting that in the future he might try putting Tricky Style into that format. The zine ethos parallels his own: "I do it for myself. I don't really have any great big aspirations. I do it because I love it. . . . All the people making zines are just doing

Figure 5.12. *Source:* Amekomi Comics. Used with permission.

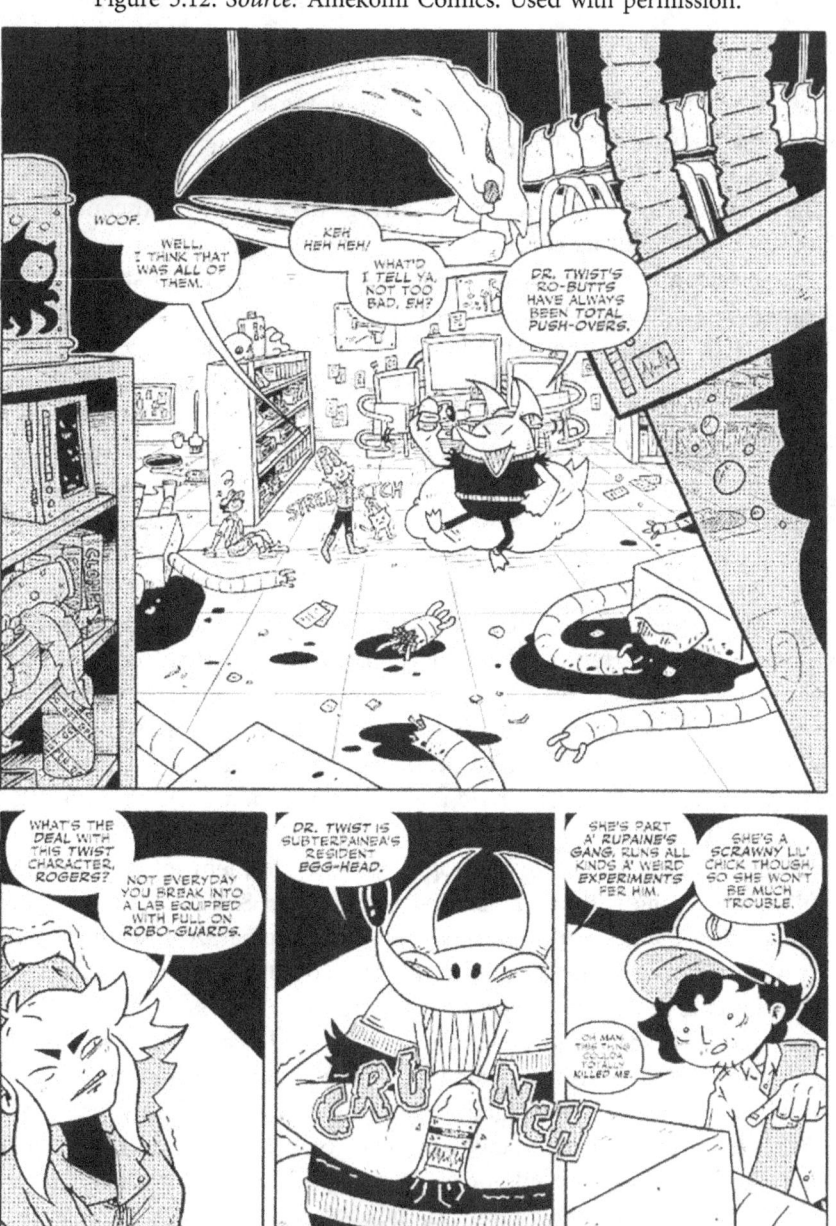

it because they love it." Sheridan notes that these fests work particularly well in areas too distant to take easy advantage of the comics conventions in major cities: "There are people I'm friends with who do comics, zine stuff, who live out of state. They'll host zine festivals, and I'll go to those. It is always like small towns—people who don't have some big New York Comic Con or something like that going on—they'll just put on their own, which is pretty awesome. That's something I feel like maybe we should do around here."

Given the plenitude of colleges and independent bookstores in the area, a Hudson River valley Zine Fest sounds like a great idea for the future. Having experienced both the opportunities and tragedies of a global lockdown, Sheridan and others who entered adulthood in the Covid era seem particularly attuned to the benefits of finding new ways to gather in person and celebrate both digital and hand-crafted creative work.

The pandemic also played a key role in the trajectories of two artists based in Newburgh, a city on the Hudson River about thirty miles due south of New Paltz. Like Sheridan, Alexis Lamb and Seth Christian Martel experienced challenges in that era that have led them to explore modes of creativity and ways of living.

Alexis Lamb: Mobility and Stability

Alexis Lamb wears many hats—artist, welder, and handywoman, just for starters—and works in many media. Like Arthur Rackham, her training and exhibited work encompasses both painting and illustration. Distinctly unlike Rackham, Lamb spent more than a year purchasing, renovating, and living in a forty-foot school bus with her fiancé (she is currently working on a graphic narrative about the experience). Born and raised in New York City, Lamb paired a formal education at Hunter College with travel and lengthy sojourns all over the country. While she notes that this kind of mobility can be "jarring," these experiences also placed her in dialogue with other places and forced her to attend carefully to her own responses to them.

"During my time in college I was thinking about starting to travel, and that's how the bus was born," Lamb recounts. She and her fiancé landed in Santa Fe, New Mexico, for a year-long sojourn that profoundly affected Lamb's work. Seeing Indigenous artists' color palettes, depictions of landscape, and representations of their own communities got Lamb thinking more deeply about "cultural identity and who owns the rights to certain cultural aspects of people." This eventually led to pieces such as *Loc'ed*, which give center stage to Black women's hair designs. Lamb and her fiancé then moved across the country and spent two years in a very different environment: a lakeside spot in Alexander, Maine, about ten miles from Canada. "I was really in the sticks," Lamb recalls, noting that the confines of the bus also made it difficult to work on large-scale paintings. Having "spent a lot of time in isolation trying to figure out what [she] was into," Lamb found herself depicting urban settings, such as the Brooklyn Bridge. She also started working more closely with Prismacolor markers as a medium, noting the value of materials that are "easy to carry around and easy to manipulate: I didn't have to have a whole paint set, with water, a whole setup and breakdown and all of that stuff, I could literally just whip out the markers any time and just go."

Lamb found herself with more space when she and her fiancé sold the bus, and she moved in with her family in Newburgh, New York. Illustrating with markers, however, remained a useful practice, now for a different reason: "Moving into the Hudson valley I feel like it transformed again because I started getting more into art shows. I had booked three or four art shows, and they were all my first time doing art shows," which put Lamb on a relatively quick timetable for producing works. Moreover, she has found that drawing needs to be a daily practice for her: "If I don't do art at least every other day, it feels like I'm dehydrated. It's like needing to drink water [or] to talk to people."

All three kinds of sustenance are offered by congenial spaces in the Hudson River valley, such as the 2 Alices coffee lounges in Newburgh and Cornwall: "They have huge tables, and I really like sprawling out on there and grabbing a coffee and a bagel and staying there for six or seven hours. [The café in Newburgh] has huge windows, and it's a social atmosphere as well. I can't tell you how many times I have my markers out with big pieces of paper, and I'm actively working, and people are constantly coming up and saying, 'Wow, that looks so great—tell me about this.'" Coupled with these moments of connection and community is the attention to detail that Lamb refined during her time in the quieter spaces of New Mexico and Maine. "There's so many little moments in Newburgh that people just kind of pass by," she says, noting that she likes to walk with her fiancé around the neighborhood. She values the small details "instead of the macro and thinking about landscapes and iconic figures and things that tourists might see. Can we zoom in on the things we see every day? Do you notice this one brick that has a whole bunch of text on it that might tell you about the building?" Lamb's piece in this volume, *Hudson Valley in a Cup*, renders those questions into vibrant linework (see figure 5.13). While the drawing contains a traditional landscape, it gives greater prominence to the animals and plants central to valley ecosystems. Paradoxically, attending to our natural environment can both bring us out of ourselves and lead to new insights. If you want to think about place, Lamb recommends, "Immerse yourself in a different situation entirely. You can learn a lot about yourself."

While Lamb's work has explored the effects of this immersion through illustration and painting as well as a graphic memoir-in-progress, another artist in Newburgh has combined a career in graphic design with comics creation. Whether through advancing the work of an area environmental nonprofit or finding new ways to tap into the valley's history of scary stories, Seth Christian Martel finds new ways to highlight the region's natural and social ecosystems.

Figure 5.13. *Source:* Alexis Lamb. Used with permission.

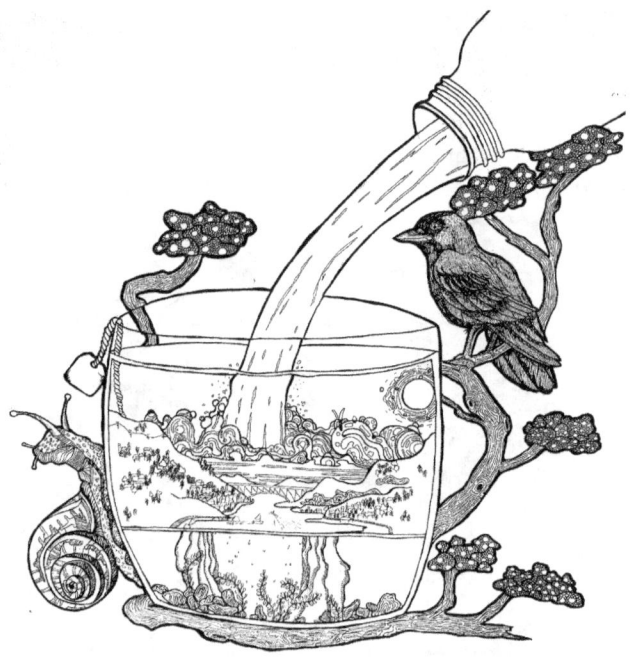

Seth Christian Martel: Riverside Thrills and Chills

Martel's ties to the region run wide and deep. Two of his aunts worked for Western Printing; he graduated with an arts degree from the State University at New Paltz; and he works as a design and creative services coordinator for Scenic Hudson, an organization dedicated to safeguarding the health and beauty of the Hudson River valley's environment. In his other professional role as a cartoonist and writer, Martel recently published *The Mare*, a graphic novel that provides a new spin on the region's longstanding association with supernatural events.

Martel had extensive experience illustrating others' books before 2020. As with Sheridan, the Covid lockdown provided Martel with the bandwidth to focus on long-postponed projects. Once he began to plot out *The Mare*'s storyline, Martel recalled what he valued about the work of legendary X-Men writer—and fellow Hudson River valley resident—Chris Claremont: "Claremont gave you emotional beats between characters where you felt truly invested in them." Within *The Mare*, these character-driven moments are complemented by the region's landscape (see figure 5.14).

As teenage protagonist Indy struggles with school, job, her alcoholic father, and mysterious night-time visitations by an unnamed entity, she finds solace in the support of her friend Kasia. In a pivotal moment in the comic, the strength of Indy's support from Kasia is complemented by

Figure 5.14. Seth Christian Martel, *The Mare*, 37. *Source:* Graphic Mundi. Used with permission.

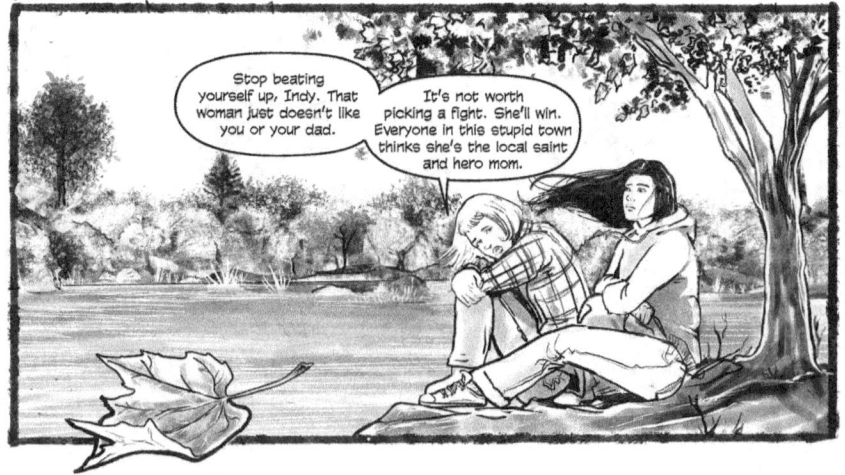

the glowing autumnal light and framed by a leaf that rests outside the panel. Like Claremont, Martel refrains from spelling everything out for readers; instead, he trusts them to connect the visually rich landscape with the emotional ups and downs of adolescent life.

Valley connections also came into play when *The Mare* went into production for Pennsylvania University Press's Graphic Mundi imprint; the project's graphic designer was a graduate of the same SUNY New Paltz program as Martel. He found this connection particularly reassuring since, as a graphic designer himself, he has strong ideas about color—in particular, the eerie dark blue that signifies the supernatural presence within the comic.

As we have seen, a blend of realism, natural beauty, and horror has pervaded depictions of the valley since Irving's time. One strand of this cultural legacy directly influenced Martel's resume, as well as his art: he worked as a makeup artist and scene painter at the Terror Dome, an interactive haunted-house attraction in Newburgh, for seven years. "It was small. We would get about a hundred people a night, but it was still fun," Martel recalls, noting that the work gave him a strong sense of place: Halloween attractions are a frequent and popular destination for visitors to the valley throughout the fall. "It was a really great experience for me . . . [I]n a haunted house you are telling a story in different spaces." Other narratives came through the encounters with performers: "Essentially when you're doing makeup, you're a therapist," he recalls.

These varied levels of storytelling—through place and space; through physical gesture and tone; and through in-depth conversation—all help to ground *The Mare*'s supernatural events in credible human relationships and environments. At times, Martel drew from specific memories as well: when he wanted Indy and Kasia to research the history of ghosts in the valley, he based their visit on a somewhat dim and "creepy" microfiche area that used to reside in the basement of the Adriance Memorial Library in Poughkeepsie before its renovation in 2009. The building's historic Market Street façade is clearly visible as the two friends enter the building, as seen in Figure 5.15.[64]

Other locations provide Martel himself with inspiration and camaraderie. He has made several visits to the drawing nights hosted by Summer Pierre at Split Rock Books in Cold Spring. "There's a good community there," Martel says, noting the value of chances to interact with artists, writers, and editors without any specific "agenda" or time-sensitive task to accomplish. Martel also notes the burgeoning artistic community in Newburgh and, like Lamb, enjoys convening with friends at the 2 Alices cafés.

Figure 5.15. Seth Christian Martel, *The Mare*, 79. *Source:* Graphic Mundi. Used with permission.

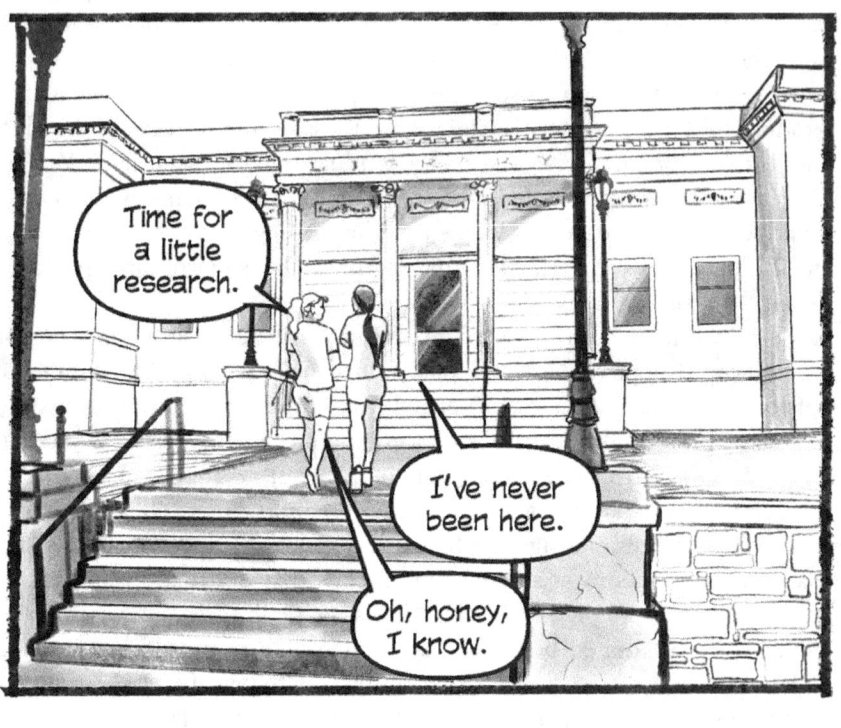

Martel's work suggests that he shares Marz's gratitude for moments of stillness and solitude. One of the full-page drawings at the end of *The Mare* offers readers a glimpse of a prosaic but lovely sight characteristic of Hudson River valley winters: the muffled glow of a streetlight during a night-time snowstorm. You can hear the flakes as they fall. The smaller scale of comics makes them ideal for conveying these everyday marvels. With that in mind, let's return to Poughkeepsie to learn about two artists who have found their own distinctive ways to engage with the environment of the valley.

Heinz Insu Fenkl, Bella Dalton-Fenkl, and the Nature of Home

The work of Heinz Insu Fenkl demonstrates the global reach of comics as well as the medium's ever-growing presence in college classrooms. A professor of English at the State University of New York at New Paltz,

Fenkl has taught comics both in literature courses and in practice-based workshops. He dates his interest in the medium all the way back to his childhood in South Korea. "Before I could even read, I would hang out in the local *manhwa-bang* [comics reading room]," he recounts. Although comics were too expensive for Fenkl and his friends to buy, they could sit in the store and read them and bring them home at night for a fee. Since the owner of the store was the father of one of Fenkl's friends, he could sit and peruse the comics for free, even though he was not yet able to decode their words. "I would sort of watch the comics. I remember timing my page turns by looking at other kids who were reading comics. I was pretending to read them too, but I was following the visual narratives. So I had a lot of *manhwa* in me before I could even read."

Fenkl and his family moved out of South Korea when he was twelve. He spent the rest of his youth in Germany and the United States. Among the comics he read then were Woody Woodpecker ones, published by Gold Key and printed by Western Printing in Poughkeepsie until the late 1960s. Fenkl's own education took him to Poughkeepsie—he attended Vassar as an undergraduate—and he eventually taught there as well. It was the planning of an exhibit on Korean comics by the Korean Society that brought him back to comics as a translator, scholar, and creator. While researching North Korean comics at the request of the exhibit's curator, Fenkl came across two works in the country's publicly available *manhwa* archives: *The Crystal Key* and *Great General Mighty Wing*, both appearing in their entirety. "I found them fascinating," he recalls. They clearly reflected the influence of Japanese artists such as Osamu Tezuka (who, as we have seen, was an important artistic model for Wendy Pini as well). Moreover, the comics functioned as political allegories. "Not only did it [*Great General Mighty Wing*] have a narrative that was allegorical, but it had explicit propaganda slogans going down the sides of each page. As you read them, they began with fairly commonplace and nationalistic things, like 'The earth of our homeland is worth more than gold.' It would begin like that. As the comic went forward, the slogans became progressively more militant and paranoid."

Fenkl's translations of the comics appeared in several venues, including *Words Without Borders* and *Korean Quarterly*. Gradually, he began to incorporate comics into his courses and to encourage students' own efforts as artists. He continued this work once he took a position at SUNY New Paltz. He has been astonished by the amount of nonsuperhero material being produced now. Unlike when he first taught comics in the early 1990s at Vassar, "Now there's so much that it's literally impossible to keep up with what's coming out."

While publishing work as a novelist (including *Memories of My Ghost Brother*) and a translator, Fenkl began to try his hand at comics creation as well. Having added a course in visual and verbal storytelling to his teaching repertoire, he put his knowledge into practice with *A Boy and His Ox: A Zen Parable Based on the Oxherding Pictures* (2013), a graphic novel which was serialized in *Korean Quarterly*. As he worked on the book, he found himself weaving together influences from both the landscapes he has called home. In addition to evoking Korean landscape painting, Fenkl incorporated elements of the Hudson River valley into his work and noticed parallels between the two places: "The Han River is very much like the Hudson River. It's also an estuary. The salt water from the ocean comes back upriver. The hills in the Han River area in Korea are also really old, like the ones in this region. A lot of the landscape for that reason is very familiar. It's very much like the place where I grew up." Fenkl came to recognize other parallels. Just as he used to cross the Han River to get from his home in the Bupyeong district of Incheon to school in the American army base in Yongsan, so did crossing the Hudson from his home in Poughkeepsie to his work in New Paltz become a regular part of his routine. "The parallels are really quite funny" (see figure 5.16).

This would not be the only instance of paths retraced in Fenkl's life. As he and his family took hikes on the Vassar College campus in Poughkeepsie, on area trails, and on the Appalachian Trail, someone else was paying very close attention to the surroundings: his daughter, Bella Dalton-Fenkl. Fenkl remembers introducing his daughter to comics with classics such as Bill Watterson's *Calvin and Hobbes* and Jeff Smith's *Bone*. Dalton-Fenkl also recalls connecting comics to her schoolwork. As her mom guided her through mathematics homework, Dalton-Fenkl developed "Space Bunny," a character whose travels through space depended on correctly completed equations. At only ten years old, she developed the character into a bilingual cartoon that ran in *Korean Quarterly* for over fifteen years.

Even as she worked on a comic set in space, attention to regional art was a crucial part of Dalton-Fenkl's coming of age. As an undergraduate at Vassar, she worked as a docent in the Frances Lehman Loeb Art Center, providing her with an ideal opportunity to engage with the museum's excellent collection of Hudson River school paintings and to speak with curators and visitors about the works: "I got to educate people, but visitors and other people also got to educate me," she recalls. "I took inspiration from the techniques in that art movement when I started doing ink drawing in my own work."

Outdoor surroundings also attracted her attention. She learned about nature photography, attended Friends of the Great Swamp's annual art

Figure 5.16. *Source:* Page from Heinz Insu Fenkl's *A Boy and His Ox*. Used with permission of the artist.

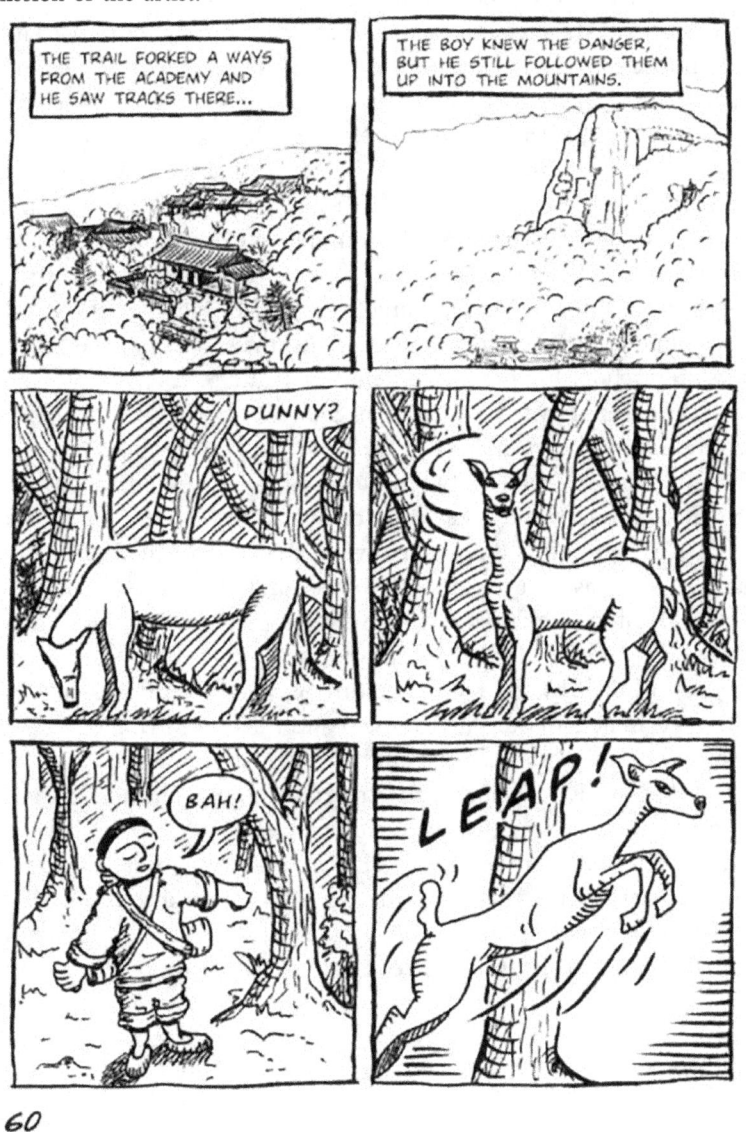

60

shows, and volunteered with the Hudson River Eel Project, which monitors the eel population in the river and facilitates their migration past dams. "I take photos of all the life in the Hudson valley area—the landscapes, the insects, everything," she notes. Although *Space Bunny* is a fantasy comic, attention to real-life animals gave her ideas for her animal protagonist.

"Even in *Space Bunny*, I do include sci-fi landscapes and landscapes based on my own lived experiences" (see figure 5.17).

Dalton-Fenkl's environmental and artistic interests merged even more closely in an earth science course project at Vassar that became a comic, *Eels of the Hudson Valley*. "I used my own photography and own experiences with the eel ladder and with the Hudson River as the framework for doing the background and settings of the comic." Local settings played a role, too; the cover recalls the view across the river from Waryas Park in Poughkeepsie. When staff at the Department of Environmental Conservation (DEC) headquarters at Norrie Point saw the comic, they expressed interest in distributing it to visitors. With the help of funding from Vassar, Dalton-Fenkl was able to get the comic printed and give it to the DEC; they, in turn, have distributed it to visiting schoolchildren and others (see figure 5.18).

Dalton-Fenkl's work spans other genres as well. She and her father collaborated on *Korean Myths: A Guide to the Gods, Heroes and Legends* (2024). But the interplay between cartooning and environmental advocacy will continue to be a key part of her work. "I want to do another eel comic-like project but about native bee species of the Hudson valley. I plan to do it as a fundraising project for the Xerces Society." Many aspects of Dalton-Fenkl's work involve reciprocity and paying it forward. Initially taught by her father, she now works alongside him as a creative colleague; inspired by the region's nature and art, she creates comics that heighten awareness of our environment and the other living beings within it. Along the way, both Dalton-Fenkl and her father help us gain a sense that the Hudson River valley and American comics production connect in important ways to natural and cultural ecosystems elsewhere in the world. Close attention to our local surroundings can, perhaps surprisingly, foster connection with geographically distant places and communities. Our final profile will feature another Poughkeepsie-area creator with a strong interest in the interplay between comics and community.

Jon Santana: Moving Forward with a Retro Approach

Born in the Bronx and a resident of Poughkeepsie since he was fourteen, Jon Santana has built a career as a comics writer and publisher while also serving full time as a major in the United States Army National Guard.[65] Even though he has collaborated with writers and artists all over the world, he "gravitate[s] toward the ones that I have coffee with." Local comics shops, conventions, and face-to-face interactions have played an

Figure 5.17. *Source: Space Bunny* cartoon by Bella Dalton-Fenkl. Used with permission of the artist.

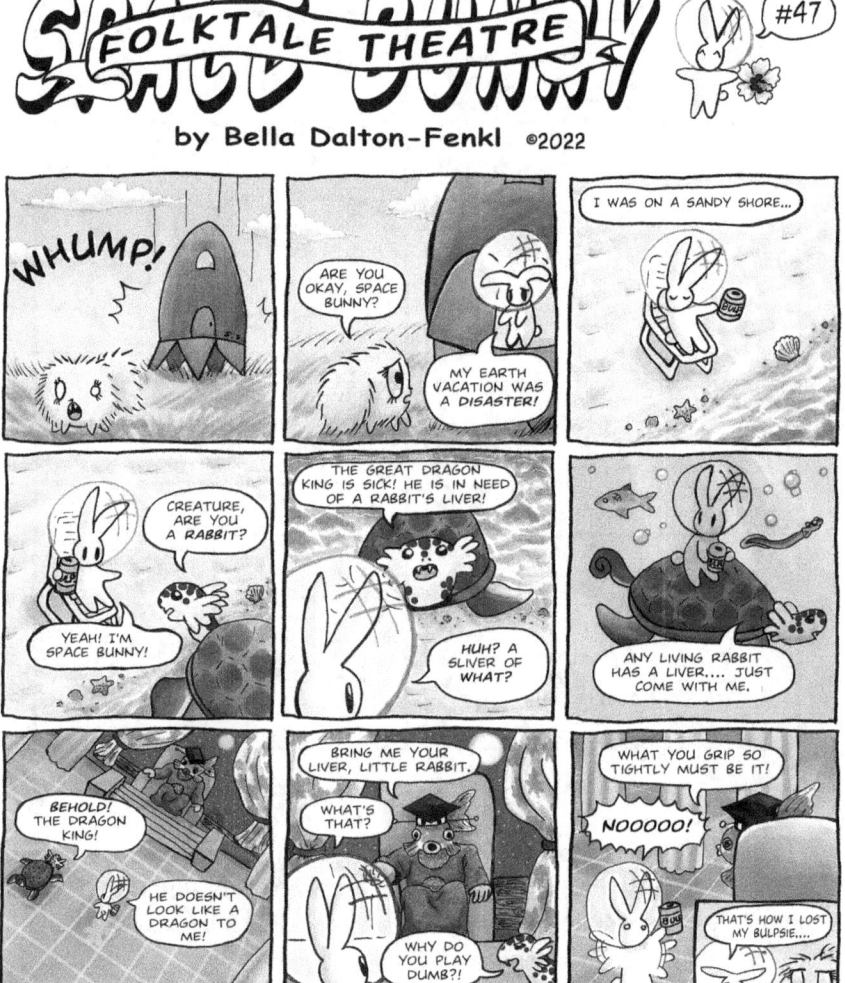

essential role in his development of Iron Age Productions, which creates comics and other media.

His involvement in the comics industry began in a brick-and-mortar setting when he began working at the Dragon's Den comic store in Poughkeepsie in the early 1990s. This experience "was fully influential" on Santana's fledgling efforts as a writer. Encountering comics profession-

Figure 5.18. *Source:* Excerpt from Bella Dalton-Fenkl's *Eels of the Hudson Valley.* Used with permission of the artist.

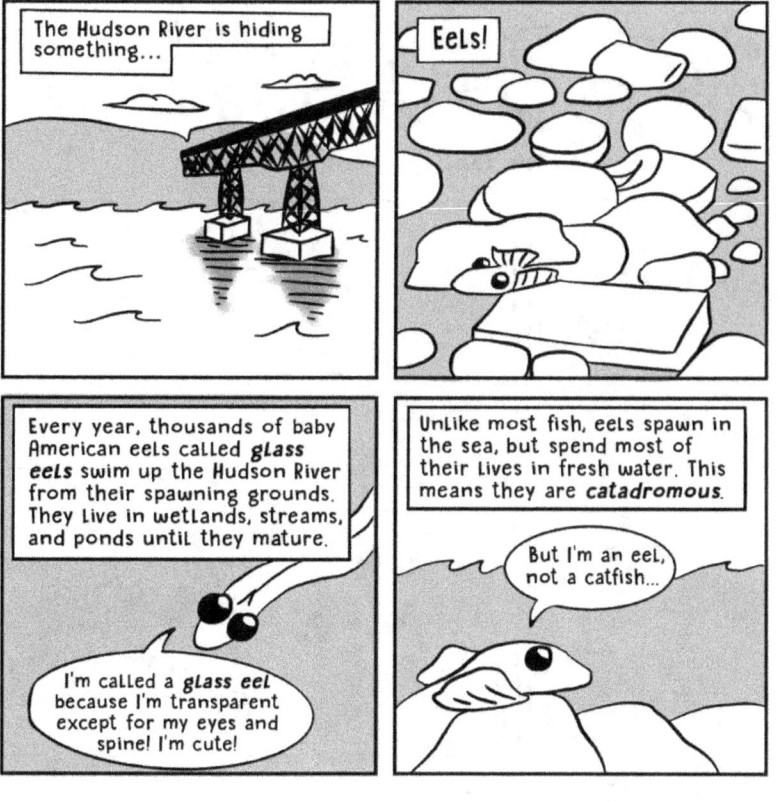

als in the store and hearing from co-workers about other creators who lived nearby was a revelation for him. He remembers thinking, "Wait a minute—regular people are comic book writers?!" Like Martel, Santana also participated in the "haunting industry" that has been a part of the region's story since Irving published his works in the nineteenth century. An abandoned correctional facility in Warwick became the site of a highly successful interactive role-playing haunted house that he produced. He and his team wrote a script, publicized the event, "cut the power and watched people scare themselves."

While Santana's career as a writer has spanned several genres, including the science fiction-influenced *Everhounds* and the action thriller *Jaded,* he has recently turned toward horror, working on the *Haunted Box* role-playing game and comic series (see figures 5.19 and 5.20). Collaborators on this

Figure 5.19. *Source:* Iron Age Comics. Used with permission.

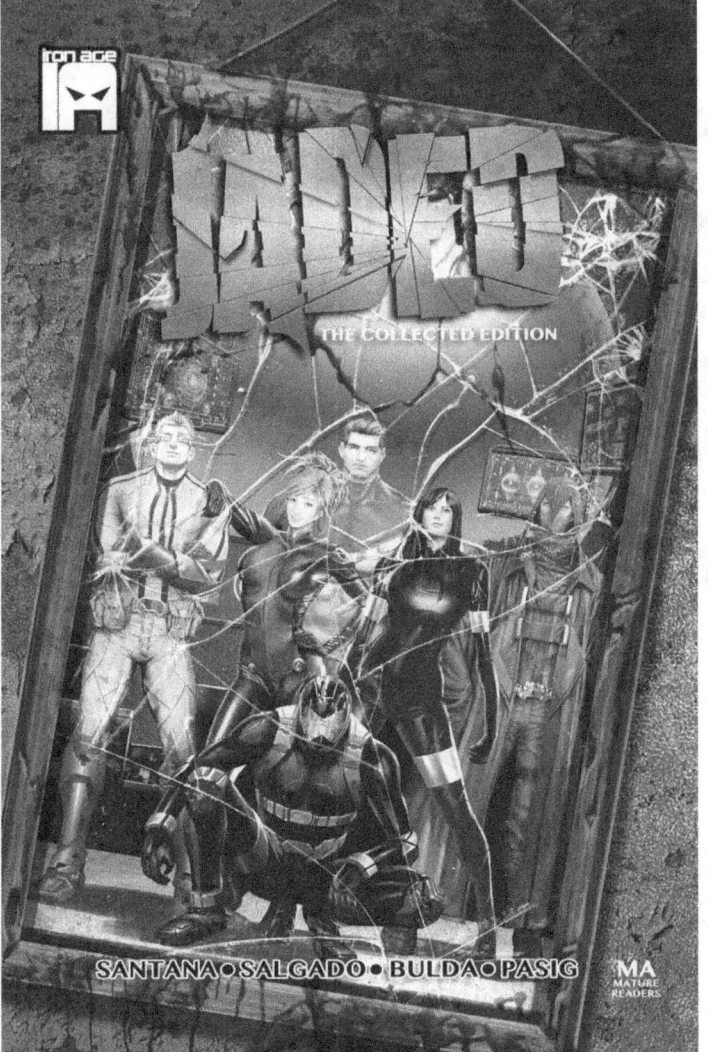

project include artist Ryan G. Browne, based in Poughkeepsie, and Mina Elwell, who works out of Cold Spring. "It's really the people I met that led me towards horror," Santana recalls. While the creative process often involves a certain amount of solitary work, ideas can really "turn into something" when you run into like-minded colleagues and begin to share your work in progress.

Figure 5.20. *Source:* Iron Age Comics. Used with permission.

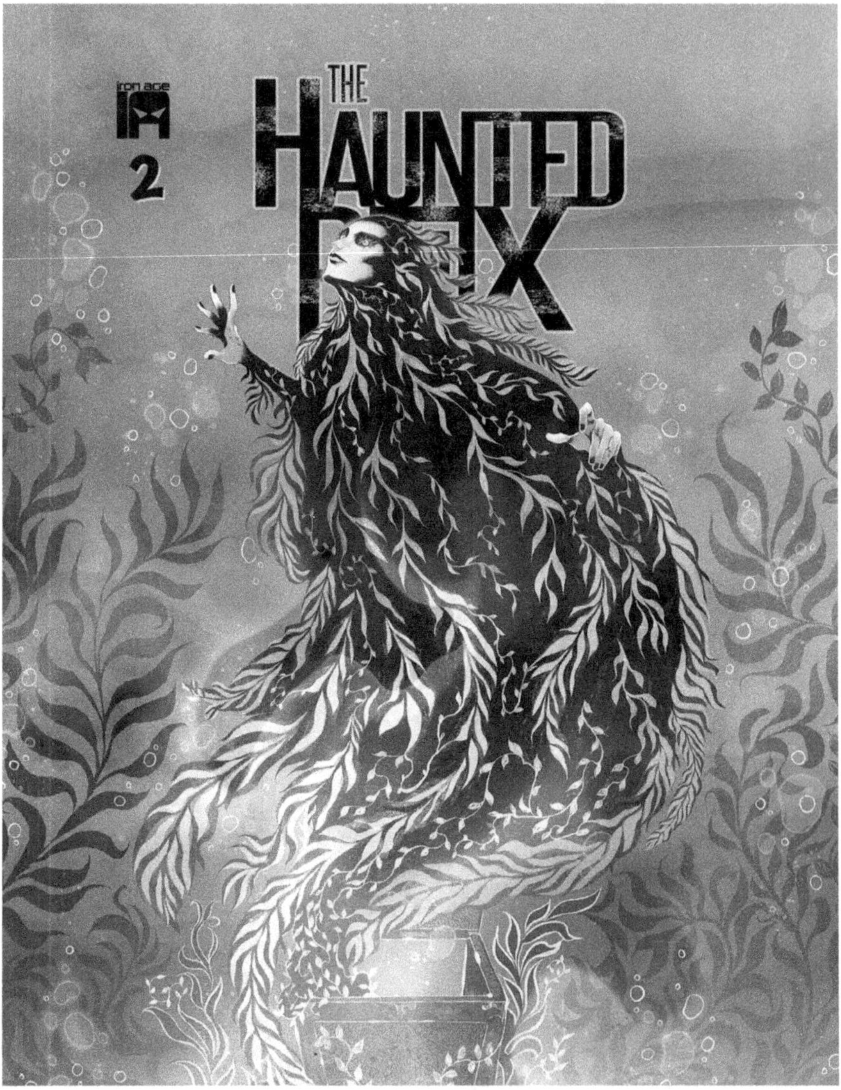

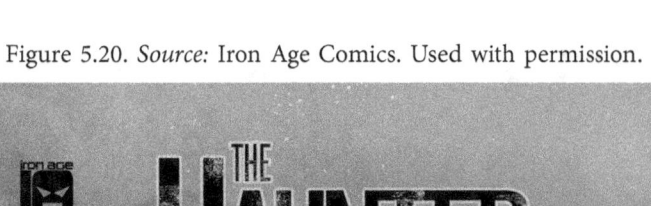

Because of these experiences, one of Santana's long-term goals is to create a space for creative collaboration in the Poughkeepsie area—a kind of "retro studio where creators could share space" with one another. Complementing his publishing efforts, the studio would gather artists in residence for discrete periods of time, rotating them in and out as projects evolve. Lamenting that "nobody sits together in a room any more," Santana argues that physical proximity can help creators "bring each other's game up . . . [Y]ou have to talk comics, talk stories, talk art—and new things come up."

Many aspects of this project recall earlier phases of the Hudson River valley's involvement in the comics industry. By envisioning that his publishing company would give at least partial ownership to creators, Santana builds upon a model that is now widely espoused and that counts the Pinis as one of the earliest and most successful practitioners. By emphasizing the need for writers, artists, colorists, and editors to work in an in-person environment, Santana's model evokes some of the interactions that took place at Western Printing in the twentieth century. Many of the other artists profiled in this chapter have also expressed their gratitude for the natural and architectural spaces that have provided them with opportunities for inspiration and interaction. It takes a great deal of patience and persistent effort to bring an initiative like this to fruition—but the area has already proved its receptiveness to ambitious creators. As Pierre suggested, the Hudson River valley offers many opportunities for "deep company" with the environment, with local communities, and with artists past and present. Given expanded opportunities for collaboration, who knows what new vistas might be imagined by comics creators in the area?

Conclusion

Dynamic Systems

I hope that our travels in this book have persuaded you that taking a place-based approach to comics and a comics-based approach to place can lead us to new ways of thinking about both fields of inquiry. While the valley is distinctive in many ways, I suspect this combination of approaches could be useful for many other regions as well.

The Hudson River valley is not one ecosystem, but many. Environmental, cultural, commercial, and social systems are just a few we have considered. There are multiple, sometimes contradictory factors within each of these systems. Accordingly, many subjects covered in this book challenge us with their complexity. Landscapes communicate and conceal. Comics generate stereotypes (both metaphorical and literal) and provide a powerful means of questioning them. Western Printing contributed a great deal to the Poughkeepsie area while extracting many human and natural resources in its turn. The Pinis' success as independent creators has depended upon the choices of thousands of readers to buy their works and to keep doing so for decades. Artists in the valley and beyond enjoy unprecedented opportunities to gain new audiences for their work, even as they also confront technological changes that could threaten their livelihoods.

Both ephemeral and resilient, the comics medium continually reshapes itself in response to internal change and external pressures. With that in mind, it is invigorating to think about how the Hudson River valley might continue to grow and change as a comics ecosystem. How might comics production in languages other than English emerge from the area in coming years? What might a Lenape-centric graphic narrative about the region add to our sense of the valley's identity? Will zines continue to grow as a medium for self-expression and community gatherings? Could comics history and creation play a more prominent role in the region's tourism industry?

There is much more to be explored about comics in the Hudson River valley and in other regional contexts. I see this book as a conversation starter rather than as the last word on the subject. Perhaps it's a good time, then, to acknowledge your own role as a meaning maker in our travels. We might think of this book as a kind of ecosystem in which comics, regional history, artists' ideas, and my analysis have interacted with your own experiences and interpretations. I appreciate your joining me in "rivering" our way through comics-related regional studies, and I invite you (in figure C.1) to draw your own conclusions.

Figure C.1. *Source:* Created by the author.

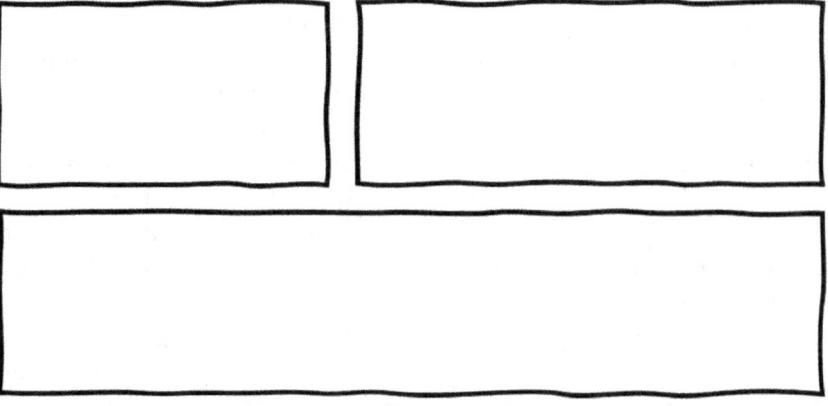

Notes

Introduction

1. See David Lumb, Poughkeepsie Pop Culture, and "Poughkeepsie Compilation V 1.1."

2. I am grateful to linguist Charlie Farrington for consulting with me about the term's phonological and morphological characteristics.

3. "Poughkeepsie History," The Poughkeepsie Public Library District.

4. Silver Sprocket Press originally published Passmore's *Your Black Friend* as a twelve-page zine.

5. For an exhilarating visual essay on this subject, see Nick Sousanis's *Unflattening*, 85–97.

6. See Kendall Whitehouse, "Stan Lee, Jack Kirby, and the Mythical Marvel Bullpen."

7. One of these trips led to a priceless anecdote. Confronted with a glorious view of the Matterhorn, Jaffee spread his arms wide and proclaimed, "Only in America" (Weisman 196).

8. See also Fraser's *Barcelona, City of Comics*.

9. For a historical and critical analysis of this term's use in comics studies, see Christopher Pizzoni in *Keywords in Comics Studies*, 121–26.

10. Chute, *Why Comics?*, 141–74.

11. Stories in recent years include Jack Howland, "HV Comic Con: Pop Culture Fans, Stars Unite"; Quinn O'Callaghan, "Many Comic Book Heroes Have Hudson Valley Roots"; and John Barry, "A Fresh Perspective on the Cape, Mask, and Superhero." The latter article described an exhibit, *Komic Kreators of the Mid-Hudson Valley*, staged by Arts Mid-Hudson in 2015. As mentioned previously, the Poughkeepsie Public Library District hosted an exhibit of local cartoonists' work in tandem with its fall 2022 Big Read selection, Thi Bui's *The Best We Could Do*.

12. See Nicolle Lamerichs, "Scrolling, Swiping, Selling," 213, 215.

13. See Hall's conversation with Hillary Chute in "Critics and Creators: The LGBTQ+ Comics Ecosystem."

14. This is also true of many of the artists profiled in Martin Salisbury's practical and theoretical guide *Drawing for Illustration*.

15. See, for example, Joe DeLessio, "Nobody Knows Where 'Upstate New York' Actually Is." For my husband, who grew up in Queens, the answer was his aunt Pat's house in Putnam County.

16. The southern and eastern reaches of Westchester County, for example, are largely beyond the scope of this book; this area once hosted the Museum of Cartoon Art and still serves as the home base of *Archie Comics*.

17. "State of the Hudson 2020," Hudson River Foundation.

18. For a helpful overview, see "Movements/The Hudson River School."

19. And in fact, as Maggie M. Cao (17) and others have noted, the designation *Hudson River school* was originally a disparaging one.

20. See Reed Sparling, "Celebrating the Scenic Hudson Decision."

21. See "Origin and Early History," Stockbridge-Munsee Community Band of Mohican Indians, and Baker, Coumans, and Whitney, eds., *Lenapehoking: An Anthology*.

22. Nature's creative agency also emerges vividly in Robert and Johanna Titus's *The Hudson River Schools of Art and Their Ice Age Origins*, which explores the geological developments that shaped the valley's distinctive vistas.

Chapter One

1. See Thomas Cole National Historic Site and Nancy Siegel, Kate Menconeri, and Amanda Malmstrom, *Women Reframe American Landscape*. Another valuable resource is the catalogue from a 2010 exhibit at the Cole site, *Remember the Ladies: Women Artists of the Hudson River School*.

2. Nancy Siegel, "Susie M. Barstow: Redefining the Hudson River School," in *Women Reframe American Landscape*, 36. To cite one instance of historical "amnesia" regarding women artists: The 1987 exhibit *American Paradise: The World of the Hudson River School* at the Metropolitan Museum of Art did not include a single work by a woman artist.

3. Important studies that place landscape paintings in dialogue with other media of the period include the anthology *Ecocriticsm and the Anthropocene in Nineteenth-Century Visual Art and Culture*, ed. Maura Coughlin and Emily Gephart; Edward S. Casey's *Representing Place: Landscape Painting and Maps*; and Maura Lyons, "Nature Defamiliarized: Picturing New Relationships between Humans and Nonhuman Nature in Northern Landscapes from the American Civil War."

4. Pratt, *The Philosophy of Comics*, 3–5. For a similar narrative in comic-book form, see *The Comic Book History of Comics*, especially 1–43.

5. Recent biographies of Irving include Andrew Burstein, *The Original Knickerbocker*, and Brian Jay Jones, *Washington Irving*.

6. For more on Irving's invocations of Chaucer's work, see Charlotte Fiehn, "Washington Irving's Mediaeval Renaissance."

7. Jeffrey Rubin-Dorsky explores the importance of visual art to Irving's work in "Washington Irving and the Genesis of the Fictional Sketch."

8. Irving does put one Black person inside the party, an "old grey headed negro" who plays the music at the event but sees him as an extension of his fiddle: "His instrument was as old and battered as himself" (1077). I see no persuasive evidence to support McCree's claim (152) that Irving characterizes the messenger and Black viewers of the party as "in on the plot" against Crane.

9. See Joseph T. Butler, *Washington Irving's Sunnyside*, 45.

10. See Schuyler, "The Mid-Hudson Valley as Iconic Landscape," 15–16; for analysis of Andrew Jackson Downing's influence on literature and art, see Schuyler, *Sanctified Landscape*, 69–91.

11. Kevin J. Avery, "John Frederick Kensett, 1816–1872."

12. See Avery, "John Frederick Kensett," and Richard C. Wiles, "The Commerce of Art in the Nineteenth-Century Hudson Valley," 216.

13. "John Frederick Kensett," National Gallery of Art.

14. Trafton, "It Is a Joint Venture," 104.

15. See Trafton, "It Is a Joint Venture," 109, and *vignette* (1a) in the *Oxford English Dictionary*.

16. Elaborately and playfully decorated capital letters have a very long history, of course; for an introduction to their use in medieval manuscripts, see Eleanor Jacks, "Off to a Good Start."

17. George Curtis, *Lotus-Eating: A Summer Book*, 24.

18. In "Gifford and the Catskills: Resort and Refuge," Kevin J. Avery comes to a similar conclusion about the book: "World traveler that he was by then, Curtis disclosed the shopworn character of some of the older resorts including the Catskills" (170).

19. Notably, Kensett avoids using Indigenous people as decorative features within his landscapes. By contrast, the title page of *The Hudson Illustrated in Pen and Pencil*, also produced in 1852, features an Indigenous man looking simultaneously historical, picturesque, and concerned about the train chugging next to the river.

20. Trafton notes that Kensett may be inviting readers to see a "gentle caricature" of tourists in images such as figure 1.5 (see 108), but this is different than the kind of dehumanizing description found in "The Legend of Sleepy Hollow" or in Curtis's remark about Indians.

21. Avery connects the subject matter of *Lotus-Eating* to Kensett's success as a landscape painter: "Some of the illustrations precede Kensett's earliest paintings of subjects for which he became most beloved and which he truly seemed to make his own: Lake George and, even more so, Newport" (170).

22. For Curtis's career as an editor, see "Harper's Weekly" and "George William Curtis."

23. The two often clashed; see Thomas Nast and John Chalmers Vinson, *Thomas Nast, Political Cartoonist*, 29, and Stella Wei, "Thomas Nast: The Rise and Fall of the Father of Political Cartoons."

24. See, for example, Nast's *Colored Rule in a Reconstructed State* in *Harper's Weekly*.

25. See "Thomas Nast, 1840–1902," in Thomas Nast: Prince of Caricaturists.

26. *Uncle Sam's Panorama of Rip Van Winkle and Yankee Doodle* can be accessed in its entirety through Yale Library's Digital Collections.

27. See "Site #8: Catskill Mountain House."

28. See also Morton Keller's discussion of Nast's use of racial caricature in "The World of Thomas Nast."

29. The montage was not Nast's only foray into landscape art. As Maura Lyons has shown in "Nature Defamiliarized," his 1863 work "The Result of War—Virginia in 1863" offers a wide-angle view of the devastation wrought on natural and human environments by the war.

30. The National Gallery owns five of Palmer's works; the Metropolitan Museum of Art owns 142. None of them is on public display as of March 2025. Her works are, however, accessible on each organization's websites.

31. See also Sarah Burns, *Pastoral Inventions*, 11–19.

32. Charlotte Rubinstein, *Fanny Palmer*, 38–43.

33. For Palmer's treatment of Hudson River valley subjects, see Rubinstein, *Fanny Palmer*, 127–35.

34. See Rubinstein, *Fanny Palmer*, 133.

35. Rubinstein, *Fanny Palmer*, 188–90. "Lithography: It's a Process" provides a useful introduction to lithographic procedures.

36. See Harry T. Peters, *Currier & Ives*, 26–29, 14.

37. *Westerner*, January 1953, 4–6. In another confluence with the development of comics, Currier & Ives also employed Benjamin Day, who in 1879 developed the "ben day dots" that became ubiquitous in comics printing in the twentieth century (Rawls 25).

38. See Charlotte Rubinstein, 199–206; Colin L. Anderson, "Imagining Racial Segregation before the Ghetto"; and John Dorsey, "Currier & Ives's America Could Be a Dark Place." Harry T. Peters celebrates the series in *Currier & Ives*, 22–24.

39. See Charlotte Rubinstein, *Fanny Palmer*, 203–4, and Harry T. Peters, *Currier & Ives*, 23.

40. See Palmer's "American Country Life" (Rubinstein, 202) and "The Mountain Pass, Sierra Nevada" (Rubinstein, 217).

41. See Edgar Allan Poe, *Tales of Mystery and Imagination*.

42. Rackham may have traveled up the Hudson River en route to Boston, but his itinerary for the trip has not been conclusively established.

43. For Rackham's engagement with Irving's work, see James Hamilton, *Arthur Rackham*, 40,67–71, 142; for his trip to America, see 134–37.

44. See Derek Hudson, *Arthur Rackham*, 171.

45. James Hamilton, *Arthur Rackham*, 59–60.

46. *The Morning Post* recorded his remarks; see also James Hamilton, *Arthur Rackham*, 90–91.

47. *The Legend of Sleepy Hollow*, illustrated by Rackham, 13. All page citations in this section are from the 1928 edition of the story.

48. *The Legend of Sleepy Hollow*, 28, 30.

49. *The Legend of Sleepy Hollow*, 67.

50. *The Legend of Sleepy Hollow*, 79.

51. "Lynchings: By Year and Race."

52. See also Didier Ghez, *They Drew as They Pleased: The Hidden Art of Disney's Golden Age*, 130.

Chapter Two

1. "Celebrating the Scenic Hudson Decision."

2. "Memorial Today for Cartoonist Dick Oldden."

3. Felix Belair Jr., "King Tries Hot Dog and Asks for More."

4. "Royalty Discards Pomp to Munch on Hot Dogs."

5. "A Guide to the Fred O. Seibel Editorial Cartoonist's Research Collection."

6. "The Lend-Lease Program, 1941–1945."

7. Eleanor Roosevelt, quoted in Swift, *The Roosevelts and the Royals*.

8. For additional information on this family and its activities in the eighteenth century, see J. Michael Smith, "The Highland King Nimhammaw and the Native Indian Proprietors of Land in Dutchess County, N.Y."

9. Other invaluable resources include Michael A. Sheyahshe's *Native Americans in Comic Books: A Critical Study* and a growing body of comics produced by other Indigenous writers and artists, such as the three *Moonshot* collections, Arigon Starr's *Super Indian* series, and the anthology *Indiginerds: Tales from Modern Indigenous Life*.

10. I am grateful to Noah DeCambra for bringing this comic to my attention in a graphic narratives course project.

11. See Eisner, *A Contract with God and Other Tenement Stories*, xxviii.

12. See Strawbalicious, "While 'Hudson Valley, New York' Isn' a Real Town . . . ," r/MovieDetails.

13. Adding to the fun are Nelle's realistic renderings of Sleepy Hollow architectural landmarks such as the high school and the Historical Society building.

14. They later admit that they did chase Ichabod Crane out of town, but only because he was greedily angling for Katrina Van Tassel's fortune.

Chapter Three

1. "About the Trail."

2. *Westerner*, April 1950, 15.

3. See Michael Barrier, *Funnybooks*, 335, and *Westerner*, 8 March 1968, 1, 4.

4. Jon B. Cooke, "Mark Evanier Interview," 87.

5. For an infrastructure-based approach to texts and writing, see Sarah Read and Jordan Frith, "Special Issue Introduction: Writing Infrastructure."

6. See "Site of the Spring."

7. See Kees-Jan Waterman and J. Michael Smith, *Munsee Indian Trade*, as well as Smith, "The Highland King Nimhammaw."

8. See William P. McDermott, "Land Grants in Dutchess County," and "Hermanse/Sanders Patent," Marist Heritage Project. The spelling of the patentees' names varies across records.

9. See Smith, "The Highland King," and Grumet, *First Manhattans*, 60.

10. See also Bruegl, "Not the Last of the Mohicans," and Grumet, *First Manhattans*, 224–34.

11. For resources in Bowler, Wisconsin, see "Arvid E. Miller Library/ Museum." Recent exhibits in the Northeast include *The Lenapehoking* at the Brooklyn Public Library in 2022; *Our Lands, Our Home, Our Heart*, at the Mission House at Stockbridge (Massachusetts) in 2023; and *Never Broken: Visualizing Lenape Histories* at the Michener Art Museum (Pennsylvania) in 2023 and 2024.

12. See James Spratt, "Milestones of Dutchess County."

13. For the relationship between the city and town of Poughkeepsie, see "Poughkeepsie History," Dutchess County, New York.

14. "Steamboats on the Hudson: An American Saga."

15. See Harvey Flad and Clyde Griffen, *Main Street to Mainframes*, 29–33. Merrilee Brown's "Before Quiet Computers, Factory Noise Prevailed" also provides an excellent overview of industrial development in the area.

16. See Stephen Edelstein, "Poughkeepsie's Lost Railroad."

17. "The Birth of Ford Motor Company."

18. Although the name was originally an acronym ("Fabbrica Italiana Automobili di Torino"), I will follow the company's current practice and write it as a regular word.

19. "Fiat Company at Fairview," 5.

20. "Fiat Company Is Coming," 5.

21. "Felice Nazzaro."

22. Butler, "The American Fiat—Built in Poughkeepsie."

23. "Willys Concern Will Take Over Old Fiat Plant"; "Old Fiat Plant on Sale Tuesday."

24. "Ponty Asserts Deal for Fiat Waits Ringling."

25. "Henry Schaffer Is Dead at 92."

26. The first attested usage of the term in the Oxford English Dictionary comes from 1931. See "Supermarket, N."

27. *Poughkeepsie Eagle-News*, 14 April 1934, 11.

28. See *Poughkeepsie Eagle-News*, 25 April 1934, 3; 4 June 1934, 2; 10 July 1934, 14; and 13 July 1934, 10.

29. "Circus Arrives in Town."

30. "Brophy Is Held for Grand Jury."

31. "Whitman Firm to Speed Work," *Poughkeepsie Eagle-News*, 8 October 1934, 1.

32. September 1962, 7, and December 1964, 4.

33. *Westerner*, 27 March 1970, 1.

34. See "The Story of Western, 1907–1962, Part I," *Westerner*, April 1962, 11–13, and "Part II" of the same series, May 1962, 2, as well as Karkowski, "Celebrating 175 Years: Western Printing," and Barrier, *Funnybooks*, 18–19.

35. *Westerner*, December 1964, 5.

36. *Westerner*, 3 December 1971, 4. See also Laurie Hagar, "Poughkeepsie Plant Started as a Warehouse."

37. The full image also incorporates the WPL Company's facility in St. Louis.

38. *Westerner* writers regularly emphasized the "five-year-old" data point in its many celebratory articles about the WPL Company's relationship with WDC. See, for example, July 1957, 2.

39. For an affectionate history of this form, see Bill Borden, *The Big Book of Big Little Books*.

40. Ed Rhoades, "George Wilson Interview: The Phantom Painter," 74.

41. *Westerner*, July 1955, 17.

42. "Western Officials to Visit Disneyland."

43. For Callender's career, see *Westerner*, December 1967, 13; for Morse, see *Westerner*, April 1958, 5. For a history of K.K. Publications, see Barrier's *Funnybooks*, 17–20,43–52.

44. For overviews of the convoluted WDC-Dell-WPL relationship, see Mark Evanier, "An Incessantly-Asked Question," and Barrier, *Funnybooks*, 49–52.

45. Barrier's *Funnybooks* (25–42) explores the achievements of Oskar Lebeck, whose editorial skill shepherded some of the strongest products of the WPL-Dell alliance. Although based in New York City, he lived for many years in the Croton-on-Hudson and regularly visited the Poughkeepsie site.

46. A helpful overview can also be found at "Little Golden Books," a summary of a 2013–2014 exhibit at the Smithsonian Museum of American History.

47. See Barrier, *Funnybooks*, 91, and Marcus, *Golden Legacy*, 49.

48. *Westerner*, September 1958, 16.

49. "Publishing Official Feted."

50. In addition to David Hajdu's work, the complexities of Wertham's ideas have been usefully explored in scholarly studies, including Amy Kiste Nyberg's *Seal of Approval* and Bart Beaty's *Fredric Wertham and the Critique of Mass Culture*, as well as in Robert A. Emmons Jr.'s documentary *Diagram for Delinquents*.

51. "New Code Banishes Racy Comic Books."

52. "Local Plant's Comics Scanned by Comics Commission."

53. See David Hajdu, *The Ten-Cent Plague*, 337–52.

54. David Hajdu, *The Ten-Cent Plague*, 310; Michael Barrier, *Funnybooks*, 313.

55. "200 Attend Pressmen's Dinner."

56. "Awards Won by Western Comics."

57. *Westerner*, June 1954, 9.

58. "Program Listed for 'Book Bazaar.'"

59. Helen Myers, "Of Making Many Books There Is No End."

60. *Westerner*, May 1951, 19.

61. *Westerner*, April 1961, 12–13, and October 1965, 8–11.

62. *Westerner*, September 1961, 18.

63. Marian College became Marist College in 1960. In January 2025, Marist College became Marist University.

64. See *Westerner*, April 1950, 16 (Vassar College); December 1959, 22, January 1960, 22, and July 1961, 17 (Marist University); and April 1962, 22 (Dutchess County Community College).

65. *Westerner*, November 1952, 16.

66. *Westerner*, February 1950, 22.

67. George Bernstein, "Western Publishing Comes Full Circle," 11C.

68. *Westerner*, July 1954, 14. The *Poughkeepsie New Yorker* covered the strike extensively throughout February and March of that year. I am grateful to Joella Hom and Emily Viesta for sharing their research on these events.

69. For an overview of John Stanley's work on *Little Lulu*, see Barrier, *Funnybooks*, 138–41, 203–6, and 329–33.

70. The artist Morris Gollub, quoted in Don Phelps, "John Stanley and the Universal Progeny," *The Little Lulu Library*, 469.

71. Schelly, *John Stanley*, 67.

72. He moved to Croton-on-Hudson in the early 1950s (Schelly, 88). He moved to New York City in the 1960s but later moved to the Hudson River Valley town of Cold Spring: *Funnybooks*, 333.

73. See Tenan, "Miss Lulu Moppet Lives at 22 Main Street," 7–8; Schelly, *John Stanley*, 60; and Michele Maki, "My 'Diry' of My Trip to Peekskill—Little Lulu's Hometown," *Michelesworld*.

74. Frank Young, *The Tao of Yow: John Stanley's World* (CreateSpace, 2015).

75. Maggie Thompson, "Marge," *The Little Lulu Library*, 643.

76. See Barrier, *Funnybooks*, 347.

77. Schelly, 96.

78. Barrier, *Funnybooks*, 131.

79. Schelly, *John Stanley*, 144.

80. "Janet DuBois' Engagement Announced by Her Parents." The couple later divorced; Tripp was married to his second wife, Phyllis, for twenty-four years before she passed away.

81. Bill Tripp, interview; Scouting item, *Poughkeepsie Journal*.

82. Hamilton, "A Tripp down Memory Lane," 17.

83. Schelly, 51; Hamilton, 17.

84. *Funnybooks*, 141; Hamilton, 14–16; Schelly, 88.

85. Bill Tripp, interview.

86. Hamilton, "A Tripp down Memory Lane," 15, 18.

87. Bill Tripp, interview.

88. *Westerner*, December 1961, 11.

89. Bill Tripp, interview.

90. *Westerner*, July 1951, 18–19.

91. *Westerner*, December 1951, 18–19.

92. *Westerner*, February 1952, 11. Two women were made journeymen in the Litho Art Department in September 1957. The first Black woman journeyman depicted in *The Westerner* appears in May 1966 (22) and worked at the WPL Company's plant in Hannibal, Missouri.

93. For Doris Mack's recollections, see "Black History Is Local History" and Sandra Foyt, "Eleanor Roosevelt Remembered at Val-Kill."

94. *Westerner*, December 1959, 18; "Glenn Henry Johnson."

95. *Westerner*, September 1963, 21; for the community activism of Rupert and Marie Tarver, see also "Former Poughkeepsie School Board President Dies."

96. *Westerner*, May 1964, 1.

97. *Westerner*, September 1963, 23; February 1966, 21; March 1960, 7; and January 1959, 15.

98. See, for example, *Westerner*, March 1955, 2–6. The representations of Indigenous culture in the WPL Company's comics and other products would be a worthy subject for a future scholarly book. The caricatures in the quality-control ads conform to several tropes listed by Raymond William Stedman in *Shadows of the Indian: Stereotypes in American Culture*. Sheyahshe's *Native Americans in Comic Books* offers brilliant and exhaustive discussions of comic books' content, while Jacquelyn Kilpatrick's *Celluloid Indians* explores depictions in film.

99. The WPL Company produced similar rapid-response publications following the publication of the Warren Commission Report (1964) and the assassination of Robert F. Kennedy (1968).

100. Michelle Miller, "Michelle's Meanderings: Days of Comic Book Chaos."

101. See Lopes, *Demanding Respect*, 63, and Barrier, *Funnybooks*, 348.

102. *Westerner*, January 1963, 2.

103. *Westerner*, November 1964, 18.

104. Ed Rhoades, "George Wilson Interview: The Phantom Painter."

105. Jon B. Cooke, "Editor's Rant: Mining for Gold," 5. Perhaps not coincidentally, Cooke himself grew up in Croton-on-Hudson.

106. Interviews with Carrington, Miller, and Robishaw.

107. *Westerner*, April 1966, 9–10.

108. Quoted in Chris Irving, "Western Civ 101," 21.

109. *Westerner*, May 1966, 3.

110. *Westerner*, 18 April 1969, 1. Those of a mystical bent might see the Jumbo Market exacting its revenge through this development.

111. *Westerner*, 30 August 1968, 1.

112. *Westerner*, 4 October 1968, 4.

113. See Evanier, "It's in the Bag!"

114. *Westerner*, 6 December 1968, 1.

115. *Westerner*, 20 June 1969, 1, 4.

116. *Westerner*, 1 May 1970, 2.

117. Jean-Paul Gabilliet, *Of Comics and Men*, 85.

118. *Westerner*, 29 January 1971, x.

119. *Westerner*, 26 January 1973, 1, and 19 April 1974, 1–2.

120. Barrier, *Funnybooks*, 348.

121. Interviewed in Cooke, "Western Goes West," 81.

122. Bernstein, "Western Publishing," 11C, and "Mattel's Western to Close a Plant."

123. Bernstein, "Western Publishing," 11C.

124. David Harris, "The News Hits Western Workers Hard"; for employment numbers, see "Mattel's Western to Close a Plant."

125. George Bernstein. "Questions Linger over Western Closing," 10C.

126. See Jon Olson, "Bernstein to Leave Western"; Sandler and Knecht, "Snyder Is Nearing Day of Reckoning"; Karkowski, "Celebrating 175 Years"; and Leonard S. Marcus, *Golden Legacy*, 209–19.

127. "A History of the Physical Plant of Marist College."

128. See John Breiner, "Western Printing Graffiti Tour Part I" and "Western Printing Factory—Graffiti Tour Part II."

129. "Superfund Site Information: Former Western Publishing."

130. For "Friends of Lulu," see Trina Robbins, *Pretty in Ink*, 142–43; for Gold Key, see "1962–1984 & Beyond."

131. See Michael Valkys, "Downsizing Puts Crimp in Loyalty."

132. "President's Message," 3.

133. *Retirees of Western*, vol. 17, no. 1, January 1996, 3.

Chapter Four

1. Wendy and Richard Pini, *The Dreamberry Tales*.

2. These include Wendy's adaptations of the 1987 through 1990 television show *Beauty and the Beast* into two graphic novels, *Night of Beauty* and *Portrait of Love*; see *Line of Beauty*, 122–29.

3. Scott McCloud, for example, recognizes Wendy Pini as one of "only a few published artists who openly acknowledged a manga influence" in the early 1980s (*Making Comics*, 242).

4. Unless otherwise indicated, all direct quotations from the Pinis are drawn from three interviews conducted with them in July and August 2023.

5. "About Warp—and W&RP," *ElfQuest* website.

6. This process involved Richard's taking a flight to Michigan and lying in wait for an editor who was practicing an early form of "ghosting." For a more detailed description of this event, see Shaun Clancy, "*ElfQuest* Behind the Scenes: A Chat with Richard and Wendy Pini," 28–30.

7. For a concise and thoughtful summary of *ElfQuest*'s publication history, see Robert Saunders, "The Identity Politics of *ElfQuest* at 40: Moving Beyond Race, Class, and Gender?" 7–8.

8. For example, Richard was part of the cohort that generated the Creator's Bill of Rights in 1988; see Scott McCloud, *Reinventing Comics*, 62.

9. See Richard and Wendy Pini, *Line of Beauty*, 214, for Wendy's self-characterization and her longtime *ElfQuest* collaborator Sonny Strait's response.

10. Shawn Taylor, "In Praise of *ElfQuest*."

11. Reactions have ranged from the dismissive ("I just don't get it. Sorry," declared one Fantagraphics editor) to the outright oblivious, as in the case of a local comics shop owner who ignored Wendy and addressed himself only to Richard (Richard Pini and Wendy Pini, interviews).

12. The documentary is *Marvel Rejected This Couple, So They Revolutionized the Comics Industry* by @mattwith4ts. Other prominent acknowledgments of Wendy Pini's significance emerge in Trina Robbins's *Pretty in Ink*; in Scott McCloud's *Understanding Comics*, *Making Comics*, and *Reinventing Comics*; in Fred Van Lente and Ryan Dunleavy's *The Comic Book History of Comics: Comics for All*; and in Marisa Stotter's film *She Makes Comics*. Incisive analyses of *ElfQuest* can be found in Saunders, "The Identity Politics of *ElfQuest* at 40"; Madeline Gangnes and Kevin Cooley, "Drawn to Reconcile"; and Isabelle Licari-Guillaume, "Women W.A.R.P.ing Gender in Comics: Wendy Pini's *ElfQuest* as Mixed Power Fantasy."

13. *Line of Beauty*, 24–27.

14. *Line of Beauty*, 198–201.

15. Ekenezar described these experiences in a segment of *Two Moons and a Microphone*, a podcast series launched in 2024 by Tanya Scott Thomas under the

auspices of SyFy Sistas, Inc., a media organization that explores fantasy, fandoms, and science fiction from the perspective of Black women.

16. Geoffrey Wilson, "Local Couple Ends Beloved Comic Series," A2.

17. Jon B. Cooke explores the Pinis' respective early experiences in "WaRP Speed with Richard Pini at the Helm" and in "Shadows & Sunlight: The Deep Sorrows and Radiant Joys of Wendy Fletcher Pini." *Line of Beauty*, 1–58, offers an illustrated account of Wendy's artistic development.

18. *Line of Beauty*, 191.

19. *Line of Beauty*, 195.

20. *Line of Beauty*, 44–51.

21. For an account of the Pinis' early relationship, see *Marvel Rejected This Couple* and Jan Gehorsam, "Zap! Wow! Comic Fantasy Comes True," 19, 22.

22. For a detailed discussion of Wendy's performances as Red Sonja, see Dwight Decker, "From Poughkeepsie to Elfland: An Interview with Wendy and Richard Pini," 137–42. Dan Gearino provides an entertaining account of Wendy's appearance on *Mike Douglas* in *Comic Shop: The Retail Mavericks Who Gave Us a New Geek Culture*, 50–51.

23. *She Makes Comics*, dir. Marisa Stotter.

24. Decker, "From Poughkeepsie to Elfland," 141.

25. See Gearino, *Comic Shop*, 26–60.

26. Inner cover editorial note, "Voice of the Sun."

27. *Line of Beauty*, 62.

28. Joellyn Auklandus, "There and Back Again."

29. "Joe Barruso," *IMDb*; Richard Pini and Wendy Pini, *The Art of "Elf-Quest*," 138.

30. Fairview Litho closed in 1990; see Kent Gibbons, "30 Jobs Lost as Fairview Litho Goes Bankrupt."

31. *The Art of "ElfQuest*," 32.

32. The final installment of the nine-issue Kings of the Broken Wheel series was published in 1992. The final issue of Hidden Years, issue 29, appeared in 1996.

33. For a discussion of the Cartoon Museum and the Pinis' support of it, see Florence Pennella, "Cartoon Museum Is a Castle of Laughs."

34. *"ElfQuest": The Audio Movie* is available on standard podcast outlets; see also " *'ElfQuest' ASL Version*."

35. *She Makes Comics*, dir. Stotter.

36. The speech was published by Pendragon Press in 1973; see *From Elfland to Poughkeepsie*.

37. *The Dreamberry Tales*, 34. This exchange serves as the frame for Decker's *Comics Journal* interview with the Pinis (127). Cooke also recounts this event in his interviews with the Pinis (34).

Chapter Five

1. Unless otherwise indicated, all quotations from artists in this chapter will come from the author's interviews with them.

2. For an introduction to John Burroughs's ideas, see "The Art of Seeing Things," his 1908 essay that still has much to teach us today.

3. Jane Tripp, interview.

4. See "Mr. and Mrs. Tripp Wed for 50 Years"; "Robert C. Tripp Dies: Railroad Employee"; and "Miss Tripp, 89, Native of City."

5. HJT, "Things Recalled."

6. "High School Holds Patriotic Exercises."

7. "Give Cafeteria Supper"; "Miss Lloyd Wed to Elmer Tripp."

8. "Elmer Lane Tripp Opens Main St. Art Studio."

9. "Sketches Feature Social at Church."

10. See John Canemaker, *Winsor McCay: His Life and Art*, 74–75, 131–37.

11. "Dutch Arms Club Host at Ladies' Night"; "Eva Effron Is Honored at Dinner Party, Shower"; "Country Club Is Scene of Christmas Party"; "Surprise Party Held for Mrs. E. Tripp."

12. "Elmer Tripp Returns from Schenectady Trip"; "Elmer Tripp Is Speaker before Bankers' Club"; Poughkeepsie Savings Bank advertisement; "Parade of Progress Exhibition"; and "Chalk Talks Given for Beacon Pupils."

13. "Scandinavian Society Entertains at Picnic"; "Business Men's Group Discusses Program"; "Medals Are Awarded to Forty Boy Scouts"; "Arlington Scouts to Receive Awards"; "Awards to Be Presented at Arlington Scout Dinner."

14. "Tripp to Instruct Course in Painting"; "Arlington Couples Slate Supper-Meeting"; "Art Association Schedules Show."

15. Jen Kirby, "See Vintage Manspreading Ads and More from the Vintage '40s and '50s Subway Courtesy Campaign."

16. "Amelia Ross Opdyke, Former Local Girl, Bride Today of Col. William J. Jones." The announcement also decorously modifies the title of her cartoon to *The Young Idea.*

17. "Morgue Visit Almost Changed Her Career."

18. Margaret Mara, "Subways Go in for Etiquette: Woman Artist Picks on Men—Women Can't Take Criticism." See also Trina Robbins, *Pretty in Ink*, 115–16.

19. "The Subway's Surrealist: The Cartoons of a New Jersey Housewife Help to Improve Commuters' Manners."

20. "Christmas Shopping for Deals at Luckey, Platt, & Company."

21. To say nothing of language and environmental awareness. Her posters helped to popularize the term *litterbug*. See George James, "Mark She Made on Subway Wasn't Graffiti."

22. Teddy Shearer, "Artists' Colony Lists Big Names." Shearer mentions Louise E. Jefferson, who worked as an art director at the Friendship Press; all the other artists in the article are men.

23. See "E. Simms Campbell," *Encyclopedia of Black Comics*, 44–49.

24. E. Simms Campbell, *A Night-Club Map of Harlem*, Library of Congress.

25. Ken Quattro, *Invisible Men*, 10. See also David Apatoff, "The Art of the Post: The First Successful Black Magazine Illustrator," *Saturday Evening Post*.

26. Other useful overviews of Campbell's work include Arna Bontemps's *We Have Tomorrow*, 1–14; "Campbell, E. Sims," in *Esquire*; and Hugh Merrill, *Esky: The Early Years at "Esquire,"* 42–43.

27. Caitlin McGurk, "Found in the Collection: E. Simms Campbell Letters," Billy Ireland Cartoon Library & Museum Blog.

28. "Memorial Service Held for E. Simms Campbell," *Crusader* (Illinois).

29. "Artworks: A Commentary on Lynching, 1935," Maryland Institute Black Archives; E. Simms Campbell, *I Passed along This Way*, Library of Congress.

30. E. Simms Campbell, "Blues Are the Negroes' Lament"; Bill Chase, "Bill Chase Around Town," *New York Age*.

31. "Noted Negro Artist Seeks to Buy Country Estate in Pleasantville," *The Daily News* (Tarrytown).

32. "Estate Sale Is Barred: Negro Loses Suit to Buy Site in Westchester County," *New York Times*.

33. "Negro Can't Buy Property: Court Denies Motion by Noted Artist," *The Daily News* (Tarrytown).

34. "About Resurfacing Main Street" and "Summer is Soap Box Derby Time," *Daily News* (Tarrytown).

35. A. A. Surrey, "Artist Builds Own Modernistic Home on Sound."

36. "Past Recipients: 2020 to Present," San Diego Comic-Con International.

37. 1920 United States Federal Census, District 0066.

38. 1930 United States Federal Census, District 0185.

39. "John F. Parker Draws for Daily News," *Daily News* (Tarrytown). A slightly edited version of the article, "Tarrytown Youth Now on Staff of Local Daily as Cartoonist," also appeared in the *New York Age*.

40. Marguerite Nixon, "Letter to the Editor," and "Editor's Note," *Daily News* (Tarrytown), 22 August 1938, 8.

41. Housed at Cornell University Library's Division of Rare and Manuscript Collections, the Mel Tapley Collection contains articles, photographs, artwork, and printing plates for comics.

42. Herb Boyd, "Mel Tapley: A Beacon of Brilliance at the *Amsterdam News*," *New York Amsterdam News*.

43. "Out-of-Town News and Other Personal Items," *New York Age*, 10.

44. Tim Jackson, *Pioneering Cartoonists of Color*, 58–69.

45. I am grateful to Nat Gertler for kindly sharing his digitized versions of *Breezy* with me.

46. It seems likely that this was Leonard Carrington, a lifelong Peekskill resident who entered the navy in 1944. After an honorable discharge he raised a family, worked at General Motors, and engaged in community and political life before his passing in 2009. See "Leonard Carrington, Obituary," *LoHud/The Journal News.*

47. This book makes no mention of the longstanding presence of Black people in the community, beyond a reference to William Lee, "the faithful colored servant and slave" accompanying General George Washington on his journey through Peekskill in 1776. A review of the book by Maureen McKernan in *The Daily Times* (Mamaroneck) notes that "Drawings are by a young Negro newspaper columnist, Melvin Tapley, whose ancestors were Peekskill people" (4).

48. "Peekskill NAACP Presidential History," Peekskill NAACP Branch 2170.

49. In "Lone Budget Defeated in School Vote," *The Reporter Dispatch: Northern Westchester Edition* notes that "In Peekskill, a Negro, Melvin S. Tapley was elected without opposition" (1).

50. "Where to Go, What to Do," *Citizen Register* (Ossining), 14.

51. "Mrs. Singer Named Fellow at Columbia," *Mount Vernon Argus*, 33; Margie Druss, "Peekskill NAACP to Honor Seven at Awards Dinner," *The Reporter Dispatch* (White Plains), 8.

52. Arline J. Tapley, who met her future husband while working at the *Amsterdam News*, was a nurse who also taught Sunday school, worked for the Peekskill Community Action Program, and led Hudson Valley Blood Services in Valhalla, New York. See "Arline J. Tapley: former NAACP Chapter President," *The Standard-Star* (New Rochelle), 4.

53. Quoted in Ken Quattro, *Invisible Men: The Trailblazing Black Artists of Comic Books*, 7.

54. The Catskill Comics website gives a sense of the plenitude of comics artists currently or recently working in the area.

55. See "The Cat, Vol. 1." This series, also known as *The Claws of the Cat*, had an unpublished fifth issue featuring art by Ramona Fradon (Fite).

56. Marz took two or three classes in the spaces converted from the Western Printing building. As indicated in chapter 3 (note 63) during Marz's undergraduate years Marist University was known as Marist College.

57. Ron Marz, "Bernie Wrightson's Halloween."

58. See also the recollections of Herb's son, Alex Trimpe, in Dewey Cassel and Aaron Sultan's *The Incredible Herb Trimpe.*

59. For the enduring influence of Fradon's work, see *She Makes Comics* and Trina Robbins, *Pretty in Ink*, 120–22.

60. See *The Incredible Herb Trimpe*, 9–10.

61. *The Incredible Herb Trimpe*, 137.

62. Herb Trimpe, "Old Superheroes Never Die, They Join the Real World."

63. "About Us," Historic Huguenot Street.

64. See Poughkeepsie Public Library District.

65. Eric Durr, "New York Army National Guard Member Has a Comic Book Alter Ego," *U.S. Army*.

Works Cited

"About Resurfacing Main Street." *Daily News* (Tarrytown), 3 June 1938, p. 6.

"About the Trail." The Northside Line Project, www.dutchesscountyurbantrail.com/about. Accessed 10 December 2023.

"About Us." Historic Huguenot Street, www.huguenotstreet.org/home. Accessed 3 March 2024.

"About Warp—and W&RP." The *ElfQuest* Reading Room, elfquest.com/reading-room/. Accessed 1 May 2023.

The Adventures of Ichabod and Mr. Toad. Directed by Jack Kinney, Clyde Geronimi, and James Algar, performances Basil Rathbone and Bing Crosby, Walt Disney Productions, 1949.

Ahrens, Jörn, and Arno Meteling, eds. *Comics and the City: Urban Space in Print, Picture, and Sequence.* Bloomsbury, 2010.

Allan, Robin. *Walt Disney and Europe: European Influences on the Animated Feature Films of Walt Disney.* John Libbey, 1999.

"Amelia Ross Opdyke, Former Local Girl, Bride Today of Col. William J. Jones." *Central New Jersey Home News*, 16 November 1934, p. 22.

Anderson, Colin L. "Imagining Racial Segregation before the Ghetto: Representations of Black Urban Space and Mobility in the 'Darktown' Comics, 1877–1900." *Journal of Urban History*, 2023, pp. 1–30.

Apatoff, David. "The Art of the Post: The First Successful Black Magazine Illustrator." *Saturday Evening Post*, 1 February 2022, www.saturdayeveningpost.com/2022/02/the-art-of-the-post-elmer-simms-campbell-the-first-successful-black-magazine-illustrator/. Accessed 20 February 2024.

"Arline J. Tapley: Former NAACP Chapter President." *The Standard-Star* (New Rochelle), 20 December 1990, p. 4.

"Arlington Couples Slate Supper Meeting." *Poughkeepsie Journal*, 25 March 1963, p. 10.

"Arlington Scouts to Receive Awards." *Poughkeepsie Journal*, 18 October 1962, p. 5.

"Art Association Schedules Show." *Poughkeepsie Journal*, 10 February 1965, p. 32.

"Artworks: A Commentary on Lynching, 1935." Maryland Institute Black Archives, www.miba.online/blog/2018/11/15/931891-a-surprise-sprung-in-baltimore-it-is-the-appointment-of-a-colored-youth-to-an-art-institute-scholarship-feay6-ag3yl. Accessed 20 March 2024.

"Arvid E. Miller Library/Museum." Stockbridge/Munsee Community Band of Mohican Indians, www.mohican.com/services/cultural-services/arvid-e-miller-library-museum/. Accessed 1 September 2023.

Auklandus, Joellyn. "There and Back Again." *The Hidden Years*, vol. 29, 1996. *ElfQuest* Reading Room, elfquest.com/reading-room/. Accessed 9 November 2023.

Avery, Kevin J. "Gifford and the Catskills: Resort and Refuge." *Within the Landscape: Essays on Nineteenth-Century American Art and Culture*, ed. Philip Earenfight and Nancy Siegel. Pennsylvania State UP, 2005, pp. 149–81.

Avery, Kevin J. "John Frederick Kensett, 1816–1872." Heilbrunn Timeline of Art History, https://www.metmuseum.org/toah/hd/kens/hd_kens.htm. Accessed 12 December 2023.

"Awards to Be Presented at Arlington Scout Dinner." *Poughkeepsie Journal*, 1 January 1962, p. 1.

"Awards Won by Western Comics." *Poughkeepsie New Yorker*, 2 April 1956, p. 1.

Baker, Joe, Hadrien Coumans, and Joel Whitney, eds. *Lenapehoking: An Anthology*. Lenape Center: Brooklyn Public Library, 2022.

Barrett, Thomas. "A Map of Poughkeepsie, 1931." Barry Lawrence Ruderman Antique Maps, www.raremaps.com/gallery/detail/55315jc. Accessed 16 October 2024.

Barrier, Michael. *Funnybooks: The Improbable Glories of the Best American Comic Books*. U of California P, 2015.

Barruso, Joe. Interview. Conducted by the author, 8 December 2023.

Barry, John. "A Fresh Perspective on the Cape, Mask, and Superhero." *Poughkeepsie Journal*, 26 February 2015, www.poughkeepsiejournal.com/story/entertainment/2015/02/25/arts-mid-hudson-comics/24001459/. Accessed 4 December 2022.

Beaty, Bart. *Fredric Wertham and the Critique of Mass Culture: A Re-Examination of the Critic Whose Congressional Testimony Sparked the Comics Code*, University Press of Mississippi, 2005.

Bechdel, Alison. *Fun Home: A Family Tragicomic*. Mariner Books Classics, 2007.

Belair, Jr., Felix. "King Tries Hot Dog and Asks for More." *New York Times*, 12 June 1939, p. 1.

Benjamin, Walter. "The Work of Art in the Age of Mechanical Reproduction." *Illuminations*, ed. Hannah Arendt, trans. Harry Zohn. Harcourt Brace Jovanovich, 1968 (originally published in 1935), pp. 217–52.

Bernstein, George. "Questions Linger Over Western Closing." *Poughkeepsie Journal*, 3 July 1983, pp. 9C and 10C.

Bernstein, George. "Western Publishing Comes Full Circle in Poughkeepsie." *Poughkeepsie Journal*, 3 July 1983, pp. 9C and 11C.

"Black History Is Local History: Theodore and Doris Mack." Poughkeepsie Public Library District, poklib.org/black-history-is-local-history-theodore-and-doris-mack/. Accessed 2 February 2024.

Bloom, David. "*ElfQuest* Creators Donate $500,000 to Columbia University Comics Archive."

Forbes, 25 February 2025, www.forbes.com/sites/dbloom/2025/02/25/elfquest-creators-donate-500000-to-columbia-university-comics-archive/. Accessed 20 March 2025.

Bontemps, Arna. *We Have Tomorrow*. Houghton Mifflin Harcourt, 1945.

Borden, Bill, with Steve Posner. *The Big Book of Big Little Books*. Chronicle Books, 1997.

Boyd, Herb. "Mel Tapley: A Beacon of Brilliance at the *Amsterdam News*." *New York Amsterdam News*, 24 May 2018.

Breiner, John. Interview. Conducted by the author, 29 September 2023.

Breiner, John. *Power Kingdom: Graffiti in Poughkeepsie, NY (1990s and 2000s)*. My Daily Habit, 2022.

Breiner, John. "Western Printing Graffiti Tour Part I." YouTube, https://www.youtube.com/watch?app=desktop&v=7JCCE9hx41I&list=PLwIn7RvUMR-jt0EM9lnkONSrk-qFjDyzI5&index=19. Accessed 3 April 2023.

Breiner, John. "Western Printing Factory—Graffiti Tour Part II." YouTube, https://www.youtube.com/watch?v=Dx8OOIwgc4E&list=PLwIn7RvUMRjt0EM9lnkONSrk-qFjDyzI5&index=23. Accessed 3 April 2023.

"Brophy Is Held for Grand Jury." *Poughkeepsie Eagle-News*, 11 July 1934, p. 2.

Brown, Merrilee. "Before Quiet Computers, Factory Noise Prevailed." *Poughkeepsie Journal*, 14 March 1999, p. 17.

Brown, Sterling A. *Southern Road: Poems by Sterling A. Brown*. Illustrated by E. Simms Campbell. Harcourt, Brace, 1932.

Bruegl, Heather. "Not the Last of the Mohicans: Forced Migration of the Stockbridge Munsee from New York to Wisconsin." *Lenapehoking*, ed. Baker et al., pp. 105–116.

Bryan, Ford R. "The Birth of Ford Motor Company." Henry Ford Heritage Association, hfha.org/the-ford-story/the-birth-of-ford-motor-company/. Accessed 9 February 2023.

Bui, Thi. *The Best We Could Do: An Illustrated Memoir*. Abrams ComicArts, 2017.

Burns, Sarah. *Pastoral Inventions: Rural Life in Nineteenth-Century American Art and Culture*. Temple UP, 1989.

Burroughs, John. "The Art of Seeing Things." Library of America Story of the Week, storyoftheweek.loa.org/2012/07/the-art-of-seeing-things.html. Accessed 5 October 2023.

Burstein, Andrew. *The Original Knickerbocker: The Life of Washington Irving*. Basic Books, 2008.

"Business Men's Group Discusses Program." *Poughkeepsie Eagle-News*, 8 July 1937, p. 16.

Butler, Joseph T. *Washington Irving's Sunnyside*. Sleepy Hollow Restorations, 1974.

Butler, Shannon. "The American Fiat—Built in Poughkeepsie." Poughkeepsie Public Library District, poklib.org/the-american-fiat-built-it-poughkeepsie/. Accessed 6 April 2024.

Calenti, Michael. Interview. Conducted by the author, 31 March 2023.

Campbell, E. Simms. "Blues Are the Negroes' Lament." *Esquire*, 1 December 1939, pp. 100–280.

Campbell, E. Simms. *I Passed along This Way*. Library of Congress, www.loc.gov/item/2015650267/. Accessed 20 March 2024.

Campbell, E. Simms. *A Night-Club Map of Harlem*. Library of Congress, www.loc.gov/item/2016585261/. Accessed 29 February 2024.

"Campbell, E. Simms." *Esquire*, October 2015, pp. 54–56.

Canemaker, John. *Winsor McCay: His Life and Art*. Harry N. Abrams, 2005.

Cao, Maggie M. *The End of Landscape in Nineteenth Century America*. U of California P, 2018.

Carrington, Barbara McGue (Jones). Interview. Conducted by the author, 5 July 2023.

Case, Jennifer. "Place Studies: Theory and Practice in Environmental Nonfiction." *Assay: A Journal of Nonfiction Studies*, vol. 10, no. 1, www.assayjournal.com/jennifer-case-place-studies-theory-and-practice-in-environmental-nonfiction.html. Accessed 23 March 2024.

Casey, Edward S. *Representing Place: Landscape Painting and Maps*. U of Minnesota P, 2002.

Cassel, Dewey, and Aaron Sultan. *The Incredible Herb Trimpe*. TwoMorrows, 2016.

"The Cat Vol. 1." Marvel Database, marvel.fandom.com/wiki/The_Cat_Vol_1. Accessed 21 March 2023.

Catskill Comics: Original & Commission Art, catskillcomics.com. Accessed 14 October 2023.

"Celebrating the Scenic Hudson Decision." Scenic Hudson, www.scenichudson.org/viewfinder/celebrating-the-scenic-hudson-decision/. Accessed 24 March 2024.

"Chalk Talks Given for Beacon Pupils." *Poughkeepsie Eagle-News*, 1 December 1948, p. 12.

Chase, Bill. "Bill Chase around Town." *New York Age*, 8 October 1949, p. 19.

"Christmas Shopping for Deals at the Luckey, Platt, & Company." Poughkeepsie Public Library District, poklib.org/christmas-shopping-for-deals-at-luckey-platt-and-company/. Accessed 11 October 2024.

Chute, Hillary. *Why Comics? From Underground to Everywhere*. Harper, 2017.

Chute, Hillary, and Justin Hall. "Critics and Creators: The LGBTQ+ Comics Ecosystem." *The LGBTQ+ Comics Studies Reader: Critical Openings, Future Directions*, ed. Alison Halsall and Jonathan Warren. UP of Mississippi, 2022, pp. 181–99.

"Circus Arrives in Town; To Give Two Shows Today." *Poughkeepsie Eagle-News*, 11 June 1934, p. 2.

Clancy, Shaun. "*ElfQuest* behind the Scenes: A Chat with Richard and Wendy Pini." *Back Issue*, vol. 75, 2014, pp. 23–28.

Cooke, Jon B. "Editor's Rant: Mining for Gold." *Comic Book Artist*, vol. 22, 2022, pp. 5–6.

Cooke, Jon B. "Mark Evanier Interview: Western Goes West." *Comic Book Artist*, vol. 22, 2022, pp. 80–87.

Cooke, Jon B. "Shadows & Sunlight: The Deep Sorrows and Radiant Joys of Wendy Fletcher Pini." *Comic Book Creator*, vol. 23, 2020, pp. 32–71.

Cooke, Jon B. "WaRP Speed with Richard Pini at the Helm." *Comic Book Creator*, vol. 23, 2020, pp. 72–76.

"Country Club Is Scene of Christmas Party." *Poughkeepsie Eagle-News*, 30 December 1936, p. 10.

Coughlin, Maura, and Emily Gephart, eds. *Ecocriticsm and the Anthropocene in Nineteenth-Century Visual Art and Culture*. Routledge, 2019.

Curtis, George William, *Lotus-Eating: A Summer Book*. Illustrated by John Frederick Kensett. Harper & Brothers, 1852.

Dalton-Fenkl, Bella. *The Adventures of Space Bunny*. Korean Quarterly, www.koreanquarterly.org/webtoons/space-bunny/. Accessed 5 October 2024.

Dalton-Fenkl, Bella. *Eels of the Hudson Valley*. Kirin, 2022.

Dalton-Fenkl, Bella. Interview. Conducted by the author, 12 September 2024.

Dauber, Jeremy. *American Comics: A History*. W. W. Norton, 2022.

Decker, Dwight. "From Poughkeepsie to Elfland: An Interview with Wendy and Richard Pini." *The Comics Journal*, vol. 63, 1981, pp. 127–51.

DeLessio, Joe. "Nobody Knows Where 'Upstate New York' Actually Is." *New York Magazine*, 29 March 2016, nymag.com/intelligencer/2016/03/what-are-the-boundaries-of-upstate-new-york.html. Accessed 2 December 2023.

Diagram for Delinquents. Directed by Robert A. Emmons, Jr. Scifidelity Pictures, 2014.

Dorsey, John. "Currier & Ives' America Could Be a Dark Place." *Baltimore Sun*, 26 June 1997, p. 1E.

Druss, Margie. "Peekskill NAACP to Honor Seven at Awards Dinner." *The Reporter Dispatch* (White Plains), 16 October 1996, p. 8.

Durr, Eric. "New York Army National Guard Member Has a Comic Book Alter Ego." U.S. Army, www.army.mil/article/68033/new_york_army_national_guard_officer_has_a_comic_book_alter_ego. Accessed 7 April 2024.

"Dutch Arms Club Host at Ladies' Night." *Poughkeepsie Eagle-News*, 22 May 1934, p. 7.

Edelstein, Stephen. "Poughkeepsie's Lost Railroad." *The Ilium Gazette*, stephened-elstein.wordpress.com/tag/poughkeepsie-hospital-branch/. Accessed 9 March 2024.

Eisner, Will. "Preface" (2004). *A Contract with God: And Other Tenement Stories. Will Eisner Centennial Edition.* W. W. Norton, 2017.

ElfQuest *ASL Version*. YouTube. Realm of Possibility Inc, www.youtube.com/watch?v=oKUWpfut1fw. Accessed 11 June 2023.

ElfQuest: *The Audio Movie*. Dir. Fred Greenhalgh. Dagaz Media and the Fantasy Network, 2021.

"Elmer Lane Tripp Opens Main St. Art Studio." *Poughkeepsie Eagle-News*, 25 February 1925, p. 5.

"Elmer Tripp Is Speaker before Bankers Club." *Poughkeepsie Eagle-News*, 22 October 1930, p. 6.

"Elmer Tripp Returns from Schenectady Trip." *Poughkeepsie Eagle-News*, 18 June 1930, p. 5.

"Estate Sale Is Barred: Negro Loses Suit to Buy Site in Westchester County." *New York Times*, 26 May 1938, p. 9.

"Eva Effron Is Honored at Dinner Party, Shower." *Poughkeepsie Eagle-News*, 5 May 1936, p. 8.

Evanier, Mark. "An Incessantly-Asked Question." News from Me, https://www.newsfromme.com/iaq/iaq07/. Accessed 19 February 2023.

Evanier, Mark. "It's in the Bag," News from Me, web.archive.org/web/20151029022218/http:/www.newsfromme.com/2007/04/29/its-in-the-bag/. Accessed 13 May 2024.

Fawaz, Ramzi. "A Queer Sequence: Comics as a Disruptive Medium." *PMLA*, vol. 134, no. 3, 2019, pp. 588–94.

Fawaz, Ramzi, Shelley Streeby, and Deborah Elizabeth Whaley, eds. *Keywords in Comics Studies*. New York UP, 2021.

"Felice Nazzaro." Vanderbilt Cup Races, www.vanderbiltcupraces.com/drivers/bio/nazzaro. Accessed 3 May 2023.

Fenkl, Heinz Insu. *A Boy and His Ox: A Zen Parable Based on the Oxherding Pictures*. 2013.

Fenkl, Heinz Insu. Interview. Conducted by the author, 18 September 2024.

Fenkl, Heinz Insu, and Bella Dalton-Fenkl. *Korean Myths: A Guide to the Gods, Heroes and Legends*. Thames & Hudson, F2024.

Fernández, Teresita, "Artist as Arsonist: Burning Down the Myth of the American Landscape." *Women Reframe American Landscape*, ed. Nancy Siegel, Kate Menconeri, and Amanda Malmstrom. Hirmer, 2023, pp. 88–91.

"Fiat Company at Fairview." *Poughkeepsie Eagle-News*, 12 July 1909, p. 5.

"Fiat Company Is Coming." *Poughkeepsie Eagle-News*, 9 July 1909, p. 5.

Fiehn, Charlotte. "Washington Irving's Mediaeval Renaissance: Chaucer's Influence on Irving's Foundational Project." *English Studies*, vol. 103, no. 6, 2022, pp. 837–52.

Fite, Linda. Interview. Conducted by the author, 26 February 2024.

Flad, Harvey, and Clyde Griffen. *From Main Street to Mainframes: Landscape and Social Change in Poughkeepsie.* State U of New York P, 2009.

"Former Poughkeepsie School Board President Dies." *Hudson Valley Press*, 17 April 2024, hudsonvalleypress.com/2024/04/17/former-poughkeepsie-school-board-president-dies/. Accessed 17 October 2024.

"For Sale—Notice to Factories." *Poughkeepsie Eagle-News*, 1 August 1918, p. 8.

Fox, Joseph M. *The History of Early Peekskill, 1609–1876.* Enterprise, 1947.

Foyt, Sandra, "Eleanor Roosevelt Remembered at Val-Kill." YouTube, www.youtube.com/watch?v=ADCQy9b46qU. Accessed 8 May 2023.

Francis IV, Lee, and Weshoyot Alvitre. *Loyalty Betrayed. Telling Stories with Pictures: Collected Comics from "Native New York."* National Museum of the American Indian, 2021.

Fraser, Benjamin. *Barcelona, City of Comics: Urbanism, Architecture, and Design in Postdictatorial Spain.* State U of New York P, 2022.

Fraser, Benjamin. *Visible Cities, Global Comics: Urban Images and Spatial Form.* UP of Mississippi, 2019.

Gabilliet, Jean-Paul. *Of Comics and Men: A Cultural History of American Comic Books.* Translated by Bart Beaty and Nick Nguyen. UP of Mississippi, 2010.

Gangnes, Madeline, and Kevin Cooley. "Drawn to Reconcile: The Queer Reparative Journey of *ElfQuest.*" *Inks: The Journal of the Comics Study Society*, vol. 4, no. 2, 2017, pp. 156–78.

Gearino, Dan. *Comic Shop: The Retail Mavericks Who Gave Us a New Geek Culture.* Swallow, 2017.

Gehorsam, Jan. "Zap! Wow! Comic Fantasy Comes True." *Poughkeepsie Journal*, 5 March 1984, pp. 19, 22.

"George William Curtis." Politics in Graphic Detail: Exploring History through Political Cartoons. Historical Society of Pennsylvania, digitalhistory.hsp.org/hint/politics-graphic-detail/person/george-william-curtis. Accessed 12 March 2023.

Get a Horse! Directed by Lauren MacMullan, performances by Walt Disney, Jimmy MacDonald, and Marcellite Garner, Walt Disney Animation Studios, 2013.

Ghez, Didier. *They Drew as They Pleased: The Hidden Art of Disney's Golden Age.* Chronicle Books, 2015.

Gibbons, Kent. "30 Jobs Lost as Fairview Litho Goes Bankrupt." *Poughkeepsie Journal*, 31 July 1990, p. 5A.

"Give Cafeteria Supper." *Poughkeepsie Eagle-News*, 16 April 2023, p. 6.

"Glenn Henry Johnson." *Poughkeepsie Journal*, 6 February 2022, p. A9.

Gray, Maggie, and Ian Horton. *Seeing Comics through Art History: Alternative Approaches to the Form.* Palgrave, 2022.

Grumet, Robert. *First Manhattans: A History of the Indians of Greater New York.* U of Oklahoma P, 2011.

"A Guide to the Fred O. Seibel Editorial Cartoonist's Research Collection." Archival Resources of the Virginias, ead.lib.virginia.edu/vivaxtf/view?docId=uva-sc/viu02380.xml. Accessed 14 February 2024.

Hagar, Laurie. "Poughkeepsie Plant Started as a Warehouse in 1934." *Poughkeepsie Journal*, 3 November 1982, p. 5.

Hajdu, David. *The Ten-Cent Plague: The Great Comic-Book Scare and How It Changed America*. Picador, 2009.

Hamilton, Bruce. "A Tripp Down Memory Lane." *The Little Lulu Library*. Edited by John Clark. Volume 16. Another Rainbow, 1985, pp. 13–18.

Hamilton, James. *Arthur Rackham: A Life with Illustration*. Pavilion, 1995.

"Harper's Weekly." Thomas Nast, Prince of Caricaturists, Ohio State University Libraries, library.osu.edu/site/thomasnast/harpers-weekly/. Accessed 14 July 2024.

Harris, David. "The News Hits Western Workers Hard." *Poughkeepsie Journal*, 3 November 1982, p. 5.

Harris, Rachel. "Imprints from Book Illustration and Advertisement: Eco-Sources in Walt Disney's Sleeping Heroine Films." *Marvels & Tales*, vol. 36, no. 2, 2022, pp. 258–83.

"Henry Schaffer Is Dead at 92; Founded Supermarket Chain." *New York Times*, 17 February 1982, p. B8.

Herb Trimpe, We Love You! Directed by Jon Michael Riley. YouTube, www.youtube.com/watch?v=vrO52WmwV4U. Accessed 2 December 2023.

"Hermanse/Sanders Patent." Marist Heritage Project, exhibits.archives.marist.edu/s/marist-heritage-project/page/Prehistory-Hermanse-Sanders. Accessed 31 October 2023.

"High School Holds Patriotic Exercises," *Poughkeepsie Eagle-News*, 23 February 1921, p. 5.

"A History of the Physical Plant of Marist College." Marist Heritage Project, exhibits.archives.marist.edu/s/marist-heritage-project/page/Written-Histories-Physical-Plant. Accessed 20 June 2023.

HJT, "Things Recalled." *Poughkeepsie Journal*, 12 November 1967, p. 16D.

Howard, Sheena C. *Encyclopedia of Black Comics*. Fulcrum, 2017.

Howland, Jack. "HV Comic Con: Pop Culture Fans, Stars Unite." *Poughkeepsie Journal*, 8 May 2017, p. A3.

Hudson, Derek. *Arthur Rackham: His Life and Work*. Charles Scribner's Sons, 1960.

The Hudson Illustrated with Pen and Pencil. T. W. Strong, 1852.

"Hudson River Graphic." National Estuarine Research Reserve System Science Collaborative, www.nerrssciencecollaborative.org. Accessed 1 August 2022.

"The Illustrating of Books: Discussion at the Authors' Club." *The Morning Post*, 1 February 1910, p. 5.

Irving, Chris, "Western Civ 101: Unlocking the Mystery of Gold Key Comics." *Comic Book Artist*, vol. 22, 2002, pp. 16–31.

Irving, Washington. *The Sketch Book of Geoffrey Crayon, Gent. Washington Irving: History, Tales, and Sketches*, ed. James W. Tuttleton. Library of America, 1983, pp. 731–1092.

Irving, Washington. *The Legend of Sleepy Hollow*. Illustrated by Arthur Rackham. George G. Harrap, 1928.

Jacks, Eleanor. "Off to a Good Start: Exploring Decorated Initials." British Library Medieval Manuscripts Blog, blogs.bl.uk/digitisedmanuscripts/2019/10/off-to-a-good-start-exploring-decorated-initials.html. Accessed 2 November 2024.

Jackson, Tim. *Pioneering Cartoonists of Color*. UP of Mississippi, 2016.

James, George. "Mark She Made on Subway Wasn't Graffiti." *New York Daily News*, 13 November 1978, p. 9.

"Janet DuBois' Engagement Announced by Her Parents." *Poughkeepsie Journal*, 15 September 1943, p. 10.

"Joe Barruso." IMDb, www.imdb.com/name/nm0057914/. Accessed 12 April 2024.

"John F. Parker Draws for Daily News: Gene Byrnes Aided Talented N.T. Youth." *Daily News* (Tarrytown), 15 July 1938, pp. 1–2.

"John Frederick Kensett." National Gallery of Art, www.nga.gov/collection/artist-info.1434.html. Accessed 12 December 2023.

Jones, Brian Jay. *Washington Irving: An American Original*. Arcade, 2008.

Jones, Elizabeth Opdyke. Interview. Conducted by the author, 7 March 2024.

Karkowski, Gerald L. "Celebrating 175 Years: Western Printing." *Racine Post*, racinepost.blogspot.com/2010/07/celebrating-175-years-western-printing.html. Accessed 13 August 2023.

Keller, Morton. "The World of Thomas Nast." Thomas Nast: Prince of Caricaturists, Ohio State University Libraries, library.osu.edu/site/thomasnast/world-of-nast/. Accessed 10 January 2024.

Kilpatrick, Jacquelyn. *Celluloid Indians: Native Americans and Film*. U of Nebraska P, 1999.

Kimmerer, Robin Wall. *Braiding Sweetgrass: Indigenous Wisdom, Scientific Knowledge and the Teachings of Plants*. Milkweed Editions, 2015.

Kirby, Jen. "See Vintage Manspreading Ads and More from the Vintage '40s and '50s Subway Courtesy Campaign." *New York Magazine*, 10 March 2015, nymag.com/intelligencer/2015/03/see-courtesy-campaign-ads-from-the-40s-and-50s.html. Accessed 10 October 2023.

Kunzle, David. *History of the Comic Strip*. U of California P, 1973.

Lamb, Alexis. Interview. Conducted by the author, 8 August 2024.

Lamerichs, Nicolle. "Scrolling, Swiping, Selling: Understanding Webtoons and the Data-Driven Participatory Culture around Comics." *Participations: Journal of Audience and Reception Studies*, vol. 17, no. 2, 2020, pp. 211–29.

"Lancia Dinner Plans Finished." *Poughkeepsie Eagle-News*, 12 January 1928, p. 1.

Lankevich, George L. *River of Dreams: The Hudson Valley in Historic Postcards*. Fordham UP, 2006.

Le Guin, Ursula. *From Elfland to Poughkeepsie*. Pendragon Press, 1973.

"The Lend-Lease Program, 1941–1945." Franklin D. Roosevelt Presidential Library and Museum, www.fdrlibrary.org/lend-lease. Accessed 12 March 2024.

"Leonard Carrington Obituary." *LoHud/The Journal News*, www.legacy.com/us/obituaries/lohud/name/leonard-carrington-obituary?id=48123899. Accessed 4 April 2024.

Lewis, John, Andrew Aydin, and Nate Powell. *March*. Three vols. Top Shelf Productions, 2016.

Lewis, Richard, Interview. Conducted by the author, 16 June 2023.

Licari-Guillaume, Isabelle. "Women W.A.R.P.ing Gender in Comics: Wendy Pini's *ElfQuest* as Mixed Power Fantasy." *Revue de recherche en civilisation américaine*, vol. 6, 2016.

"Lithography: It's a Process." The Columbia Museum of Art, www.columbiamuseum.org/news/lithography-its-process. Accessed 19 January 2024.

"Little Boy Hit by Fiat Machine." *Poughkeepsie Eagle-News*, 3 January 1912, p. 5.

"Little Golden Books." Smithsonian Albert H. Small Documents Gallery, americanhistory.si.edu/documentsgallery/exhibitions/goldenbooks/index.html. Accessed 30 March 2024.

"Local Plant's Comics Scanned by Comics Commission." *Poughkeepsie New Yorker*, 13 June 1950, p. 10.

"Lone Budget Defeated in School Vote." *The Reporter Dispatch: Northern Westchester Edition*, 5 May 1965, p. 1.

Lopes, Paul. *Demanding Respect: The Evolution of the American Comic Book*. Temple UP, 2009.

Lumb, David. "Poughkeepsie Compilation V 1.1." YouTube, www.youtube.com/watch?v=NptUnbIEr4o. Accessed 31 October 2023.

Lumb, David. Poughkeepsie Pop Culture, www.poughkeepsiepopculture.com. Accessed 7 July 2022.

Lumb, David. "Poughkeepsie Compilation V 1.1." YouTube, www.youtube.com/watch?v=NptUnbIEr4o. Accessed 31 October 2023.

"Lynchings: By Year and Race." University of Missouri at Kansas City Law School, http://law2.umkc.edu/faculty/projects/ftrials/shipp/lynchingyear.html. Accessed 21 November 2024.

Lyons, Maura. "Nature Defamiliarized: Picturing New Relationships between Humans and Nonhuman Nature in Northern Landscapes from the American Civil War." *Panorama: Journal of the Association of Historians of American Art*, vol. 1, no. 1, 2015, n.p.

Maki, Michele. "'My Diry' of My Trip to Peekskill—Little Lulu's Home Town." Michelesworld, michelesworld.net/dmm2/lulu/peekskil.htm. Accessed 2 April 2024.

Mara, Margaret. "Margaret Mara, "Subways Go in for Etiquette: Woman Artist Picks on Men—Women Can't Take Criticism." *The Brooklyn Daily Eagle*, 9 August 1946, p. 11.

Marcus, Leonard. *Golden Legacy: The Story of Golden Books*. Golden Books, 2017.

Martel, Seth Christian. *The Mare*. Graphic Mundi, 2023.

Marz, Ron. "Bernie Wrightson's Halloween," *The Comic Book Review*, 27 October 2011, www.cbr.com/bernie-wrightsons-halloween/. Accessed 7 July 2023.

Marz, Ron. Interview. Conducted by the author, 7 June 2023.

"Mattel's Western to Close a Plant." *New York Times*, 23 November 1982, p. D5.

@mattwith4ts. *Marvel Rejected This Couple, So They Revolutionized the Comics Industry*. YouTube, www.youtube.com/watch?v=w-Pygh3A4bY, 2024. Accessed 29 August 2024.

McCloud, Scott. *Making Comics: Storytelling Secrets of Comics, Manga, and Graphic Novels*. William Morrow Paperbacks, 2006.

McCloud, Scott. *Reinventing Comics*. HarperCollins, 2000.

McCree, J. Woodrow. *Washington Irving's Critique of American Culture: Sketching a Vision of World Citizenship*. Lexington Books, 2021.

McDermott, William P. "Land Grants in Dutchess County: Settlements or Speculation?" *Transformations of an American County*. Dutchess County Historical Society, 1986, pp. 27–40.

McGurk, Caitlin. "Found in the Collection: E. Simms Campbell Letters." Billy Ireland Cartoon Library & Museum Blog, the Ohio State University Libraries, 28 February 2013, library.osu.edu/site/cartoons/2013/02/28/found-in-the-collection-e-simms-campbell-letters/. Accessed 14 February 2024.

McKernan, Maureen, "Judge Fox's History of Peekskill Gives Intimate Historic Link to Westchester." *The Mamaroneck Daily Times*, 14 August 1947, p. 4.

"Medals Are Awarded to Forty Boy Scouts." *Poughkeepsie Eagle-News*, 25 January 1936, p. 10.

"Memorial Service Held for E. Simms Campbell." *The Crusader* (Illinois), 17 February 2971, p. 6.

"Memorial Today for Cartoonist Dick Oldden." *Los Angeles Times*, 26 February 1995.

Merrill, Hugh. *Esky: The Early Years at* Esquire. Rutgers UP, 1995.

Miller, Kayla, and Jeffrey Canino. *Besties Work It Out*. Illustrated by Kristina Luu. Houghton Mifflin Harcourt, 2021.

Miller, Kayla, and Jeffrey Canino. Interview. Conducted by the author, 19 July 2023.

Miller, Michelle. "Michelle's Meanderings: Days of Comic Book Chaos." *Comic Book Artist* 22, 2000, pp. 12–14.

Miller, Susan. Interview. Conducted by the author, 16 October 2023.

"Miss Lloyd Wed to Elmer Tripp." *Poughkeepsie Eagle-News*, 29 June 1925, p. 3.

"Miss Tripp, 89, Native of City." *Poughkeepsie New Yorker*, 3 November 1958, p. 28.

Montgomery, Imani. Interview. Conducted by the author, 11 March 2024.

Moore, Alan, and Dave Gibbons. *Watchmen*. DC Comics, 1987.

"Morgue Visit Almost Changed Her Career." *New York Daily News*, 2 May 1954, p. 278.

"Movements/The Hudson River School." The Art Story, www.theartstory.org/movement/hudson-river-school/. Accessed 2 November 2024.

"Mr. and Mrs. Tripp Wed for 50 Years." *Poughkeepsie New Yorker*, 9 September 1941, p. 8.

"Mr. Sague Becomes Rash." *Poughkeepsie Eagle-News*, 17 October 1929, p. 6.

"Mrs. Singer Named Fellow at Columbia." *Mount Vernon Argus*, 11 October 1966, p. 33.

Murphy, Cullen. *Cartoon County: My Father and His Friends in the Golden Age of Make-Believe*, Macmillan, 2017.

Murray, Hannah Lauren. *Liminal Whiteness in Early U.S. Fiction*. Edinburgh UP, 2021.

Murray, Laura J. "The Aesthetic of Dispossession: Washington Irving and Ideologies of (De)Colonization in the Early Republic." *American Literary History*, vol. 8, no. 2, 1996, pp. 205–31.

Myers, Helen. "'Of Making Many Books There Is No End.'" *Poughkeepsie New Yorker*, 24 November 1946, p. 2A.

Nast, Thomas. "Colored Rule in a Reconstructed State," *Harper's Weekly*, 14 March 1874, Library of Congress, www.loc.gov/item/91705051/. Accessed 8 January 2024.

Nast, Thomas. "Sketches among the Catskill Mountains." *Harper's Weekly*, 21 July 1866.

Nast, Thomas. *Uncle Sam's Panorama of Rip van Winkle and Yankee Doodle*. Yale Library, collections.library.yale.edu/catalog/2002798. Accessed 14 July 2024.

Nast, Thomas, and John Chalmers Vinson. *Thomas Nast, Political Cartoonist*. U of Georgia P, 2014.

"Negro Can't Buy Property: Court Denies Motion by Noted Artist." *Daily News* (Tarrytown), 25 May 1938, p. 1.

"New Code Banishes Racy Comic Books." *Poughkeepsie New Yorker*, 2 July 1948, p. 20.

"New York Bank Made Receiver in Lancia Case." *Poughkeepsie Eagle-News*, 18 April 1929, p. 1.

"1962–1984 & Beyond." Gold Key Comics, goldkeycomics.com/blogs/news/1962-1984-beyond. Accessed 2 February 2023.

1930 United States Federal Census, District 0185.

1920 United States Federal Census, District 0066.

Nixon, Marguerite. "Letter to the Editor." *Daily News* (Tarrytown), 22 August 1938, p. 8.

"Noted Negro Artist Seeks to Buy Country Estate in Pleasantville." *Daily News* (Tarrytown), 24 May 1938, p. 1.

Nyberg, Amy Kiste. *Seal of Approval: The History of the Comics Code*. UP of Mississippi, 1998.

O'Callaghan, Quinn. "Many Comic Book Heroes Have Hudson Valley Roots." Hudson Valley One, 26 February 2020, hudsonvalleyone.com/2015/01/24/

many-comic-book-heroes-have-roots-in-the-hudson-valley/. Accessed 12 March 2023.

Olana. www.olana.org. Accessed 14 April 2024.

Oldden, Rick. "That's the Hudson River School, Son." *New Yorker*, 22 June 1968, p. 31.

"Old Fiat Plant on Sale Tuesday." *Poughkeepsie Eagle-News*, 1 October 1921, p. 5.

Olson, Jon. "Bernstein to Leave Western." *Milwaukee Journal-Sentinel*, 7 September 1995, p. D1.

"The One with the Girl from Poughkeepsie." *Friends*, created by David Crane and Marta Kauffman, season 4, episode 10, Warner Bros. Studios, 1997.

Oravetz, Kenneth. "The Comics Shift: Modifying Material Rhetorics of Bookstores for Collaborative Category and Community Change." *ImageText*, vol. 12, no. 1, n.p.

"Origin and Early History." Stockbridge-Munsee Community Band of Mohican Indians, www.mohican.com/brief-history/. Accessed 2 September 2023.

"Out-of-Town News and Other Personal Items." *New York Age*, 16 May 1936, p. 10.

"Parade of Progress Exhibition." *Poughkeepsie Eagle-News*, 23 September 1940, p. 12.

Parker, John F. "The First Half Champs." *Daily News* (Tarrytown), 23 July 1938.

Parker, John F. "I Was Here First." *Daily News* (Tarrytown), 15 July 1938.

Parker, John F. "Those Soap Box Derby Boys Are at It Again." *Daily News* (Tarrytown), 25 July 1938.

Passmore, Ben. *Your Black Friend and Other Strangers*. Silver Sprocket, 2018.

"Past Recipients: 2020 to Present." San Diego Comic-Con International, www.comic-con.org/awards/eisner-awards/past-recipients/past-recipenties-2020s/. Accessed 1 March 2024.

"Peekskill NAACP Presidential History." Peekskill NAACP Branch 2170, www.peekskillnaacp.org/about_us. Accessed 5 April 2024.

Pennella, Florence. "Cartoon Museum Is a Castle of Laughs." *Poughkeepsie Journal*, 22 August 1986, pp. 1D & 13D.

Pete, Alina, ed. *Indiginerds: Tales from Modern Indigenous Life*. Iron Circus Comics, 2024.

Peters, Harry T. *Currier & Ives, Printmakers to the American People*. Doubleday, Doran, 1942.

Phelps, Don. "John Stanley and the Universal Progeny." *The Little Lulu Library*, ed. Bruce Hamilton. Volume 18. Another Rainbow, 1985, pp. 467–69.

Pierre, Summer. *All the Sad Songs*. Retrofit Comics, 2018.

Pierre, Summer. Interview. Conducted by the author, 26 July 2023.

Pierre, Summer. *Paper Pencil Life: Comics & Diary Comics*. Numbers 1–9. *Summer Pierre: Comics & Illustration*, summer-pierre.com. Accessed 21 April 2024.

Pini, Richard, and Wendy Pini. *The Art of "ElfQuest."* Flesk, 2015.

Pini, Richard, and Wendy Pini. Interviews. Conducted by the author, 22 June 2023, 28 June 2023, and 10 July 2023.

Pini, Richard, and Wendy Pini. *Line of Beauty: The Art of Wendy Pini*. Flesk, 2017.

Pini, Wendy. *Beauty and the Beast: Night of Beauty*. First Comics, 1990.

Pini, Wendy. *Beauty and the Beast: Portrait of Love*. Marvel Comics, 1989.

Pini, Wendy, and Richard Pini. "The Dreamberry Tales." *Original Quest*, no. 7. The *ElfQuest* Reading Room, elfquest.com/reading-room/. Accessed 1 May 2023.

Pini, Wendy, and Richard Pini. "The Forbidden Grove." *Original Quest*, no. 10. The *ElfQuest* Reading Room, elfquest.com/reading-room/. Accessed 5 May 2023.

Pini, Wendy, and Richard Pini. *Hidden Years*. The *ElfQuest* Reading Room, elfquest.com/reading-room/. Accessed 10 November 2023.

Pini, Wendy, and Richard Pini. *Kings of the Broken Wheel*. The *ElfQuest* Reading Room, elfquest.com/reading-room/. Accessed 10 November 2023.

Pini, Wendy, and Richard Pini. "The Lodestone." *Original Quest*, no. 9. The *ElfQuest* Reading Room, elfquest.com/reading-room/. Accessed 1 May 2023.

Pini, Wendy, and Richard Pini. "The Quest Begins." *Original Quest*, no. 6. The *ElfQuest* Reading Room, elfquest.com/reading-room/. Accessed 7 May 2023.

Pini, Wendy, and Richard Pini. "Voice of the Sun." *Original Quest*, no. 5. The *ElfQuest* Reading Room, elfquest.com/reading-room/. Accessed 1 May 2023.

Poe, Edgar Allan. *Poe's Tales of Mystery and Imagination*. Illustrated by Arthur Rackham. George G. Harrap, 1935.

"Ponty Asserts Deal for Fiat Waits Ringling." *Poughkeepsie Eagle-News*, 14 July 1930, p. 1.

"Poughkeepsie History." Dutchess County, New York, www.dutchess.org/poughkeepsie/poughkeepsie_history. Accessed 1 March 2024.

"Poughkeepsie History." The Poughkeepsie Public Library District, poklib.org/learn/local-history-genealogy/poughkeepsie-history/. Accessed 2 October 2023.

"Poughkeepsie, N.Y." (map). Library of Congress, www.loc.gov/resource/g3804p.pm006211/?r=0.097,0.463,0.177,0.095,0. Accessed 27 September 2023.

Poughkeepsie Savings Bank advertisement. *Poughkeepsie Eagle-News*, 27 August 1927, p. 2.

Pratt, Henry. *The Philosophy of Comics: What They Are, How They Work, and Why They Matter*. Illustrated by Kurt F. Shaffert. Oxford UP, 2023.

Pratt, John Lowell. *Currier & Ives's Chronicles of America: Color Plates Reproduced from the Original Hand-Colored Stone Prints of N. Currier and Currier & Ives*. Promontory Press, 1968.

"President's Message." *Retirees of Western*, vol. 19, 1998, p. 3.

"Program Listed for 'Book Bazaar.'" *Poughkeepsie New Yorker*, 13 November 1955, p. 8.

"Publishing Official Feted." *Poughkeepsie New Yorker*, 24 September 1955, p. 12.

Quattro, Ken. *Invisible Men: The Trailblazing Black Artists of Comic Books*. IDW, 2020.

Rawls, Walton. *The Great Book of Currier & Ives's America*. Abbeville, 1979.

Read, Sarah, and Jordan Frith. "Special Issue Introduction: Writing Infrastructure." *Communication Design Quarterly*, vol. 10, no. 3, 2022, pp. 4–9.

"Regions of the Hudson River Valley." Maurice D. Hinchey Hudson River Valley National Heritage Area, www.hudsonrivervalley.com/regions. Accessed 12 March 2024.

Rhoades, Ed. "George Wilson Interview: The Phantom Painter." *Comic Book Artist*, vol. 22, 2002, pp. 74–75.

Robbins, Trina. *Pretty in Ink: North American Women Cartoonists 1896–2013*. Fantagraphics, 2013.

"Robert C. Tripp Dies: Railroad Employee." *Poughkeepsie New Yorker*, 28 October 1957, p. 18.

Robishaw, Jim. Interview. Conducted by the author, 19 July 2023.

"Royalty Discards Pomp to Munch on Hot Dogs." *Poughkeepsie Eagle-News*, 12 June 1939, pp. 1–2.

Rubin-Dorsky, Jeffrey. "Washington Irving and the Genesis of the Fictional Sketch." *Early American Literature*, vol. 21, no. 2, 1986, pp. 226–47.

Rubinstein, Charlotte Streifer. *Fanny Palmer: The Life and Works of a Currier & Ives Artist*. Edited by Diann Benti. Syracuse UP, 2018.

Salisbury, Martin. *Drawing for Illustration*. Thames & Hudson, 2022.

Sandler, Linda, and G. Bruce Knecht. "Golden Books' Richard Snyder Is Nearing Day of Reckoning to Turn Around Publishing Firm." *Wall Street Journal*, 23 March 1998, p. C2.

Santana, Jon. Interview. Conducted by the author, 20 March 2024.

Santana, Jon, et al. *The Haunted Box 2*. Iron Age Comics, 2024.

Santana, Jon, et al. *Jaded: The Collected Edition*. Iron Age Comics, 2016.

Santana, Jon, Michael Oppenheimer, and Bunny Pasig. *The Everhounds*. Iron Age Comics, 2019.

Satrapi, Marjane. *The Complete Persepolis*. Volumes 1 and 2. Pantheon, 2007.

Saunders, Robert. "The Identity Politics of *ElfQuest* at 40: Moving beyond Race, Class, and Gender?" *Journal of Graphic Novels and Comics*, vol. 10, no. 1, 2019, pp. 3–27.

"Scandinavian Society Entertains at Picnic." *Poughkeepsie Eagle-News*, 29 August 1932, p. 5.

Scarpero, Pamela A. Interview. Conducted by the author, 11 March 2024.

Schelly, Bill. *John Stanley: Giving Life to Little Lulu*. Fantagraphics Books, 2017.

Schuyler, David. "The Mid-Hudson Valley as Iconic Landscape: Tourism, Economic Development, and the Beginnings of a Preservationist Impulse." *Within the Landscape: Essays on Nineteenth-Century American Art and Culture*, ed. Philip Earenfight and Nancy Siegel. Pennsylvania State UP, 2005, pp. 11–42.

Schuyler, David. *Sanctified Landscape: Writers, Artists, and the Hudson River Valley 1820–1909*. Cornell UP, 2012.

Scouting Item. *Poughkeepsie Journal*, 25 November 1956, p. 4C.

"Series MT. Mel Tapley Collection." Division of Rare and Manuscript Collections, Cornell University Library, rmc.library.cornell.edu/EAD/htmldocs/RMM08084BMT.html#MT. Accessed 14 March 2024.

Shearer, Teddy. "Artists' Colony Lists Big Names." *New York Age Defender*, 22 August 1953, p. 3.

She Makes Comics. Dir. Marisa Stotter. Respect Films and Sequart Organization, 2014.

Sheridan, Harry. Interview. Conducted by the author, 23 February 2024.

Sheridan, Harry. *Tricky Style: Vampire vs. Werewolf . . . Round Two!* Amekomi Comics, 2020.

Sheyahshe, Michael. *Native Americans in Comic Books: A Critical Study*. McFarland, 2008.

Siebel, Fred O. "The Essence of Democracy." *Richmond Times-Dispatch*, 11 June 1939, p. 44.

Siegel, Mark. *Sailor Twain: Or, the Mermaid in the Hudson*. First Second, 2012.

Siegel, Nancy. "'We the Petticoated Ones:' Women of the Hudson River School." *The Cultured Canvas: New Perspectives on American Landscape Painting*, ed. Nancy Siegel. U of New Hampshire P, 2011.

Siegel, Nancy, and Jennifer Krieger. *Remember the Ladies: Women Artists of the Hudson River School*. Thomas Cole National Historic Site, 2010.

Siegel, Nancy, Kate Menconeri, and Amanda Malmstrom. *Women Reframe American Landscape: Susie Barstow & Her Circle/Contemporary Practices*. Hirmer, 2023.

Singsen, Doug. "Teaching Comics and Graphic Novels as Art History." Art History Teaching Resources, arthistoryteachingresources.org/2017/04/teaching-comics-and-graphic-novels-as-art-history/. Accessed 17 April 2024.

"Site #8: Catskill Mountain House." Hudson River School Art Trail, www.hudson-riverschool.org/catskill-mountain-house. Accessed 14 January 2024.

"Site of the Spring." Town of Poughkeepsie, www.townofpoughkeepsie.com/350/Site-of-Poughkeepsie-Spring. Accessed 9 March 2023.

"Sketches Feature Social at Church." *Poughkeepsie Eagle-News*, 7 June 1923, p. 6.

Smith, Andrew. "There's the Good, the Bad, and the So-Bad-It's Good." *The Commercial Appeal*, 18 January 2004, p. F6.

Smith, J. Michael. "The Highland King Nimhammaw and the Native Indian Proprietors of Land in Dutchess County, NY: 1712–1765." *Hudson Valley Regional Review*, vol. 17, pp. 69–107.

The Smurfs: The Legend of Smurfy Hollow. Directed by Stephan Franck, performances by Melissa Sturm and John Oliver, Sony Pictures Entertainment, 2013.

Sousanis, Nick. *Unflattening*. Harvard UP, 2015.

Sparling, Reed. "Celebrating the Scenic Hudson Decision." Hudson Valley Viewfinder, www.scenichudson.org/viewfinder/celebrating-the-scenic-hudson-decision/. Accessed 21 March 2024.

Spider-Man: Into the Spider-Verse. Directed by Bob Persichetti, Peter Ramsey, and Rodney Rothman, performances by Shameik Moore and Jake Johnson, Sony Pictures and Marvel Entertainment, 2018.

Spiegelman, Art. *The Complete Maus: A Survivor's Tale*. Pantheon, 1996.

Spratt, James. "Milestones of Dutchess County." The Hudson River Valley Institute, www.hudsonrivervalley.org/milestones-of-dutchess-county. Accessed 9 February 2024.

Stanley, John, and Irving Tripp. *Little Lulu: All Dressed Up*. Edited by Dave Marshall. Dark Horse Books, 2006.

"The State of the Hudson 2020." Hudson River Foundation, www.hudsonriver. org/state-of-the-estuary#report. Accessed 8 December 2023.

"Steamboats on the Hudson: An American Saga." New York State Library, nyslibrary.libguides.com/steamboats/newspapers#s-lg-box-wrapper-34974906. Accessed 11 June 2023.

Stedman, Raymond William. *Shadows of the Indian: Stereotypes in American Culture*. U of Oklahoma P, 1982.

Strawbalicious. "While 'Hudson Valley, New York' Isn't a Real Town, Spiderman: Into the Spiderverse Shows It Next to the Real New York State Route 32 and Reservoirs That Run through the Region." r/MovieDetails, Reddit, www.reddit.com/r/MovieDetails/comments/b4wg4p/while_hudson_valley_new_york_isnt_a_real_town/. Accessed 3 November 2024.

"The Subway's Surrealist: The Cartoons of a New Jersey Housewife Help to Improve Commuters' Manners." *New York Times*, 19 September 1948, p. SM58.

"Summer Is Soap Box Derby Time." *Daily News* (Tarrytown), 3 June 1938, p. 6.

"Superfund Site Information: Former Western Publishing." United States Environmental Protection Agency, cumulis.epa.gov/supercpad/CurSites/cadminrecord.cfm?id=0206423&doc=Y&colid=63694. Accessed 1 October 2022.

"Supermarket, N." *Oxford English Dictionary*. Oxford UP, July 2023, https://doi.org/10.1093/OED/7326853785.

"Surprise Party Held for Mrs. E. Tripp." *Poughkeepsie Eagle-News*, 26 February 1927, p. 14.

Surrey, A. A. "Artist Builds Own Modernistic Home on Sound." *Daily News* (Tarrytown), 9 June 1938, p. 6.

Swift, Will. *The Roosevelts and the Royals*. MJF Books, 2004.

Tapley, Melvin. *Breezy*. About Comics, 2022.

Tarbell, Harlan. *How to Chalk Talk*. T. S. Denison, 1924.

"Tarrytown Youth Now on Staff of Local Daily as Cartoonist." *New York Age*, 30 July 1938, p. 12.

Taylor, Shawn. "In Praise of *ElfQuest*." The Nerds of Color, 21 April 2021, thenerdsofcolor.org/2021/04/21/in-praise-of-elfquest/. Accessed 7 November 2023.

Tenan, Bradley. "Miss Lulu Moppet Lives at 22 Main Street." *The Stanley Steamer for Lulu Collectors*, vol. 24, n.d.

Thomas Cole National Historic Site, thomascole.org. Accessed 2 June 2023.

Thompson, Maggie. "Marge." *The Little Lulu Library*, ed. Bruce Hamilton. Volume 18. Another Rainbo, 1985, pp. 641–44.

Titus, Robert, and Johanna Titus. *The Hudson River Schools of Art and Their Ice Age Origins*. Purple Mountain, 2024.

Trafton, Melissa Geisler. " 'It Is a Joint Venture': John Frederick Kensett's Images for *Lotus-Eating*." *American Art*, vol. 25, no. 2, 2011, pp. 104–19.

Trimpe, Amelia. Interview. Conducted by the author, 23 February 2024.

Trimpe, Herb. "Old Superheroes Never Die, They Join the Real World." *New York Times*, 9 January 2000, pp. EL25–46.

Tripp, Bill. Interview. Conducted by the author, 10 July 2023.

Tripp, Jane. Interview. Conducted by the author, 26 July 2023.

"Tripp to Instruct Course in Painting." *Poughkeepsie Journal*, 26 December 1962, p. 11.

Turner, Sue. Interview. Conducted by the author, 28 June 2023.

"200 Attend Pressmen's Dinner." *Poughkeepsie New Yorker*, 14 February 1955, p. 13.

Valkys, Michael, "Downsizing Puts Crimp in Loyalty." *Poughkeepsie Journal*, 14 March 1999, p. 21.

Van Lente, Fred, and Ryan Dunleavy. *The Comic Book History of Comics*. IDW, 2012.

Van Lente, Fred, and Ryan Dunleavy. *The Comic Book History of Comics: Comics for All*. IDW, 2018.

"Vignette, N." *Oxford English Dictionary*, Oxford UP, December 2023, https://doi.org/10.1093/OED/9958873075. Accessed 2 November 2024.

Wanzo, Rebecca. *The Content of Our Caricature: African American Comic Art and Political Belonging*. NYU Press, 2020.

Waterman, Kees-Jan, and J. Michael Smith. *Munsee Indian Trade in Ulster County, New York, 1712–1732*. Syracuse UP, 2013.

Watters, Shannon, and Branden Boyer-White. *Hollow*. Illustrated by Berenice Nelle. Boom! Box, 2022.

Wei, Stella. "Thomas Nast: The Rise and Fall of the Father of Political Cartoons." *Illustration History*, www.illustrationhistory.org/essays/thomas-nast-the-rise-and-fall-of-the-father-of-political-cartoons. Accessed 2 January 2024.

Weisman, Mary-Lou. *Al Jaffee's Mad Life: A Biography*. Illustrated by Al Jaffee. It Books, 2010.

Wertham, Fredric. *Seduction of the Innocent*. Rinehart, 1954.

Westerfeld, Scott. *Spill Zone*. Illustrated by Alex Puvilland. First Second, 2017.

Westerfeld, Scott. *Spill Zone Book Two: The Broken Vow*. Illustrated by Alex Puvilland. First Second, 2018.

"Western Officials to Visit Disneyland." *Poughkeepsie New Yorker*, 12 July 1955, p. 22.

Whitehouse, Kendall. "Stan Lee, Jack Kirby, and the Mythical Marvel Bullpen." On Technology and Media, ontechnologyandmedia.com/2013/02/13/stan-lee-jack-kirby-and-the-mythical-marvel-bullpen/. Accessed 20 March 2024.

"Where to Go, What to Do." *Citizen Register* (Ossining), 23 March 1986, p. 14.

Whitted, Qiana J. "*All-Negro Comics* and Counterhistories of Race in the Golden Age." *Desegregating Comics: Debating Blackness in the Golden Age of American Comics*, ed. Qiana J. Whitted. Rutgers UP, 2023, pp. 181–206.

Wiles, Richard C. "The Commerce of Art in the Nineteenth-Century Hudson Valley." *America's First River: The History and Culture of the Hudson River Valley*, ed. Thomas Wermuth, James Johnson, and Christopher Pryslopski. State U of New York P, 2009, pp. 209–18.

"Willys Concern Will Take Over Old Fiat Plant." *Poughkeepsie Eagle-News*, 25 June 1919, p. 5.

Wilson, Geoffrey. "Local Couple Ends Beloved Comic Series," *The Poughkeepsie Journal*, vol. 25 April 2018, p. A2.

Young, Frank. *The Tao of Yow: John Stanley's World*. CreateSpace, 2015.

Index

www.ingramcontent.com/pod-product-compliance
Lightning Source LLC
Chambersburg PA
CBHW072140290526
45794CB00004B/1371